Just an Ordinary Girl

H. J. Samuel

Heather Samuel

H J Samuel

ISBN:
ISBN-13:

To my mother, a very precious soul,
and to my incredible son, whom I love
to the moon and back,
in all ways, always

CONTENTS

ACKNOWLEDGMENTS

Cover design:

Cover photo: Katelyn Butcher, www.ExpansionPhotography.com

Author photo: S. Pandya

"Il faut cultiver notre jardin."
Voltaire, *Candide ou L'Optimisme*

PROLOGUE

Earlier today, everyone's cell phone in the state pinged with this chilling text: BALLISTIC MISSILE THREAT INBOUND TO HAWAII. SEEK IMMEDIATE SHELTER. THIS IS NOT A DRILL.

I called my son in Europe to tell him I loved him and to say goodbye. Then I walked outside and began watering my garden.

On her deathbed, my mother told me, "When things get difficult, be sure to water your garden and that way you will always leave something good behind. Heather, always operate from a place of kindness. Remember, never let other people make you ugly. Learn to rise above the pain and seek joy in everything."

"Joy" was the middle name she had given me.

My mother's words have sustained me throughout a lifetime of misery and emotional abuse. I have never talked about exactly what I have endured. Kindness and grace, in the face of cruelty: that is how I have tried to live my life.

One day, I told myself, I will get what I truly deserve.

CHAPTER 1

MAKE THE BREAK

I was into my fifties before I admitted that I hated my father. When I did, I felt nothing but shame—shame that I could harbor such an ugly feeling. By then, he had been dead for almost seven years.

My hatred probably began when I found him in the bathroom, his hands closed tightly around my mother's slender neck. I was six years old. Of course, as with most children, my feelings for my father were mixed and confused. I may have hated and feared him but I tried desperately to gain his approval and his love. When I failed, endlessly, I simply told myself to try harder. He is probably why I became an overachiever and a perfectionist.

Unfortunately his death did not free me. His toxic legacy has made it challenging and almost impossible for me to have the kind of loving, trusting relationship I crave with a man. It is only now, as I dig up my deeply buried feelings of worthlessness and pain that I am finally coming to terms with it all.

That journey begins on a sweltering mid July day when I decide to give up my chaotic life in Toronto and move to Maui— on my own. I am fifty-four years old. I am battling an autoimmune disease triggered by treatment for fetal cancer fifteen years earlier. I am physically exhausted from overwork to support an indigent partner, a son studying for his second university degree and a home in one of Toronto's most prestigious neighborhoods. I am also drained from decades of offering emotional and often financial support to a large entourage of family and friends who depend on me to fix their problems and manage their lives. My disappointing second serious relationship is all but over, my partner permanently away chasing one questionable scheme after another, leaving me to contend with a steady stream of collection agencies. I am convinced that if I do not make a radical change to my life, I will not survive.

My friends and family are aghast that I am abandoning them, but I am resolute. The decision to leave has been building for years. Making a life in another country is a daunting prospect, but I know I can do it. I have triumphed over the many adversities that life has thrown my way. Once I make a decision, the switch is flipped—irrevocably.

Three years earlier, it took every fibre of my being but I made, and kept, a different but equally daunting resolution: to cut off all communication with my father. No more emotional abuse, no more whipping girl, no more holidays together at my expense, no more dinners, no more calls, no more talking, no more words. My son was living on his own, in college, and would not be affected by the tremendous chasm between me and my father.

I changed my phone number, locked my doors, pulled down the blinds and closed off my heart—to finally protect myself. I was ill then, too. After decades of subservience, being subjected to impossible expectations, brutal insults, incessant badgering, limitless financial demands and total neglect, I was done. It took me almost four months to be able to breathe again, to feel unburdened and healed. Then the unthinkable happened.

My Best Laid Plans

One Sunday morning in late August the phone rings. It is the police. My father has been found in a neighborhood coffee shop, disoriented and slurring his words. After following him the two blocks home, the police watched as he drove down the ramp of his underground garage, hit the door, banged into and the side of the garage and then passed out in his car. The police officer managed to rouse him and tell me that he is now sitting in a chair in the lobby of his condo.

As I listen to the officer, I feel tears and nausea welling up inside me. "I'll be there in a few minutes," is all I can manage. I reach for my car keys, purse and cell phone and dash out of the house. On the way, I suddenly remember that I, along with my siblings have never been permitted inside my father's condo. In the more than twenty years my father has lived there, I have never, ever, passed beyond the security gate. So, how will I be able to deal with this mess?

When I turn into the driveway of his condo, I can see the police and security guard waiting for me at the gatehouse. They escort me into the lobby. How surreal never to have set foot here before. But this is no time to perseverate over why and how a father could prohibit his eldest daughter from entering his home.

I find my father where the police have left him, in a chair in the lobby, disheveled, which is so unlike him as he is normally fastidious about his appearance. He smiles at me, asks if I have come to visit and invites me to come upstairs. At that moment, I am sure he has had a stroke.

The police officer and I help him up. He stumbles to the elevator. We ride up, the officer and I supporting him on either side. I have no idea what floor he lives on. When the door opens, he steps out and looks down the hall. I thank the police officer, telling him that I will take it from here and give him my contact information. He hands me his report, places a firm hand on my shoulder and, sensing that I am shaken, asks if I am okay. I thank him again and ask my father to hand me his keys. I follow him down the corridor until he stops, debating which of two doors is his. I brace myself, put the key in the lock and step inside.

A flood of emotion overwhelms me as I drop my purse and hang my coat on a dining room chair. I take a cursory look around, noting a few familiar pieces from my past: my original wedding photo hanging on the wall in the living room and a large portrait of my mother. I am heartsick. Almost a whole lifetime has passed with no explanation why he closed the door on his heart and his home. I push aside my thoughts, knowing that I have to concentrate on the vicissitude of this situation and deal with it.

My father is uncharacteristically affable and so confused that he obviously requires medical attention. I call my father's elder and only brother and request that he meet me at my father's condo. I rummage through my father's chest of drawers and bedroom closet for clean clothes, a bath towel and a suitcase. I pack his bag with pajamas, toiletries, a robe, slippers and a change of clothes, assuming that a hospital will admit him for tests and observation. I walk him into the bathroom, run the shower for him and wait outside for him to emerge. I pull out some clean clothes from his closet then help him dress and groom while attempting to give him some privacy.

I sit my father in the living room to wait for my uncle to arrive and go to the kitchen to make him some herbal tea. As I fill the kettle with tap water, I am stunned when I walk into his kitchen. The walls are splattered with a rainbow of what seems to be orange, cranberry and grapefruit juice. When I open a cupboard for a mug, I find at least a dozen drinking glasses half-full of soda pop. I am horrified.

The state of the kitchen alone is atypical. Where is the obsessively, compulsively clean and controlling father I grew up with? Something has gone terribly wrong. The knock at the door as the kettle whistles is a welcome relief.

My uncle and I sit on either side of my father, explaining that he needs to go to the hospital as a precaution. He is so complacent that my uncle and I fear a brain tumor. I open my father's bathroom medicine cabinet and night table, searching for prescriptions to take with us. I find several vials of a drug I do not recognize. I know that his family doctor has prescribed blood thinners and one baby aspirin to be taken daily for years but this is something else.

I sit in silence and gesture to my father to drink his tea but he pushes it away and asks for Diet Coke. He drinks one glass, then a second, a third and a fourth. His insatiable thirst is another red flag.

As we drive to Emergency at Mount Sinai Hospital, I make a few phone calls to alert the support staff that we are on our way and why. My hope is that my many years of chairing major fundraising events for the hospital and having a position with the Women's Auxiliary will help my father get seen immediately. As we pull in under the hospital's *porte cochère*, my father mentions that he had a car accident the day before in his bank's parking lot. "A woman drove into my car. Nothing to worry about," he says, but her lawyer has called him. The details are garbled. Did this really happen or did he imagine it? I learn much later that he drove his car into hers and there was a fair amount of damage. Just another mess for me to take care of.

In record time, my father is taken to a small draped cubical, hooked up to a heart monitor and IV and given an EEG and EKG. Doctors scurry around ordering tests. It certainly helps to have connections in the medical community, I think to myself.

I leave to get a coffee at the hospital's café and when I return, the doctor is waiting for me. "We need to admit your father. He is addicted to Lorazepam and is in acute kidney failure. We are looking at a brain contusion among other things but won't know what else until we do further tests."

This is too much for me to take in. "What's Lorazepam?" I query.

"It's an anti anxiety drug and your father has been taking very large amounts of it, perhaps ten times the recommended dose. It's toxic, highly addictive and has caused his kidneys to shut down, pollute his brain and God knows what else."

I collapse. A nurse brings me a bottle of water and a chair. I sign all the paperwork to admit him. There are no beds available on the ward so I ask that an armchair, pillow and blanket be brought into his cubicle in Emergency where he and I will spend his first night. I call home to let my husband know that I am staying overnight at my father's bedside and send my exhausted uncle home to get some rest.

The night nurses shackle my father's chest, hips, arms and legs to the bed with straps, warning me to brace myself for a rocky night. This is to detoxify him, to wean him off the drugs, they explain. As the hours creep by, he swings from amenable to restless, exhausted, cantankerous, verbally abusive, and, by 3 a.m., to violent. His body convulses. Every time he screams my name, I place my hand gently on his chest and murmur, "It's okay, dad. Heather is here. It's okay." He finally slips into a state of delirium with high fever. Throughout the night, I stroke his chest and try to calm him with soothing words. A social worker assigned to my father's case unexpectedly appears. When I politely explain that he does not need a social worker, she places her hand on my shoulder and says she is there for me. "I think you deserve some support. This is more than anyone should have to endure on her own."

In the morning, the night nurse departs as he's finished his shift and my father rallies. He appears more alert and I place my hand reassuringly on his chest once more. His eyes narrow. With brute force, he breaks the arm strap closest to me, grabs my wrist and twists it with all his might. I hear a crack. The pain is instantaneous. After X-rays, the radiologist confirms that he has broken my wrist. Another doctor resets it but nothing can repair my broken heart.

The next few days with my father in the hospital are nightmarish. He twitches, roars and thrashes against the restraints, which chafe and create open wounds on his trunk, arms and legs. His words drip pure vitriol. "You were a mistake, Heather. We didn't want you. I hope you get hit by a huge truck. You are no good, you never were. I told your mother to get rid of you."

I hold back tears as the nurse calls for the attending physician. My father's condition seems to worsen. "Don't pay any attention," the attending doctor advises when she hears the cursing. "It's the delirium talking, not your father." She does not know is how cruel and vicious my father could be; how he could reduce my mother to tears with a single word or his passive-aggressive indifference. In response to his cruelty, she became a master at disguising her wounded heart.

While my father recovers in hospital, I pick up some personal items and sundries for him from his condo. Since I am uncomfortable going there alone, I ask my uncle to accompany me. While there, I notice a stack of mail on the dining room table. Concerned not wanting to miss any bills that need to be paid, I also empty his mailbox and bring his mail upstairs. As I begin opening envelopes, I find receipts for wire transfers to Nigeria in amounts ranging from two hundred to eight hundred dollars, sent under different aliases, in the name of various business partners and family—even my late mother! These wire transfers total tens of thousands of dollars.

"Do you know what this about?" I ask my uncle. He hangs his head and mumbles that he does but offers no explanation or apology for harboring this secret. "I can't deal with this; it's making me physically ill," he says as he throws up his hands and walks out.

Left to my own devices, I quickly figure out what has happened. A month before my father's hospitalization, he called my sister, ranting unintelligibly about Africa. While it made no sense at the time, the pieces fall into place now when I turn on his computer. His inbox is full of messages from someone purporting to be a European woman; she is pleading for more money. The email exchange confirms that my father intends to marry her! The money my father has been sending "her" has been going to Nigeria. He has fallen prey to one of those notorious online Nigerian scams!

When I confront my father in hospital a few days later, he has only a vague recollection. He admits that the day before his "episode," he was supposed to send another lump sum for this woman's airfare to Toronto but had run out of cash. So, he filled a suitcase full of the mint U.S. coins that he had been collecting since I was a child, he drove across the border to Buffalo, New York, some sixty miles away, and converted these valuable coins into cash. Upon his return to Toronto, he wired the entire amount to Nigeria from a Money Mart location in the name of one of his business partners. How could he possibly have driven to Buffalo and back in his drugged state? That's a mystery to me. "There is a receipt for the coin exchange somewhere in my night table," he confesses.

Because of his folly, my father is in a precarious financial situation and I have no choice but to pay his bills until he recovers enough to return to work. I question how realistic it is for him to be well enough or able to earn an income again. Yet, at seventy-four, he still does enough to collect commissions on sales with his former business partners.

My financial load is already onerous. My partner, in a futile attempt to establish yet another business venture, has been incurring huge expenses. In order to protect my house from his creditors, I must pay my partner's bills as well.

I spend the next three weeks at my father's hospital bedside until he is finally free of his addiction and rehydrated, his kidneys and other bodily functions restored to normal. "It's a happy combination—a miracle and the care of a very loving daughter," says the chief of geriatric psychiatry, who tells me my father's recovery is worthy of a write-up in a medical journal.

A few days before my father's release from hospital, I load his fridge with healthy fresh food, replace his cooking utensils with new ones, buy him new bathroom accessories, make up his bed with fresh linens and scrub his condo from top to bottom. Even though I feel an overwhelming sense of animosity and sadness, I want him to be comfortable, safe and healthy in the weeks ahead. I arrange with the hospital social worker for a health care worker and nurse to visit him daily to help prepare meals, tidy, monitor his blood levels and administer the medicines he now requires.

Although the hospital releases my father with a clean bill of health, his driver's license had been temporarily suspended because of his initial delirium. No surprise that I become his designated driver, errand girl and go-to person. His medication comes in one-week blister packs that only I am authorized to pick up due to his prior substance abuse. I find myself at my father's beck and call once again and loathe it. He expects me to come by every day to take him shopping, to the bank and on errands; he demands that I keep him company at mealtimes. He becomes totally dependent on me. This becomes my new and unfamiliar reality.

Julia, my closest friend, who has known me and my family since I was five, is horrified that I would turn my life upside down to care for someone who has consistently treated me so cruelly. But I have to do what I think is right. I could never live with myself if I turned my back on my father when he needed me most. My sense of duty and honor would not allow it.

Caring for my father keeps my days full from late August until Christmas but when his complete recovery is imminent, I book a February flight to Maui. I need the break of a few months away and have never missed a winter in Maui in more than twenty years.

Part of my father's treatment involves weekly psychotherapy at the hospital. When I take my father to his second to last session, the chief of geriatric psychiatry informs us that he will authorize the reinstatement of my father's driver's license in a week. I almost weep in relief, finally sensing the end of my servitude. As we conclude the session, the doctor asks my father about his winter plans now that he has made such a miraculous and full recovery. I interject that I am going to Maui for a month or so. "Fantastic!" the doctor says to me. "You must be so happy to be heading for sun and warm weather."

"Well, *I'm* certainly not happy about it," my father complains. "I need her close by. She should not be leaving me now."

"Nonsense. You are in perfect health and about to regain your independence. You'll soon be able to drive yourself around and even travel if you wish."

"No. I need her here!"

"I know you are used to having your daughter with you all the time but she deserves a break."

"What are you talking about?" I blurt out in exasperation, looking from one to the other. "I was never welcome in my father's house—ever—until this health crisis.

The doctor looks mystified. "Is she serious? Why was she was never allowed in your home?"

"I have no idea why," mumbles my father.

"You must know," insists the doctor but my father unwavering repeats, "I have no idea."

I am shocked to the core. I always believed that I was not allowed in my father's home for the same reason that he never remembered or acknowledged my birthdays or any of my accomplishments: that I was not worthy. What makes this moment especially devastating is that I secretly hoped for an explanation that would make sense of why my father had belittled me my entire life. A reason why, when I was a young despite how hard I tried to please him, achieve high grades in school,   pander to his

unreasonable demands, he was so emotionally unavailable to me."
Why he never had a kind word for me and why nothing I did was
ever good enough.

It is only then that I realize that there is no reason. The truth is
of little comfort. Sadness washes over me as I acknowledge the
enormity of my father's mental dysfunction, the tragedy of it all.
The man I thought was so steely, successful, self-assured,
commanding and controlling is actually the most unhappy,
insecure and lost person I know. My mother's words resonate
within me: "hurt people hurt people, remember that when you
commit your heart to someone". Thankfully, I know that in a few
short days I will be far away and out of reach.

Until I am on the plane for Maui, I do not realize how
emotionally and physically drained I am. Julia travels with me,
intending to stay for a few weeks. As usual, I have arranged for us
to stay at my favorite hotel. We spend the first day relaxing by the
infinity pool and then linger over a light dinner on our lanai,
enjoying an epic sunset. My son is back at college, safe and happy.
All is right in my world. I know I will sleep well that night, lulled
by swishing palm fronds and the muted rumble of the waves. This
is my happy place, my cocoon of safety, where no one can hurt me.

I am blissfully asleep when the phone rings in our room early
the next morning. Julia answers, then wordlessly hands me the
phone. Still groggy, I take the phone onto the lanai, Julia following
close behind.

"Dad is dead," I hear my sister say. "What?" I cry, too stunned
to say more. She repeats, "Dad's dead."

Then a man comes on the line, identifying himself as a police
officer. "We found your father on the floor between his bedroom
and bathroom, a contusion on his forehead. We think he had a heart

attack. When your father didn't answer his door this morning, his housekeeper called the security guard and building superintendent to check on him. He was already dead. We are waiting for the coroner. He will provide your sister with the death certificate and his conclusions about the cause of death."

My sister comes back on the line. "Dad is dead and you are not here." "I'm coming. I'm coming now" is all I can say.

Cruising with My Aunt

Two years after his death, I still have not come to terms with my troubled relationship with my father but I do what I do best: I moved forward burying my grief. Sundays have always been "open house" at my Toronto home. Friends and family know they can drop in unannounced for coffee and freshly baked treats (after all I am a pastry chef) so it is no surprise when my "aunt" (an old family friend) drops by for coffee and my signature warm pear and almond custard tart, thumbprint jam cookies and fresh berries one Sunday afternoon. We start to joke about how I should celebrate my upcoming fifty-fifth birthday in August. Perhaps a quick trip to Paris to visit friends, lunch at Fauchon, a visit to the Louvre, shopping at Galeries Lafayette or a train ride to the Palace of Versailles? She knows my love of travel and how comfortable I am doing it on my own.

"In view of your upcoming move to Maui, we'd like to celebrate your birthday in a special way," my aunt suddenly announces. "You never ask for anything so I'd like to take you to Paris, at my expense." Overwhelmed, I thank her profusely but decline. "All I want for my birthday is everyone to drop by, as usual."

At eighty-three, my aunt is a four-foot, ten-inch dynamo who attends daily kickboxing and boot camp classes. Always dressed to the nines and impeccably groomed, she has been keeping herself in top shape through exercise, vitamins and organic food choices long before they became fashionable. She loves beautiful things and adventure, although traveling is becoming more difficult due to her husband's recent health problems.

"This is my last chance to go to Europe and it would be so much fun to go with you," she insists. Sensing that she can overcome my reluctance, she perseveres. "If you don't want Paris, I'll come up with an alternative plan!" I shrug and say nothing, hoping that her enthusiasm will fizzle.

The following Sunday, my aunt and her husband arrive for coffee and sweets as usual. When they present me with a brochure for a five-star European cruise, I am speechless and begin to weep. I walk out of the kitchen to collect myself. I am not comfortable accepting gifts. Gifts from my father and husband always came with a punishing price so, like Pavlov's dog, consequently I do not want to accept this one from my aunt.

She intends to book us on a luxury Mediterranean cruise with an upgraded suite complete with our own butler to tend to our every need. Its twelve-day itinerary in early October will take us to many of the places she knows I long to visit or revisit: Barcelona, Valencia, Palma de Mallorca, Marseille, Aix-en-Provence, Monte Carlo, Santa Margherita, Portofino, Florence and Rome.

"This is a gift for both of us." She grins. "You'll be gifting me because you speak several languages and can navigate through different countries with ease."

I smile inwardly as I recall an incident five years earlier when Julia and I celebrated our fiftieth birthdays together in Italy. We had just landed at Rome's airport and, as I wheeled my luggage toward the taxi sign, I heard Julia calling me over the cacophony. "Stop, Heather!" She gestured for me to follow her. "I've found someone to take us into Rome for less." I ignored her and continued toward the long taxi queue.

Before leaving Toronto, I had researched all the fares and costs for the various legs of our Italian month long journey, but Julia was insistent so I left the queue and asked her ride, in Italian, where his vehicle was parked. When he pointed to a large bus parked in front of the taxi sign, I shook my head. "Why would we want to save ten euros to take a fifty-passenger bus that stops multiple times en route to our hotel? We could be on this bus for hours!"

As we slid into the next available taxi, I felt myself transforming into the competent, self-confident traveler I had become since my first European experience in my late twenties. Chatting in Italian to the driver, I asked him about the weather and traffic conditions, the usual small talk foreigners make with locals. Julia remained silent.

Before my aunt and her husband leave that day, he disappears to their car and returns with a small tissue-wrapped birthday gift. "You'll need this for our dinners on the ship," my aunt explains as she hands me ten euros in coins. It is a black vintage Chanel evening bag with a small mother-of-pearl handle. "Be sure to keep these coins tucked away in the small satin pocket for luck." Who was I to doubt the woman who had won the first million-dollar lottery in Ontario?

A few weeks before our cruise, I lay out my casual lightweight clothes for each day and my elegant European formal dresses for each evening. After years of packing and unpacking, I have become a proficient packer. I usually pack for Julia on our travels so I offer to pack for my aunt. She buys brand new suitcases for the cruise and brings me her finery, which I press, organize and pack into her cases. I even make a list of everything I have packed.

Before I know it, it is the day before our departure and four of my girlfriends drop by with a *bon voyage* gift. "Study this on the plane," one of them advises. I giggle at the title on the cover of the book: *Why Men Love Bitches*. Then the girls begin to coach my aunt. "Heather is far too sweet and is taken advantage of far too often. It's time she met a man who treats her with the love and respect she deserves." They assure my aunt that she is in good hands with me and that she will have the trip of a lifetime but that her real mandate is to find me a wonderful man. "An Italian or an Aussie," they tease. I laugh at them but slip the book in my carry-on.

The next evening, my aunt and I fly business class to Barcelona, arriving the next morning around ten o'clock, twenty-four hours before our ship departs. After a quick taxi ride to our boutique hotel and three cups of espresso later, I urge my exhausted, jet-lagged aunt to rally and we head into the centre of Barcelona for a daylong shopping spree that soon has me laden with dozens of heavy shopping bags. After a short break to refuel with more coffee and sweets, we continue our retail therapy in my favorite European style: buying without trying.

The next morning, our heavy oversize luggage barely fits into the trunk of our prearranged taxi to the port. My pint-size aunt squeezes in between two large bulging bags in the back seat. I sit upfront with the driver, my large designer purse slung across my chest. It contains our most important documents: passports, boarding passes for the ship and, of course, my new bible, *Why Men Love Bitches*.

When we board, a handsome porter escorts us into a large reception area where we register, confirm all our dinner reservations, spa arrangements and excursions. From there, we are ushered into a large anteroom with floral-silk-paneled walls, crystal chandeliers and butter-yellow striped-velvet bench seats. I feel as if I have been transported to an elegant salon from an earlier century. White-clad waitstaff circulate with silver serving trays bearing crystal flutes of champagne. This kind of privilege, sophistication and opulence feels foreign, yet familiar. It reminds me of the stately Plaza hotel in New York, where I stayed for months at a time before opening my Fogal of Switzerland boutique twenty-five years earlier.

No Sleepovers

As a little girl, I was painfully shy. There were no sleepovers with friends for me. I was more comfortable staying close to home. Very attached to my mother and lacking self-confidence, I was happy to invite friends over to my house but dreaded their reciprocating invitations.

Every Sunday morning I attended Hebrew school at the synagogue across the street from my paternal grandparents house. Afterward, I would walk over to their place for lunch and anxiously wait for my mother to pick me up. Each week, I dreaded the menu since my grandmother was not "a gourmand in the kitchen", to say the least. What ten-year-old girl likes canned cream of celery soup? But, like a good little girl, I would choke it down, praying that my mother would arrive early.

One winter Sunday, my grandmother had a long heart to heart conversation with my mother about my lack of social confidence. As usual, my mother listened politely but dismissed her concerns and criticisms, firm in the belief that only she had the right to speak critically of her children.

My well-bred but cold grandmother assumed the role of family matriarch when the occasion suited her, which it did for this particular matter. She simply went over my mother's head and demanded my father take some action to deal with me. A few weeks earlier, she informed him, the Sunday school principal had asked my grandmother to pick me up so he could speak privately with her. "Heather is being chased by the boys in class," the principal had told her. "She cowers at any attention. She is painfully shy and needs some help to come out of her shell—a confidence boost."

Within days, my parents had enrolled me in a modeling-self-improvement program in Toronto at the Walter Thornton Model Agency. I was one of the youngest girls in the class. Every Saturday, I put on white cotton dress gloves, walked with books balanced on my head to improve my posture, practiced my diction and learned to curtsy. Every Saturday, I would beg my parents to let me stay home and play with my friends in the neighborhood ravine, ride my bicycle and walk our dog, but they always insisted I attend my three-hour modeling class.

One day, I thought I had caught a lucky break. While driving me to class, my father suddenly began to perspire and writhe in pain. He pulled over to the side of the road, telling me that he thought he was passing a kidney stone. I quickly volunteered to accompany him to Emergency and "sacrifice" my modeling class but he would not hear of it.

Finally, after six months of torture, I graduated, posed for catalogues and did a few fashion runway-modeling jobs . My grandmother assured me that this experience would stand me in good stead, that it had taught me grace. "When you are older, this will set you apart, give you the self confidence boost you will need for your future. You will be able to carry yourself with poise in any situation and with anyone. You won't be just an ordinary girl."

When my aunt and I enter our balconied stateroom, our luggage is lined up by our beds. I quickly unpack our six suitcases and carry-on bags, new purchases and arrange our clothes and sundries, shoes and bags in the closet, drawers and dressing tables. The closet is bursting.

We freshen up and begin to explore, taking the ship's central staircase connecting the seven decks because the glass elevator is full of passengers on their way to the fourth deck where the theater and reception are located. On the next level, the aroma of espresso and sweet smell of freshly baked cookies wafts from the European cafe bar on the fifth deck mid ship. We work our way to the top after investigating the library, spa, hair salon, gym, workout room, art gallery, shops, six restaurants, casino and games room. An elevated running track loops above the open-air top deck and pool.

We spend most of the afternoon lounging at the pool, enjoying the sun and, in my aunt's case, an aperitif or two. perhaps three. When we return to our stateroom to shower and dress for dinner, our suitcases have disappeared, like magic. The cream and taupe matelassé bedspread has been removed and replaced with a new one, with the word "welcome" stitched on it. We find a large bowl of fresh fruit, Veuve Clicquot champagne and a bar fully stocked with bottled water, mineral water, soft drinks and a variety of juices. Artisan chocolate truffles wrapped up with a delicate soft pink ribbon fastened with a gold seal have been carefully arranged on the living room coffee table and bar area. Splayed across our beds is the ships information packet, the next day's itinerary, excursion options and a tourism brochure for Valencia, our first port stop.

Since excursions are included in the price of the cruise, we discuss tour options for Valencia. The organized tours depart at eight o'clock, far too early for my jet-lagged aunt, so we opt for a leisurely onboard breakfast and the shuttle into Valencia to explore the charming small city on our own. (The cruise line offers a roundtrip shuttle service between the port and the city centre every half hour for self-guided tours.)

Because I have never been to Valencia, I leave her in front of the shuttle stop and head to the port's tourist kiosk for directions to the old synagogue that my aunt wants to visit. "Please don't talk to anyone while I'm gone," I tell her. I know its my responsibility to keep her safe and she does not speak or understand Spanish. More importantly, she had been experiencing some memory lapses and confusion just weeks prior to our departure so I need to be extra vigilant.

The woman at the kiosk hands me a map, stars the street corner where we need to be dropped and tells me that the taxi fare from the port to the synagogue should be no more than fifteen euros. As I walk back to my aunt, I see that she is smiling and gesturing for me to hurry. "We've just missed the shuttle," she informs me, "but it's okay." I wave my hand at the taxi line but she stops me. "That nice man says we can share a taxi with him." She points to a man with a full grey beard and a curly salt-and-pepper ponytail. He is wearing a casual dove-grey shirt with rolled-up sleeves, shorts and tan leather sandals. Looks like a local, I tell myself.

Ignoring my aunt, I walk up to a taxi and show the driver the map indicating where we want to go. He nods. "Sixty euros." I laugh at this common ploy foisted on unsuspecting tourists. In my rusty Spanish, I begin negotiating, letting him know that his obvious attempt to overcharge us will not work, but he refuses to budge. Behind me, my aunt continues to insist that we share a taxi with "that man." Frustrated, I turn to her. "We are *not* getting into a taxi with a stranger. He could be a **terrorist**!"

"But he's nice," she implores. It takes all my self-restraint not to explode.

As I continue to deal with the driver, the "terrorist" walks over and pokes his head into the open passenger window. "Hey amigo," he says, and in perfect Spanish informs the driver that we are only going a short distance. "It's not nice to cheat tourists so take the fifteen euros and take us there." The terrorist turns to me and smiles. "Shall we share a taxi now, love?" he says in Australian-accented English.

Stunned and embarrassed, I slip into the back seat of the taxi with my aunt. "See! I told you he was nice," she says with a smug smile. I am praying that he is hearing-impaired and has missed my reference to him as a terrorist. Deciding it is best to avoid eye contact, I sit quietly in the back of the taxi and stare out the window.

"Do you want the driver to point out where the shuttle picks up in central Valencia to take us back to the ship?" he asks me from the front seat. Oh no, he is a passenger on our cruise! Now I am certain that he heard me call him a terrorist. He offers to split the taxi fare. Thoroughly humiliated, I merely nod in agreement.

When we pull up in front of the synagogue, the terrorist discovers he has no change so he asks me if I can pay the fare, promising to get some change right away to reimburse me. I agree and tip the driver. The terrorist wishes us a pleasant day and then struts off. Fuming, I turn to my aunt. "He has no intention of paying!" She laughs. "Forget about it. It's only a few euros. You're not paying for it anyway so let it go."

But I cannot. Thanks to the going-away gift from my girlfriends, my new bible on men, I am determined not to let anyone, particularly a man, take advantage of me ever again. "I'll hunt that man down like a dog to collect those seven and a half euros," I retort. My aunt merely shakes her head. She knows how generous I am normally and how ridiculous I sound.

After a quick visit to the *Synagogo mayor* in the Medieval Jewish Ghetto, we spend a lovely afternoon in the city, sightseeing and shopping for shoes, clothes and jewelry. Careful to keep my aunt hydrated and nourished so she does not pass out in the heat despite her robust constitution, I insist we stop mid-afternoon in the main piazza for a snack and a cappuccino, a European tradition I have come to appreciate. As we walk toward the centre of the piazza, I spy the terrorist flirting with a pretty young waitress at a small outdoor café. On a mission, I sprint toward him with steely resolve, my dozens of packages flapping around me. Behind me, I hear my aunt shouting, "What are you doing? Have you lost your mind?"

"Getting my money," I shout back as I approach the terrorist. "Hey amigo, you owe me seven and a half euros!" He grins sheepishly, admits he has forgotten and asks me if I'd be prepared to wait while he gets some change from the café. I wait, while my aunt remarks how out of character I am behaving. He returns promptly and hands me the money. I thank him, turn on my heels and walk away, feeling totally empowered. It is a decisive moment. I have finally stood up for myself! Victory, I think, beaming.

After a quick cappuccino, calamari salad and salted-caramel gelato, we take the shuttle back to the ship. The early October weather is still balmy so we change into swimsuits, grab our beach bags and head up to the top deck for a poolside drink and some late-afternoon sun. As we review the highlights of our day and discuss dinner plans, I catch sight of the terrorist jogging on the running track above us, glaring down at me. I feel queasy and try to ignore him.

"This evening we have 7:30 dinner reservations at the most formal restaurant so we need time to shower, dress and do our makeup," I remind my aunt. She asks me to bring her a last Bloody Mary and when I return with her drink (a "virgin," unbeknownst to her), I find the terrorist seated on my lounger next to her, oozing his terrorist-like charm. What is he up to now? After he introduces himself and enquires about our dinner plans, my aunt invites him to join us. Of course she does! I quickly remind her we that we have a pre-booked shared table and that there are no empty seats available. He understands and asks if we have plans for tomorrow in Palma de Mallorca, our next stop. "Perhaps we can have coffee or lunch together," he suggests. "Thank you, but we have plans," I respond dismissively, as I grab our bags and my aunt and flee to our stateroom.

Showered, perfumed and ready to step into a black fitted backless Moschino dress and black-patent Chanel heels, I check on my aunt. She is clad in colorful Pucci swirls accented with elaborate costume jewelry. I carefully apply her makeup. For a woman in her eighties, she looks formidable. While she puts on her dress shoes and organizes her evening bag, I dry my hair and wind my long reddish-gold curls around my finger to style them into something appropriate for evening. Just as we are about to leave, my aunt reminds me to take the little Chanel evening bag she gave me for my birthday. I fasten my three-stranded pearl necklace and as we walk down the corridor, I put on my diamond-and-pearl earrings and apply more red "man-catcher" lipstick, as my girlfriends call it. Normally, I bound up the stairs two by two but now is not the time, so we wait for the elevator like genteel ladies.

The intimate black-tie restaurant on the sixth floor is dimly lit, with seating for about seventy-five guests at round tables set for four or eight. We join a fascinating couple from London and soon become engrossed in conversation. When the white-garbed tuxedoed waiter pops the cork of our Dom Pérignon, we toast our new friendship and our Mediterranean voyage. Over a first course of fresh oysters and shrimp cocktail, there is more champagne, chatting and a discreet waiter reconfirming our entrées of lobster and veal tenderloin, both my favorites. I am so captivated by our new British friends that I fail to notice that the other diners are slipping out. Just as our entrées arrive, our friends get up and apologize for leaving before the end of the meal. Stunned, I ask if something I said is prompting their departure. They laugh and explain that a special concert, the premier performance of the cruise, is about to begin in the theater.

When I look around, I see that everyone has already left. My aunt insists that we leave as well. She complained of fatigue and shortness of breath that afternoon, I am worried that she is overdoing it and not eating enough so I strike a bargain with her: the concert after we finish our entrées.

An hour or so later, after a scrumptious, beautifully plated meal, we quietly slip inside the five-hundred-seat theatre where I spy two empty seats front row centre. If we are going to make an entrance, why not sit in the best seats? As we walk down the aisle, the room grows silent. The solo performer on stage is standing still, at attention, waiting for us to take our seats. I am embarrassed that our late arrival has interrupted his performance and even more embarrassed that he has chosen to draw attention to it. Horrified, I suddenly realize that the performer is none other than the terrorist. On cue and loud enough for everyone to hear, my aunt exclaims, "I told you he was nice!"

Once we are finally seated, the terrorist carries on with his classical-guitar performance. He plays two or three more pieces but I am so mortified that I barely pay attention. I fervently hope that he will leave the ship at the next port. After several rounds of thunderous applause and a standing ovation, the concert is finally over, to my great relief.

As I escort my aunt back to our stateroom, I beg her not to mention the terrorist. I leave her to get ready for bed and decide to walk off my humiliation. I stroll toward the shops on the fifth floor —and run headlong into the terrorist! I can barely look him in the eye. "How did you like the performance you interrupted?" "I loved it." "Do you have anything else you'd like to say to me?" he queries. I ponder a moment. "I have a tip for you!"

He looks at me curiously as I open my Chanel evening bag, count out seven and a half euros in coins and hand them to him. He laughs, his expression softening. He admits he was embarrassed not to have had any change but always intended to pay his share of the fare. "No more so than I am now," I say.

He invites me to join him for a glass of wine on the top deck. We spend the next two hours sharing our histories and stories, exchanging experiences of Europe, speaking in English, Italian and Spanish. We are the last two passengers awake on a ship of five hundred. As midnight approaches, we hug and bid each other good night. I wish the terrorist a wonderful day tomorrow in Palma. He tells me that he will be leaving the ship the day after next.

Barefoot, my high heels in hand, and a little tipsy after more Amarone than I am used to, I descend the main staircase, tiptoe into our stateroom, peel off my dress in the bathroom and fall into bed. As I drift off, I am not quite sure if the past few hours have been real or a lovely dream.

The next morning, as the sun shines brightly through the open sliding glass doors of our balcony, I feel someone nudging me. I look up to find my aunt standing over me, urging me get up and get dressed. "We are in Palma de Mallorca. Don't you have a friend here?" I nod. Groggy and hung over, I roll out of bed. Squinting in the light, I step onto the balcony and see the island of Mallorca in clear view.

A few days earlier at my aunt's insistence, I had sent my "friend" a quick email letting him know that I would be in Palma, without specifying where or when I would arrive. Given that our only encounter had been relatively brief six years earlier on a plane from Maui to San Francisco, I did not expect to hear back from him and I did not.

My aunt and I dress in light casual linen sundresses, grab a quick breakfast at the ship's coffee bar and disembark in Palma. As we step into a wide cobblestoned street just beyond the port, I hear a familiar voice shouting from across the street. "Heather, love, would you like to meet for lunch?" Before I can respond, a car pulls up directly in front of me, parks and the handsome driver jumps out, grinning. I suddenly feel flushed and faint.

"Gingy, you are here, my Gingy is here," my "friend" cries, as he embraces me and kisses me tenderly on the cheek. Overcome, I struggle to respond but only manage a feeble, "Yes." When he asks me to spend the day with him, I explain that my aunt and I are here only for the day. Caught between two men on either side of the street, I do not know what to do so I take the path of least resistance; I grab my aunt's hand and bid both men good-bye.

As we walk the winding road to the castle in central Palma, my aunt begins to scream. "That's him, isn't it? The marine biologist, the man you've been obsessed with for years." I smile, say nothing and keep walking. She knows it is him but does not pursue it, sensing my reluctance to say more. My aunt and I spend the rest of the day exploring this magical island where history melds with modernity.

Later that afternoon, I lie down exhausted in our stateroom while my aunt enjoys her end-of-day cocktail ritual on our balcony. My head spins as I mull over my morning encounter with the marine biologist, regretting a missed opportunity to spend time with a man to whom I am terribly attracted.

Change of Flight

The ocean has always fascinated and frightened me. Despite swimming lessons as a girl, I never became a confident swimmer. My son, on the other hand, took to the water from the time he was a baby. He loved spending hours splashing around the pool at our Maui condo. When he outgrew the pool, I took him to the beach. He swam, boogie-boarded, tried surfing and became an avid snorkeler. He would run to my lounge chair and excitedly recount the fish, turtles, coral and marine life he had seen underwater.

Somewhat frustrated by my fear of the ocean, I was thrilled when the Maui Ocean Center opened in March of 1998 because I could finally see what my son saw underwater. The two of us visited the Ocean Center often and used it for a school project about sharks. I was so impressed with the center that I wrote to the director, thanking him for creating this underwater world for non-snorkelers like me.

Ten years later, after my son began college, I decided to spend two months on my own in Maui to escape the worst of Toronto winter. On the last day of my stay, friends invited me to a party. When I declined because I was leaving that night, they insisted I delay my departure.

By then, Maui had been our winter home for more than a decade and I had established relationships with the agents at the United Airlines/Air Canada counter at the Kahului airport. The agents were now familiar with my pattern of last-minute flight changes to gain a few more precious vacation days in my island paradise. This time, the agent told me I could leave a day later if I were willing to reroute through San Francisco and endure a long layover. I grabbed it but decided to ditch the party.

The next evening, I drove with the convertible roof down under twinkling stars to the airport in Kahului where I returned the car to the rental office, proceeded through agricultural inspection and had the curbside porters tag my luggage and take it to the drop-off. After my name was called three or four times at the boarding gate (I was always the last to board, reluctant to leave until the very last possible moment), I wheeled my oversize, overweight carry-on bag into business class teary eyed. As I struggled to lift it into the overhead bin, a man from across the aisle offered to help but I shook my head in silence, ashamed to let him see me sobbing. When I realized that there was no one else in my row, I scooted over to the window and fastened my seatbelt for takeoff. I was still weeping as I looked out at the tarmac, heartbroken to be leaving Maui yet again.

After serving glasses of sparkling water in tall flutes and warm rolled hand towel to me and the gentleman across the isle ironically the only two passengers in business class, the flight attendants strapped themselves into the jump seats facing us. One attendant asked the gentleman about his time on Maui. He explained that he had been working on "a little project" for three months while in Maui. She probed further, asking him about his final destination, and I overheard him say that he was flying to Palma de Mallorca. That piqued my interest, as did his dark swarthy good looks, his Missoni wool scarf and, most of all, his accent that I could not quite place (unusual given my proficiency in several languages). Was he European ... American ... Argentinian? None of those. Intrigued, I listened more intently.

While the flight attendants prepared a light dinner for us in the galley, he put on tiny headphones and began listening to a miniature MP3 player. He caught me staring and offered me the headphones with a gesture. When I did not react, he unbuckled his seatbelt and made his way across the aisle to sit next to me, placing the headphones on my ears so I could hear the smoky sensual sounds of Spanish guitar. "You seemed upset when you boarded. This will calm you."

Then it clicked. "*Ani medaberet ivrit*" — I speak Hebrew — I told him. Raised in a Conservative Jewish home with Orthodox Jewish grandparents, I attended Hebrew school twice a week after school and on Sunday mornings from the age of six until my confirmation at nineteen. I could effortlessly read a Hebrew prayer book and still carry on a very basic conversation in that language.

He grinned, took my hand in his, stroking it in an effort to calm me down and we talked nonstop throughout the night. I learned that he was a marine biologist associated with the Maui Ocean Center. Intrigued by this fascinating, gentle natured man, I was disappointed that our time together was over when we landed in San Francisco in the early morning. We disembarked, wished each other well and went our separate ways. He was off to the international terminal for his flight to London and connecting flights to Barcelona and his final destination of Palma de Mallorca. I had four hours until boarding for my flight bound for Toronto from the domestic terminal.

Groggy and caffeine deprived, I rolled my heavy carry-on down the hallway, stopped at the first café along the way and sat down at a small table with my coffee. A few minutes later, I felt two hands gently squeeze my shoulders. Startled, I looked up to find the marine biologist standing over me, smiling. "Why would I go to the other terminal when I could spend more time with you, Gingy?" I was thrilled. We drank coffee, laughed and exchanged more details about our families and our Maui experiences.

Time seemed to speed by and before I was ready to let him go, he reached into his stylish European wallet and pulled out a fish-shaped business card. "My phone number and email is on this. We will keep in touch. You will come to Palma and stay with me, yes?" Stunned, I muttered a simple "Yes." When he stood up to leave, he bent over and kissed me tenderly but with warm intention.

Despite the fact that Palma had never been on my must-see list, I was sure that I would get there one day. I also expected that our paths would cross again, perhaps in Maui, since he spent a month each year on various projects at the Ocean Center.

I sat for a few more minutes after we parted, nursing my coffee. Then my cell phone rang. It was a girlfriend checking to see if I was on my way back to Toronto. I told her about meeting the marine biologist. She was a journalist and the moment I mentioned his name, she began screaming. "I've met him. He's fantastic. He's perfect for you! Go get him!" I laughed as she urged me to run after him, not to let him get away. No need, I thought. One day he will come to me ... if it is meant to be.

Introducing the Terrorist

When the phone rings in our stateroom, I am jolted out of my daydream. "Absolutely he can join us," I overhear my aunt say. Not knowing to whom she is speaking or to what she is agreeing, I motion to her to pass me the phone. "There is a gentleman here, Ms. Heather, asking if he can join you tonight for dinner," the maître d' explains. Confused, I ask for clarification. Then the terrorist comes on the line, apologizing for creating a fuss. "Impossible," I tell him. "Our table and the restaurant is fully booked." My aunt rips the phone out of my hands and instructs the terrorist to cancel our reservation and make a new one for eight o'clock at any onboard restaurant that can accommodate the three of us. Then she quickly hangs up.

I am furious and refuse to go to dinner with her. My aunt reminds me that she promised my girlfriends to find me a man on this trip. Begrudgingly, I acquiesce but send her off ahead to meet him. She lectures me, making me promise to wear something beautiful and not to be too late.

When I finally arrive at the Italian restaurant, the terrorist, to my surprise is dressed in a black silk tuxedo-like suit; he cleans up quite nicely I say to myself. He takes my hand and guides me towards the back of the restaurant, through glass sliding doors onto the outdoor deck of the ship. A small table covered in crisp white linen set with a vase of fresh fuchsia-and-white flowers placed in the center of the table, a bottle of Tuscan red and two wine glasses awaits us. He gestures to a seat with the best view and pulls out my chair like a real gentleman. Chivalry is still alive and well I am reminded. We drink a glass of wine and when our indoor table is ready, we join my aunt who has been waiting patiently in the dining room for dinner. After polishing off her veal entrée in record time, my aunt informs us that she is, tired and going to bed. She hugs us both. "You two enjoy your evening and be sure to stay out very late!" The terrorist asks the waiter to serve our dessert and *digestif* at our private outdoor table.

That evening we begin to build a bond of friendship as the terrorist starts to open up. He is melancholy despite his cheerful demeanor. "I am heartbroken. The girl I intended to marry told me she no longer wants to see me. That it's over."

I am desperately trying to think of something consoling and wise to offer but simply say, "I don't understand why you are so blue. The world is full of girls and she is only one girl." He smiles and squeezes my hand in gratitude.

As we talk and sip vin santo into the wee hours of the night, the ship sails into the port of Monaco. It is a magical backdrop with its multi million dollar yachts dotting the marina and looks like a screen shot from Fellini film. There is a light mist in the air which creates an ethereal quality to the entire scene. I have no idea what tomorrow will bring but at that moment I know that I will never forget this extraordinary evening. I suspect that this is just the beginning of something, although I am not sure of exactly what.

After the terrorist leaves the ship, the rest of the cruise passes by in a blur. I concentrate on looking after my aunt, making sure that she enjoys every moment without getting fatigued. She is having a wonderful time but every night I change into the silk La Perla nightgown I had saved for this special trip, climb into bed and pull the blankets tight around my ears in an effort to ward off the air-conditioned chill my aunt requires to ease her breathing. Because of my sensitivity to cold, for a few nights I sleep on a lounge chair on the balcony, where the night air even though it's now fall in Europe is much warmer. I enjoy waking up in the middle of the night adrift in the middle of the sea, not anchored anywhere but headed to a new and perhaps exciting adventure. There is a certain freedom in not being rooted in one place; for now.

An Exit Full of Roadblocks

As soon as we return to Toronto, I begin to prepare my house for sale, arranging for touch-ups to baseboards and some minor bathroom repairs. I dispose of my possessions so lovingly collected over the years on my travels—the multiple sets of Italian dishes, the thick Oriental rugs and the Louis XVI chairs and settee shipped home from a French chateau. I give some pieces to my son to furnish his apartment, store others and send the best items out for consignment. My son chides me that I've provided him with enough to set up his house times two. When I offer him a set of hors d'oeuvre plates that he can use to serve an "amuse bouche", he rolls his eyes, shakes his head. Ah yes, a reminder to simplify.

At the same time, I continue to work furiously to complete my various design projects for clients: gutting and renovating, choosing color schemes, sourcing carpets and furnishings, selecting artwork and designing bathrooms and kitchens. My clients have faith in me so I work diligently to deliver as promised, despite Murphy's Law. Suppliers often disappoint and make mistakes, as they often do but it is my job to make it right. My stock response to any client request, no matter how outlandish, is "My pleasure; it is not a problem." This makes for long hours and seven-day workweeks—a pace I have maintained for years.

Each time the doorbell rings at home, I cringe, wondering if it is another bill collector in pursuit of my absent partner. His bills are substantial and, as they erode my savings, I work even harder, resolved that nothing will prevent me from leaving behind the city of my birth, the city that constantly reminds me of the pain and loss I have experienced throughout my life.

Not surprisingly, my health is compromised. At my last doctor's appointment, after complaining of inflammation that often makes it difficult to bend my fingers or fit into my shoes, I ask for the game plan. The doctor shakes her head. "There's nothing more we can do for you, Heather, unless you take steroids for the rest of your life, which you have refused to do."

Shocked, I realize that I have to take charge of my own health and help myself. Prednisone was the drug my doctor prescribed to get things under control and just the mere mention of that drug brought back horrible memories of my mother jumping out of her skin, terribly bloated and uncomfortable when she was taking them to deal with cancer. Instead of using medication, I decide to change my diet and eliminate all gluten and dairy, convinced they have contributed to some weight gain. I begin exercising myself back to health. I make time to work out with a personal trainer at a local gym for several hours a day and begin twice-weekly aerobic classes. This is a new initiative for me—doing something solely for myself—and I am nothing if not determined. By the time I land in Maui a few months later, I have shrunk my size four body to a zero, a size I have maintained ever since. The next time I see my Toronto doctor (by then I have been living in Maui for a few years), she is stunned to find no sign of inflammation. "Only you could do this," she says, shaking her head in amazement. "Keep it up!"

Unfortunately, selling my Toronto house is taking much longer than I expected despite its pristine condition and highly desirable neighborhood. My agent has not been able to engineer the kind of bidding war that has seen other properties in my area sell well above the asking price or even produce a credible buyer. When her listing agreement expires, I let her go.

Then, three days before Christmas, the worst ice storm in living memory hits Toronto. Massive power outages throw the city, and my area, into chaos. This does not help my selling prospects! Without an alternate heat source, my house soon grows bitterly cold, causing my hands and feet to swell due to my autoimmune condition. Fortunately, a friend offers at the last minute to whisk me away to the Turks and Caicos for a week's reprieve. I return to frozen gas lines and no telephone or internet service. After I attend to these problems, I immediately hire a new agent.

In the New Year, huge snowfalls and bone-chilling cold plague Toronto and the entire East Coast. I buy multiple bags of salt to keep the walkway, driveway and stairs to the front door clear of ice for potential buyers. When all of my worldly possessions have been either packed, given away or sold, I can wait no longer and finally board the plane to Maui in February. Despite my Toronto home's designer touches, move-in condition and highly coveted location, no offers have been forthcoming. The housing market has stalled and I begin to fear that despite the Herculean effort I have made to move to Maui, I might be forced to return to Toronto. In the end, my house sells in April, at a price much lower than I had hoped but, by then, I am committed to never return.

When I arrive at the hotel in Maui, I feel as though I can breathe again. I have spent months at this resort every winter since coming to Maui on my own and I know almost everyone who works on the property. They are so welcoming that I feel safe and cared for there. They treat me like *Ohana*. Because I am a long-stay guest, they note all my preferences and my suite reflects their attention to detail.

A New Agenda

Unlike previous years when I was here on vacation, I now have an agenda: to recover my health, find a house, make Maui my home and then be open and receptive to meeting a man with whom I can finally have a loving , long term relationship.

My first priority is to put a roof over my head. I identify two areas in am interested in living, contact several rental agents and discover, to my surprise, that the rental market is as difficult here as in Toronto. "Sorry, there is absolutely nothing to lease in your price range and very little for sale," they all tell me, eager to abandon a fruitless quest.

Some agents never show up to scheduled appointments. I have no choice but to take matters into my own hands.

One day, skimming *The Maui News*, I notice an ad for a house to lease in my preferred area. I immediately call the listing agent to view the house. Since she is driving and unable to take down my number, she suggests I drive by on my own to take a look at the exterior. When I agree but tell her I still need to see the interior, she reminds me that it is Friday afternoon and instructs me to call her back on Monday. I am dumbfounded. In what universe do real estate agents not work on weekends? Should have been my first clue that this island is "unique". I drive by the house after she texts me the code to gain entry into this gated neighborhood. I like what I see on the exterior and on the street and call the agent back on Monday to arrange a visit. To her chagrin, she is forced to change her plans to fit me into her busy schedule.

The interior of the house is very, very dirty and neglected-looking, with old furniture in a mishmash of unattractive styles. The double-car garage is packed with tools, a large safe that could store a body upright and a heap of useless junk. Undaunted by its unappealing condition, I can envision how it could look once I clear out the owner's things and furnish and redecorate it. After all, I have gutted and redesigned a dozen homes in Toronto in the past year alone. As I walk through the house, the agent sits in the family room ignoring me, fixated on her cell phone. She does not look up once until I say, "I'll take it!"

I sign the lease and give the agent a large deposit and an additional security deposit. The move-in date is the first of the month, a few weeks away. This gives me time to purchase linens, towels, kitchen essentials, cleaning supplies, basics like lightbulbs (none of the dozens of pot lights have working bulbs), lamps and food staples. I pack up my belongings in the hotel suite, move into the house and, with the help of a housekeeper and her husband, scour every nook and cranny of this four-bedroom, five-bathroom, thirty two hundred square-foot house.

A few days later, my cell phone rings as I am pushing a shopping cart around Safeway, the neighborhood supermarket. It is the agent calling, requesting a meeting. When I tell her that I am shopping to stock the fridge, she breaks the news. The owner has good friends from Texas whom he promised could stay in his house if they ever came to Maui. They want to come in a few days for three weeks with their five children. I start to laugh, assuming she is joking. "So sorry, but the owner has promised, he went to college with his friend and wants to offer his family the house, so would you mind going back to the hotel and moving in again a month from now?"

I am beside myself. How could they have taken my certified cheques, countersigned the lease and not given me an inkling of such an arrangement? "That is totally unacceptable," I retort. Undeterred, she then asks if I could arrange for a couple of suites for this family at the hotel at my preferential rate, an alternative option she could propose to the homeowner. I am stunned by her audacity "No way, you can't be serious" I reply.

I hang up, walk to the back of the supermarket and begin to weep. Why is everything always so difficult? Just once I would like things to be easy, or at least easier. I think for a moment and come up with an idea. I drive to the real estate office to confront the agent in person. When I arrive, I discover she is not there but the agent manning reception is happy to help me.

"I'm Canadian so forgive me if this seems like a silly question, but is it customary to sign a lease, provide a certified cheque for rent and security deposit, move in and then be asked to vacate for a period of time to accommodate the owner's guests? Is this common practice in Hawaii?"

She looks at me, perplexed. "I've never heard of such a thing in all my years in real estate. Which property is it?" I tell her but ask her simply to let my agent know that I want to see her.

Within minutes, I receive a scathing call from the listing agent. "The owner is very private. He will be very upset when he finds out that you've discussed his lease with the agency."

How private can he be since he has left drawers full of family photos, old bills and his personal belongings in all the cupboards? He has even refused to let me switch the telephone and other utilities into my name, insisting that they stay in his. This makes no sense at all. Again, another clue that things on this island are a little unusual!

As it happens, I had planned to visit my son in Toronto and then spend several summer months in Europe. If I am going to be forced out of my newly leased home, I may as well turn the owner's need to accommodate his friends to my advantage. "I'll give them a month provided the owner gives me two additional months rent free. You have greatly inconvenienced me and now I have nowhere to live. Take it or leave it!" The agent promises to discuss my proposal with the owner. A few hours later, an addendum to the lease is ready for me to pick up. The owner has agreed to my terms.

I carefully wrap and store all my new purchases for the house in a friend's garage, make final travel arrangements and put my housekeeper and the agent in touch with one other. I may have agreed to temporarily vacate but I insist that my now spotless home be in the same condition when I return at the end of the summer.

Not long after the owner's guests leave, I check my email from Europe and find a disturbing message from my housekeeper. "Miss Heather, I went to the house to clean but it is impossible. I cannot clean it in one or two days. It is filthy!" She describes how the guests have left every pot and pan dirty, the kitchen counters and sinks full of leftover food, the beds and bathroom floors full of sand, the towels wet and mildewed, and food wrappers everywhere.

Frustrated and angry, I forward her message to the agent, instructing her to meet my housekeeper at the house, assess the condition and pay her whatever it takes to make the house shine again. "I have bent over backwards to accommodate the owner, his friends and you, so make this right." She assures me she will.

I fly home from Europe at the end of the summer, arriving in the late afternoon. Exhausted from the long trip, I unpack my cosmetics, a nightgown and some sundries. Most of my luggage, filled with designer clothes, shoes, hand-painted dishes and regional foods, will arrive later by UPS. I plug in a cordless telephone I find in the office and charge my cell phone. After I take a cursory look around, it is obvious that more cleaning will be needed to measure up to my standards. Tomorrow, I tell myself, I will start cleaning, pick up the new things I stored and start buying some basic furniture to replace the dingy pieces here.

I brush my teeth in the master bathroom and apply a hydrating facial masque, a sample I picked up at Kiko, a popular Italian cosmetic chain. I place a towel on the bare mattress, lie down and fall into a deep sleep, awakening early the next morning to the sounds of chirping birds outside my bedroom window. My first night back in my new Maui home—check; my first morning in my new Maui home—double check.

Feeling empowered, I grab the cordless phone from the office and call my son in Toronto to let him know I arrived and survived. I sit on the ugly stained off-white sectional sofa and shudder at the ancient end tables, the mismatched Asian lamps with torn silk shades, the oversize television mounted on the opposite wall and the "artwork" of stretched and mounted Tahitian sarongs, random prints and some scary-looking African inspired wooden plaques.

When my son finally answers, I try to make myself more comfortable, cringing as I sit on the lounger section of the soiled sofa. Out of the corner of my eye, I detect motion down the hallway between the master bedroom and the kitchenette leading into the family room. Suddenly, a huge black rat scurries up the side of the sofa, runs past me and burrows into the crease between two sofa cushions. I screech, drop the phone on the tiled marble floor and take flight, flinging open the sliding glass doors and almost flying out to the patio and pool area.

The house next door is under construction. My screams are so loud that, before I can catch my breath, two well-built construction workers hurdle over the dust fence separating our properties to my rescue. They come to an abrupt halt and start chuckling.

"Get it out!" I cry. "Why are you laughing? Take it out!" When I point to the sofa in the family room, I catch a glimpse of my reflection in the glass doors. I am pink from head to toe—pink facial masque, pink nightgown and pink socks. Never mind, I tell myself. "There is a rat in that sofa. Get rid of it. Please!"

The two men respectfully remove their construction boots and begin pulling apart the sofa. "What are you doing?" I can barely contain my exasperation.

"We are looking for the rat."

"Take the sofa," I scream, "not just the rat! I don't want it or anything else in this room!"

They must think I have lost my mind but they load all the family room furniture into their truck and drive off.

An hour later, I am standing in a large empty room with a bucket of hot soapy water and bleach, wiping down every surface; floors, walls and doors. I call the agent and explain that I just shared a sofa with a huge black rat who has probably been living here for quite some time. She agrees with my prudent decision to dispose of the furniture. Reluctantly, she admits that the house has had a rodent problem but that a monthly contract with a local pest control company is finally in place. "Perhaps now would be a good time to call them," I suggest.

The next morning, there is a knock at the door. A stocky man with a crooked smile and a few missing teeth greets me warmly and hands me his business card. "I'm John, the exterminator. I hear you have a rat."

"Not anymore. But you and I will become best friends, John. We will be the dream team that keeps this house rodent and pest free, so give me you cell phone number, your office phone number, your email address, your home address, your wife's name, your children's names, your entire immediate family's coordinates and any other information that may be useful for us to bond." I could sense immediately that this kind, gentle man would become part of a small group, my island *Ohana*, on whom I would be able to count to keep me safe.

Three years later, the owner unexpectedly decides to sell, offers me the house to purchase at an outrageous price and I decline now familiar with all the issues that plague this house and what it would cost to fix them. The appliances are all in need of repair or upgrading, the electrical was not all up to code in some areas and the house had been neglected terribly until I moved in. So now I am forced to vacate the house that I have transformed into an immaculate designer home worthy of its upscale neighborhood and lofty price tag. Julia and several other girlfriends from Toronto have reveled in its comfort and amenities during their extended winter visits.

In the final week of my lease, I follow to the letter the owner's exit instructions to put back everything exactly the way it was. After packing up all my belongings, I singlehandedly drag the owner's original hideous, shabby furniture (which I had shrink wrapped and stored in the garage, but for the family room furniture) back into the house. I wash every surface and plug, plaster and paint over every nail hole I made to hang my paintings before rehanging all of the owner's artwork in the exact spots in each room where it originally hung. I put back the tattered dirty mock Persia carpets and line up his grimy worn kitchen appliances on the counter. I spend my final day doing an industrial cleaning and white-glove inspection on a house I have been forced to return to a dated looking mismatched mess.

As I finish emptying the kitchen pantry, a big black rat scurries out from under a cabinet. My mother used to say, "You finish the way you begin so make sure that you are happy with the beginning." The sage (a dear Maui friend and my spiritual guru) would have told me that this is a message. It is clearly time to go!

CHAPTER 2

FIRENZE, MI AMORE MIO

Firenze (Florence) first captured my heart thirty years ago when I accompanied my husband on a business trip. Three decades have passed and am here again, on my own, and enjoying every moment.

On the second morning at my boutique hotel, I take my cappuccino into the garden to avoid the throng in the breakfast room. As I read an international Italian newspaper, only two pages long—clearly, Italy is not overly concerned with world events that occur outside of the country—a woman approaches me. "Are you a producer, a director, screen writer or an author?" she asks in an Australian accent.

Unsure why she is enquiring, I confess to simply traveling in Italy. She introduces herself and explains that she is in Florence to attend a prestigious professional writing workshop. We chat for a bit and as she leaves the garden she turns and asks, "Do you write?" I feel like I have been struck by lightning, wondering how she knew. All I do is write, scribbling notes, thoughts, stories and incidents that I tuck away in the hope of one day weaving them together into something worthwhile. For years, I have been writing much as I pray, in private, convinced that whatever I have to say will not have much importance, make an impact or be of value to anyone.

Then it hits me. Just as I have raised my son to believe, *if you can see it, you can be it*, what really matters is what my writing means to *me*!

From that brief serendipitous encounter with a woman at a writers' conference, I am reminded that we all have the strength and wisdom to realize ourselves if we make the effort. Only you can write our own story! I can curate my own life!

Italy's Language is More Than Italian

From year to year, I forget just how Italy works—or does not work, by some standards. After touring a fair bit of Italy, I wonder why I bother judging the country by North American standards at all.

Italians are endearingly unique! They are administratively *particolari* (rules constantly change without notice), directionally challenged and disorganized but it all seems so *non importante*, of no concern whatsoever. It all seems woven into the fabric of their culture and lifestyle.

Words are not their true or ultimate form of communication. The gestures and actions accompanying the words, even a non-response, are what inform the meaning. As I study Italian with my outrageously handsome young tutor (who cannot quite understand my fascination with his language), I realize that I am better off listening and observing behavior than concentrating on the words.

This has forced me to adopt a different strategy to deal with what frustrated me initially. It has helped me realize what is truly important. We North Americans thrive on order, on a prescribed plan, and we like to control every aspect of our lives and the lives of those around us. For us, control is as essential as breathing.

But here in Italy, if a glitch means that people take a little longer to arrive at their destination—if a shop unexpectedly closes without notice for a wedding celebration, or a car stops in the middle of the strada so the driver can speak with a friend while holding up traffic—Italians readjust, find an alternative and do not make a fuss over such a slight inconvenience. Everyone here is more concerned with the perfect espresso, a warm greeting or cleaning their home, shop or even the streets, which to my delight seems to be Italy's national pastime.

Lifestyle is key for Italians, much as it is for Hawaiians. Italy is a country scented with floral Dolce & Gabbana perfume, Fabuloso cleaning detergent and the rich aroma of espresso—a heady combination that makes the country truly special, an anomaly. Italians revel in the details and acknowledge them with animated gestures.

Yesterday, a friend invited me for an afternoon "refresher," which I assumed was a cold shower or a swim but to my delight turned out to be freshly extracted peach juice over crushed ice, served with a kumquat garnish and a chilled spoon, garnished with a white Dendrobium orchid. With a series of graceful gestures, my dear *amico* instructed the bartender to prepare my refresher by touching his mouth, pointing to the shiny chrome designer juicer and waving to the garden. My handsome tutor did not teach me this!

Ah ... language. I am learning! I hope I do not end up with a roasted pigeon and a train ticket to Palermo instead of a cappuccino and *cantucci* when I use my newly acquired skills of the gesture! *Mi auguro buona fortuna!*

The Art of Traveling Alone As a Woman in Italy

After many years of traveling *sola* in Italy, I have compiled a list of what has worked for me. I keep it in what I call my "I deserve La Perla lingerie" drawer.

Do's

*Carry at all times: a photocopy of your passport, a credit card, lipstick in a man-catcher shade of red, a cell phone with a local Sim card, a bottle of water or, even better, Limoncello.

*Place your baggage cart next to a strong-looking middle-aged, preferably handsome, Italian man when picking up your luggage at the airport carousel. He will offer to load your bags onto your cart. In fact, he will insist upon it.

*Keep a Venetian fan handy for use in art galleries, churches and synagogues in the summer. They never have air conditioning. You can expire without one!

*Walk with an air of confidence even when you feel hopelessly lost and forlorn.

*Linger over breakfast and read a foreign-language newspaper even if you have no idea what you are reading. It will force your brain cells to re-engage from the vacation fog.

*Treat yourself to lunch or dinner at the best restaurant *once*, and savor each and every bite.

*Introduce yourself to the manager of every hotel at which you stay and insist on not being referred to as "Madame.

*Order a white-peach Bellini every chance you get.

*Dance when you hear music playing in the street, no matter who is watching.

*Find the best hair salon and go at least twice. This is the best source for local gossip and information. Plus, you will emerge looking Italian chic.

*Make every effort to speak the language, gestures included.

*Smile from the deepest part of your heart at everyone you meet. People will see the joy. It will lift their spirits, yours as well.

*When you enter a store, introduce yourself to the shopkeeper and ask their name. This usually takes them by surprise and forges a connection. It is not what you purchase but where and from whom. That means everything!

*Try something totally unplanned or random. Change course at least once and embrace the mystery and adventure of it.

*Eat local cherry tomatoes like candy while sightseeing. They are so sweet and juicy. Nature's candy.

*In your hotel suite, sleep in the middle of the king-size bed and enjoy both *cantucci* left by the turndown service.

*On the train, keep your purse and belongings close to you at all times.

*Order and enjoy black truffles in season.

*Feel free to weep openly at concerts and operas, artwork and scenery, or whenever you feel overcome by beauty. Remember that this is *your* journey.

Don'ts

*Don't ask an Italian man for directions. He will send you anywhere but where you want to go. Misdirection is a national sport!

*Don't correct people if they assume your husband is dead. Italians seem more comfortable with widows in their forties and fifties than single women that age!

*Don't order an *espresso freddo* (iced coffee). You will end up with a hot espresso accompanied by a single ice cube in a bowl!

*Don't worry about what anyone says or thinks about you. Remember that you are special!

*Don't walk on the cobblestones clad streets all day in high heels.

*Don't accept an *aperitivo* from anyone named Mario or Antonio unless you are saying "yes" to sex.

*Don't miss a single opportunity to enjoy gelato and try every single flavor!

*Don't rely on an Italian to order dinner for you unless you want six courses—a *primo*, a *secondo*, three *contorni*, a *dolce*, an espresso and a *digestivo*—and *poi*, we begin again, *sì*?

*Don't drive to, or in, Naples.

*Don't miss the opera.

*Don't forget to take photos every day.

*Don't purchase from street vendors in major cities unless you want goods made anywhere but in Italy.

*Don't take "no" for an answer. Find a way to arrive at a "yes."

*Don't let the hotel do your laundry. Hand wash and hang it outside to air dry. If necessary, use a hair dryer, which you won't need for your hair since you've already booked an appointment at the salon.

*Don't stress if you can't connect to Wi-Fi. Live in the moment and leave the rest for later.

I think I will tuck this list back into my lingerie drawer for now.

You Learn Best When Things Go Off the Rails

At eight o'clock, I get a *bonjourno* wake-up call. Today, I plan to go to the beach via local train, which stops at every small town along the way. I have checked online and learned that the closest beach by train from Florence is Viareggio, a hundred or so kilometers away and takes approximately one hour and twenty minutes to arrive there.

Viareggio is a classic seaside resort with architectural roots in the early 1900s. Its wide promenade, the Passeggiata Margherita, sprawling sidewalk cafés, ice-cream parlors and private beach clubs make it the Tuscan Riviera's most popular beach resort. Viareggio also has other attractions: a carnival museum displaying miniature reproductions of the city's allegorical floats, a museum of musical instruments and an archaeological museum. In the nearby town of Torre del Lago, Puccini is honored in a museum housed in the composer's former lakeside residence, Villa Puccini. But today I intend to bypass all of these and head for the beach. The shallow water is perfect for kids—and for me, timid swimmer that I am. The beach is long enough to find a spot even if crowded, although renting a cabana for the day will cost me a king's ransom.

The ride from Florence will deposit me at a train station a half kilometer from the beach. For me, this day trip is like getting back on the horse after a fall. I refuse to give into the trepidation of traveling alone into the unknown. I am determined to do this!

Return to Italy

Although I know that local Italian trains are slow, unreliable and, more often than not, late, but I was not prepared for what ensued on the northbound local train from Rome to the beach in Ladispoli two years earlier. I can recall every detail.

By then, I had a great deal of experience traveling in Europe and had no fear moving around Italy on my own. I knew how to avoid the *zingare*, pickpockets and beggars. I learned to never carry my passport, only a photocopy. My purse contained either my atm card or my credit card, never both, and never more than a few euros.

As much as I love the adrenaline rush of a large sophisticated city like Rome, I still longed for the sea, the mountains and nature and decided to treat myself to a day at the beach. So, with my beach bag packed and zipped, I ran across the street from my hotel and bounded down the stairs two at a time to catch the early morning train. The concierge at the hotel suggested I take my cell phone to capture the beautiful countryside along the way. Instead, I tucked my brand new mini iPad into my beach bag, thinking it would do double duty for photos and my daily journal writing.

On the bustling train platform, I squeezed my way into the ticket queue. As the train came to a halt on the platform, I rushed up, boarded and grabbed a seat.

I've learned that you need to be quick once the train doors open in the station. After several stops, a blue-uniformed conductor walked through the cars, punching a hole in everyone's ticket—a little late, I thought, given the distance already traveled but I reminded myself that this was Italy, where everything often seemed a little, shall we say, dysfunctional.

I pulled out my iPad and became engrossed in journaling about this inefficient system of checking tickets. After a few more stops, I glanced up and noticed that the crowd in the car had thinned. The revelation came too late. One stop later, I was the only woman, the lone Caucasian, in a car with a group of swarthy looking men. Suddenly, I was surrounded. Someone began tugging at my hair. Another man sat close, too close, beside me, his breath heavy on my neck. He reached over and gripped my iPad. "*Donnez le moi*," he ordered in what I recognized as a North African accent. Frantically searching out the empty car with my eyes, I realized that I had no choice. I silently handed over my iPad and held my breath, praying the next stop was close. As soon as we came to a halt, the men rushed off the train.

Furious, my only thought was how to recover my new iPad. Fortunately, I had registered it on the app that tracks its location. The next day I had a flight booked to Tunisia.

As I walked through Carthage International Airport, it hit me; beyond my impulsive flight, I had no game plan. The signage was in French so I could at least navigate my way to the taxi stand outside the terminal. Now what? As I crawled into the back seat of the taxi, the French part of my brain fired and I instructed the driver to take me to the *poste de police*. I will start there, I decided, since I had the location of my stolen iPad.

At the Tunis police station, a disgruntled *gendarme* sauntered over from behind a desk, giving me the once over before uttering a word. I, on the other hand, began babbling and stammering like a petulant schoolgirl, explaining that I had come to reclaim my new iPad, stolen on a train in Italy and tracked to a location in Tunisia. In response, the officer physically turned me around and marched me back to the entrance. "Go back to Italy, *Mademoiselle*. There is nothing for you here." I put up my hand to interrupt him but he simply repeated slowly and emphatically, "*Retournez en Italie.*" Like magic, a taxi was waiting for me curbside. When the driver dropped me at the airport, he refused to let me pay; the police had apparently taken care of the fare.

This was a first for me, a lesson that sometimes no matter how tenacious I am, no matter how hard I try, there are some things I must let go. I used to think that "no" meant try again later but that day I learned that it often means walk away ... and *do not* look back! That's the lesson.

Getting off Track

Two years later, I am again off to the beach on my own on a local train in Italy. I carry a small bag with my swimsuit, towel wallet and cell phone, (no iPad this time) and walk the few short blocks to the Florence train station. Figuring out how to purchase a train ticket to Viareggio is more complicated that an appliance manual but with perseverance, luck and assistance from a local teenage boy, I manage it. I spend the trip reading, enjoying the scenery and studying the map marking all the stops along the way.

When the train arrives in Viareggio, I walk up the stairs and into the sunlight. I find myself on a street festooned with dozens and dozens of multicolored triangular flags. Old-fashioned lampposts border the street where tables covered in red-and-white-checked cloths offer household items, clothing and food for sale. I feel like I have been transported back to the 1940s. Time seems to have stopped in this charming but quirky seaside resort town.

On the corner I spot a sign indicating the way to the beach. I walk a half-dozen blocks to a wide boulevard where I find the first signs of modernity—the large and familiar retail chains with outlets in all of the country's major cities. Just beyond the boulevard, another sign indicates the beach ahead. When I finally step onto a pebbly beach, I see an endless array of bright orange and striped blue-and-white umbrellas dotting the long shoreline.

No one is in the water. Odd, I think, but I quickly change into my swimsuit in the private cabana I have rented for the day. The little change room might be somewhat antiquated and not particularly well appointed but at least I can store my personal items safely and, despite my petite stature, reach the shampoo and soap dispenser in its stall shower.

I take a quick dip in thigh deep water that is surprisingly cold. Then I remember that it is only June. When I look around, I realize that everyone has come to the beach to sun themselves and socialize; there is no swimming involved. I spend the day lounging on my beach chair, enjoying somewhat of a show. The Italians slather themselves in suntan oil while wearing enough gold necklaces, rings, bracelets, watches and anklets to fill the shops that line the Ponte Vecchio. No one seems bothered by the *zingare* combing the beach for buyers to sell their Turkish towels, knock-off sunglasses and kitschy hair clips. The Italians simply wave off the gypsies when approached.

When it is time to head back to Florence, I quickly change, load up my bag and walk back to the train station. I suppose I should have paid closer attention and noted the platform number when I arrived in Viareggio, but no matter. I am sure I will find someone who can give me directions back to Florence. Luckily, a young girl offers to help me buy my return ticket and guides me through the machine's instructions, since train stations no longer have ticket agents, only automated ticket machines. I hand her a few euros for her help, wait on platform No. 4 and jump on when the train pulls in and opens its doors.

I make myself comfortable, pick up a local newspaper left on the seat across from mine and struggle with the Italian. Although my Italian is quite serviceable, perfecting it is an ongoing process. An hour passes and I lose track of the train stops. Then another hour goes by. By now, surely we must be approaching Santa Maria Novella, my Florence train stop. I glance up and see that we are pulling into a station so I grab my bag and wait in front of the double doors. When the train finally pulls into the station, I am shocked at the sign: Siena. I am already far south of Florence, obviously heading in the wrong direction! When the doors finally open, I rush off the train. Momentarily flustered, unsure how this has happened, I take a deep breath and decide to do as the Italians do when they are confused or in a quandary—head to a little caffe order an espresso and a couple of pistachio *cantucci* and regroup.

Siena is one of my favorite towns so I decide to turn this mishap to my advantage. It is fresh porcini season in Italy and I recall a delicious meal of *bistecca* with fresh earthy porcini at the Tre Cristi restaurant a few summers back. The maître d' had seated me next to a man and his daughter from London and we immediately began to chat. They were heading to Florence the next morning to register the daughter at the prestigious Florence Design Academy. "Their interactive design program takes you to see the city's period and modern architecture, its artisans and manufacturers. You get to see everything firsthand," the daughter told me, obviously thrilled at the prospect. She and her father continued to extoll the virtues of the school's program and its high standards as I savored every bite of my entrée, the full-bodied Tuscan red wine and my dessert, a rich creamy *pannacotta*.

That encounter, by happenstance, planted a seed. I decided then and there that I would return to Florence and go back to school, not just to any school but to the Florence Design Academy. Over the next two summers, I completed two three-month courses in interior design, furniture placement and design, lighting, and principles in architecture. These courses honed my skills and deepened my understanding, especially of contemporary design, as I continued to renovate upscale Toronto homes.

My dinner at Tre Cristi is just as good as I remembered and well worth the impromptu stopover in Siena. Later that evening, without too much fuss or bother, I find my way back, unscathed, to my Florence hotel, relieved that this local train journey to the beach turned out better than the other one.

The "New Italian"

In the past few weeks, I have studied hard to learn the gestures and the Italian language despite the different dialects and rhythms. But the biggest challenge to my guessing abilities has been deciphering what I like to call the "new Italian."

For days I have shopped in a frenzy because, as every Italian will tell you, *tutti* is on sale only for a short time and then the shops close for the month of August! So, in one week, I commit to fourteen-hour shopping days in a serious effort to visit every single shop in Florence. Let us not forget, I still need my beauty sleep!

Every time I ask for my size, the salesclerks ask, "*Provare, Madame?*" I quickly understand this to mean, "Would you like to try it on?" So I do. When I leave the fitting room to find a mirror (because mirrors are not a typical fixture in the makeshift fitting rooms created from a curtain fashioned from Nona's oldest tablecloth hanging from a century-old rod and stuffed with merchandise piled ceiling high so that anyone weighing more than seventy pounds has to try on the clothes by turning sideways!), I am met with a disgusted look. "Madame, you are too *zmall*," with the emphasis on the "z"! So, assuming I have understood, I repeat, "You mean 'small'?" "No, Madame, *zmall*," comes the retort with an expression of disgust.

Discouraged, I decide to stop for a glass of fresh-squeezed orange juice. The barista at the *pasticceria* asks if I want *isa* in my juice! I assume this means ice and feeling clever and empowered by my ability to understand, I respond in English, "No ice, please." The juice comes with ice and when I ask why, the barista explains in Italian, "When I asked if you wanted *isa*, you told me 'no ice'." There is nothing to be done but shrug. Obviously, the sole purpose of this "new Italian" is to communicate to tourists in a nonsensical combination of English and Italian. Later that day, when I stop at a market to pick up a bottle of sparkling water, I ask for an *acqua frizzante*, as is clearly printed on the label, as opposed to still water or *acqua naturale*. By now, I suppose I should have been prepared for that familiar blank look on the salesclerk's face. When she asks me if I want *gaz* or *niente gaz* with emphasis on the "z," I laugh, compliment her on her English, pay for my *acqua gaz* and continue my hunt for more new Italian.

Language and Linguine

Grano, a popular neighborhood Italian resto, was one of my favorite Toronto eateries. I loved its excellent house red wine, succulent *calamari fritti*, its signature decadent white-chocolate raspberry-pistachio tart and its creamy rich cappuccino dusted with dark cocoa.

As yummy as its Italian fare was, the best part of dining there was interacting with its owner, a robust, warm, effusive and intelligent Italian—a soft spoken soul whose family had roots in Italy. Roberto not only owned and operated the restaurant but was an unofficial ambassador in the Toronto community for everything Italian. I always looked forward to listening to him speak his lyrical Italian to his staff and his siblings as I sipped my wine.

After a brief trip to Italy with my husband almost twenty years earlier, I had vowed to return, to Florence in particular, but with the ability to speak Italian. So it seemed like divine providence when, one evening at Grano, Roberto approached our table and asked if I would be interested in taking their *Language & Linguine* conversational Italian classes at the restaurant. Before he could finish his pitch, I said, "Sign me up!"

I ordered the Italian language textbook and workbook and paid the course fee. Each weekly lesson was accompanied by an *aperitivo*, mineral water, a glass of *vino* and a surprise of small bites. What could be better? We learned the basic vocabulary for traveling in Italy and touched on some of its cultural aspects, such as opera, music, art, architecture, fashion, wine and, of course, regional cuisine. I was so captivated by this beautiful language that I repeated the course, despite Roberto's insisting that I had moved past the beginner level. On my third attempt to enroll, Roberto kindly suggested that I meet with the director of the Columbus Center, Toronto's Italian community and cultural center, to discuss the options for more advanced language classes.

I enrolled in a weekly night class at the Columbus Center and sharpened my Italian skills, this time *senza aperitivo*, *vino* or even a cappuccino. At the end of the term, confident that I could now communicate in Italian, I booked a five-day trip to Florence. I was elated that I could now order a meal, ask for the restroom, order a taxi, purchase a train ticket—and ask the most important question for a girl who loves fashion: *Quanto costo per favore?* Mission accomplished, all thanks to *mio caro* Roberto!

At each luxury hotel, I have grown accustomed to finding finely wrapped candies, hazelnut *cantucci*, individually wrapped handmade truffles or even a French *macaron* perfectly placed on my pillow every evening. More often than not, these treats are left for two as *sola* appears to be an incomprehensible concept to the average Italian. Today, all that changes! It is the first of August and time to try something new.

Arrivederci to plush terry robes bearing hotel logos, cellophane wrapped monogrammed slippers, embossed stickers on toilet paper and nightly turndown services. *Bonjourno* to my new apartment in San Frediano that I leased from a friend, a middle-class neighborhood where young professional Florentines live, walk their dogs, take their children to the park, shop, dine out and enjoy a rich social life late into the night.

At first, I am slightly uneasy. Who will wish me *bonjourno* the moment I step foot into a beautifully appointed breakfast room? Prepare my *doppio espresso con crema*? Open and close doors for me? Make my train reservations? Schedule my hair and manicure appointments? Organize my dinner reservations?

Momentarily ignoring the "uniqueness" of Italy, whose quirks you must figure out as you go along, I blithely give the hotel's driver my new address. He is dressed in long sleeves in the 38^0 C (100^0plus F) heat and I can tell that the prospect of loading and unloading my six heavy suitcases is not helping his mood. He is less than thrilled when, after delivering me to the apartment building and loading half my bags into an elevator designed for a small child, he discovers that there are two streets in Florence with identical addresses—and this is not the right one!

Tomorrow, I will prepare my own *doppio espresso con crema* and revel in drinking it on my beautiful rooftop garden overlooking the city, make my own hair appointment and chance my Italian, hoping I do not end up asking for groceries instead of a trim. I will explore my new neighborhood, pick up a newspaper at the corner market and live like a Florentine. Here is to new beginnings and new adventures—and finding my balance once again.

It is Sunday. After sleeping until the disgracefully indulgent hour of eleven o'clock, I decide to abandon my agenda for the day and simply take my lead from the Florentines, who have perfected the art of ambling. I watch them stroll across the *ponte* to soak in the beauty, sightsee and warmly greet friends with a tight embrace and double *baci*, stopping constantly to answer their phones with a very self-assured yet relaxed *pronto* or *dimi*. Fueled by a potent jolt of caffeine, I bid my barista a quick *grazie mille* and meander along the banks of the Arno.

Restos and trattorias are buzzing but at a less frenetic pace than on weekdays. The air is thick and heavy and everyone is remarking *più caldo oggi*—how much warmer it is today—and hoping for rain to "make Firenze a fresh complexion." How much fresher can Firenze get, I wonder, since this city washes its streets more often than I clean my house, and that is saying a lot!

I wander the streets, cross bridges and then retrace my steps. I see locals sitting idly for what seems like hours over pasta and a glass of *vino*, appearing "fresh" or maybe "refreshed." I decide to join them and am greeted with a typical Florentine welcome at Golden View Open Bar, my favorite resto on the Ponte Vecchio, where I order a lunch so late in the day that it could pass for a *cena anticipata*.

Just as my *insalata pera* arrives, an artful plate of butter lettuce, *rucola*, a cored then reconstructed abate pear, taleggio cheese and walnuts drizzled with honey and a balsamic dressing, the heavens open, as if on cue. It pours and pours, torrentially, but I do not mind. Like my local friends, I am engaged in the art of living a Sunday in Florence: a cappuccino followed by a meal while watching this beautiful city's complexion become "fresh."

This magical gentle place reflects beauty not just in its brightly shuttered terra cotta buildings, its soul-gripping music played on every street corner and its breathtaking artwork but in its reflection in the Arno, reminding us to look beyond the complexion to see all the beauty within.

Florentines Celebrate the Art of Making Art

Since my first day in Florence, I have been awestruck by this magical city: the tangerine, magenta and gold in the sky as the sun begins to set over the Ponte Vecchio; the subtle greens of cypress and fig; the beautiful centuries-old buildings; even the haute couture that Florentines wear so proudly.

No wonder this city has inspired the great artists over the centuries. Florence is like a fine painting, its light, hues, shadows, depths, perspectives and subtleties creating a mood of passion or an impression of understated elegance and grace. You find artists on every street corner, piazza, bridge, park and church step. These *plein air* painters inhale the city's life and exhale it back with their masterful portrayals on canvas in reciprocation. Florentines celebrate the art of making art.

This small city, which residents often refer to as a village, is passionate about the aesthetics of every detail, no matter how *zmall*, as my *amici* say. I see this in the careful and proud way a Florentine painter wraps up a masterpiece for the purchaser, no matter its size or the price it has yielded. Street vendors set up their wares in the most artistic manner. Paper shops sell wrappings that are themselves handmade works of art, as are the daily chalkboard trattoria menus with their fine Italic calligraphy.

Every morning I take pleasure in watching a florist artfully load his fragrant flowers in the cargo bed of is bright green truck to simulate a garden. The waiters in a neighborhood trattoria methodically set up elaborate place settings with crisp-pressed linen, embossed white china, crystal, perfectly polished flatware and fresh multicolored flowers, all for the sole purpose of creating an artistic tabletop for a simple meal. Even my barista, who strives daily to create a *fantasia* in my cappuccino cup, has mastered the glorious practice of making art in a cup.

Yesterday evening on the way to my little apartment in San Frediano across the *ponte*, I stopped in the Piazza della Repubblica for a ride on an old-fashioned carousel. A nearby street musician was singing "Moonshadow," a 1970s Cat Stevens's song. I watched, fascinated, as he worked his artistry to draw mock seats on the cobblestone in different colored thick pieces of chalk to denote the sections and proximity from his guitar stand. Carefully, he took the time to number the ground seats in a fancy script. It was as much about creating a beautiful environment for spectators to enjoy his musical performance as it was about the performance itself. This is the essence of Florence; a feast for the eyes and a passion for the art of creating art!

"She like it, *Madame?*" my barista at Caffè Gilli asks me every day. Just 1.40 euros for this steamy hot, creamy, chocolatey marbleized work of art in a fine bone china cup, accompanied by a mother-of-pearl and sterling-silver demitasse spoon and delicate chocolate-dipped hazelnut *cantuccio* on a lacy embossed monogrammed doily. A perfectly placed sugar container and extra, embossed napkins complete the presentation. Notwithstanding my well-appointed kitchen complete with espresso maker in my magnificent apartment on the chicest street in the *centro*, like most Florentines, I prefer the ritual of taking my morning *caffè* out.

In Firenze, this caffeinated delicacy is a matter of pride, passion and priority. No wonder that cafés, tearooms, *ristoranti* and *trattorie* invest sums akin to a college tuition on an ever so beautifully designed espresso/cappuccino machine. Taking up an area that could house a Vespa, this machine is the heart and soul of every food establishment in Italy.

Like any delicacy, taste, temperature and artistic sensibility are essential to the preparation of the *cappuccino perfetto*. Heaven forbid a foreigner should utter the word "decaf," a term usually met with a dismissive gesture. (I am now schooled in the language of gestures.) If you are fortunate to get a barista who has taken a liking to you, you may find your cappuccino delivered with a heart shape floating amidst the dusting of dark cocoa.

I have figured out that the Italian obsession with coffee has little to do with coffee at all. Rather, it represents a way to break up the day, to take a moment to savor life, to connect with friends, to slow down and reflect. The accompanying *cantuccio* represents a sweet commitment to the enjoyment of life's small pleasures. Clever Italians! They have learned how to stitch together their lives with small sweet moments of quiet pleasure.

Perhaps my next acquisition should be a cappuccino machine instead of a new pair of Ferragamo shoes or an Italian-made dress since I now know that this machine is more than a coffeemaker—it is a lifestyle. But how will I coax my favorite baristo to accompany my new cappuccino machine back to Maui? Worth a try. *Domani, baristo mio!*

Memories of Meals Past

Traveling in Italy over the years on my *viaggio da sola*, I have sampled and enjoyed many regional delicacies: creamy roasted chestnuts, *pappardelle* garnished with earthy decadent shaved black truffles, fried Roman artichokes served with a zesty lemon *aioli*, orange-scented *arancini*, grilled calamari drizzled with the liquid gold of first-pressed olive oil, rich buffalo mozzarella and candy-sweet cherry tomatoes topped with fragrant peppery *basilico* the size of small lettuce leaves, fresh *porcini focaccia*, rich rare *bistecca*, lightly battered stuffed zucchini flowers, ricotta-filled agnolotti—and gelato, gelato and more gelato.

Good food is something I cherish, partly because it connotes nurturing and recalls a happier time when my mother was alive. She was a wonderful cook who delighted in lavishing affection on her three children and their friends through the meals she prepared.

By the time I went to elementary school, we lived in a relatively new Toronto suburb. Like my parents, most of our neighbors were first-time homebuyers with two or three children. All the neighborhood children played together in their unfenced backyards, which formed a large shared playground. The boys played street hockey after school until their mothers called out "dinner time" or the streetlights came on, whichever came first. The girls roamed the area in a pack.

Playing outdoors one day, I met a cute brunette, a shy girl with dark brown eyes who was five years old like me. Julia lived on our street, a few houses away, and we instantly became best friends. When we turned six, we discovered that we were born a month and two days apart, making her a Libra and me a Leo. True to our astrological signs, we could not have been more different yet our close friendship has endured for more than half a century.

Every morning on her way to school, Julia would knock at our side door at 7:30 a.m., even though our school was located in the opposite direction. When my mother invited her to join us for breakfast, Julia always smiled and shyly shrugged and replied, "Yes, please." After a quick breakfast, she and I would walk together to school. I occasionally wondered why she did not eat breakfast at home but I assumed that since we were best friends and playmates, she simply preferred to eat with me. Years later Julia confessed that she ate at home first and then came to us for "a tastier breakfast." Funny how habits are formed and traditions created. More than fifty years later, Julia still comes knocking for a second repast!

My mother ran her kitchen much like a restaurant, catering to each of our likes and dislikes at mealtimes. She was a self-taught home cook but had a creative flare and a desperate desire to please so she signed up for cooking classes with a well-known Toronto cookbook author to improve her skills.

Each week we were her guinea pigs as she shopped, unpacked the groceries and measured out a little of this and a lot of that to replicate the new recipes she had learned in class. One day, when I was eight years old, I watched her spend an inordinate amount of time cutting, chopping and dredging something for the main course. When I asked what was for dinner, she said, "It's a surprise. Whatever she put in the oven soon filled the house with a wonderful aroma. I helped set the table and returned to my bedroom to finish my homework.

When my father returned from a long day at work at his parents' variety store, my mother informed him that dinner was ready whenever he was. As always, we waited until he took a quick shower and changed his clothes before we all sat down for dinner. My mother served each of the children a generous portion and an extra generous portion for my father, who always had a hearty appetite. He lifted his fork and plunged it into the layered entrée covered in bubbling tomato sauce and a golden, crispy layer of baked Parmesan cheese. "Be careful," she warned, clearly proud and excited to share her new dish. "It's very, very hot. Blow on it, kids."

When my father swallowed his first bite, his eyes narrowed. I assumed he had not heard my mother's warning and had burned his tongue or the roof of his mouth, but no. Without a word, he turned his dinner plate upside down and slammed it onto the table. "I told you *never* to serve me eggplant," he hissed at my mother. I *hate* it!"

We all sat frozen at the table, fearful, shaking and stunned, yet familiar with his childish, cruel and sporadic outbursts. He shoved his chair back and stalked out of the kitchen. We knew better than to speak to him until he resurfaced the next morning.

Despite my distaste for eggplant, I licked my plate clean in a desperate attempt to let my mother know how much I loved her and appreciated her efforts. I silently vowed that one day I would serve my father eggplant disguised in a dish and take pleasure in seeing him eat crow, so to speak. But, at eight years of age, how could I suspect that only fifteen years later, my mother, the foundation of our family, would be dead and that my life would never be the same.

Final Goodbye

I stand silent in front of the stainless steel kitchen sink of our family home. My mother's closest friend gently places a hand on my shoulder. "It's time to go," she murmurs. I dig my heels into the cold stone tiled floor and grip the counter, resolved not to leave our house, deluding myself that this horror is not real. There is no way I am going to say a final goodbye and bury my mother today.

After resisting two or three gentle appeals by family friends, I am forced to put on my heavy winter coat and walk outside to the limousine parked in the driveway. The stretched black car is filled with family but I feel totally and utterly alone.

The car pulls up to the back entrance of the funeral home's chapel. We walk in single file into a makeshift parlor to have a talk with the rabbi. I sit stone like, unable to cry, speak, hear or move.

"You can't cry, don't you dare cry Heather," my father had admonished me earlier. "We are counting on you. This is not the time to fall apart. We need you to be strong. No tears!" How could he expect that of me, today of all days? As the rabbi respectfully gathers the family together, I walk past him without a word, force open the door to the larger chapel and slam it shut behind me.

I stand in front of the small, simple wooden casket and ask that it be opened. I drape my mother in the fuzzy white wool coat she loved and in which she specifically requested to be buried. How she loathed the cold! I make sure her wig covers her small bald head so she can be buried with pride and the modicum of dignity she deserves.

As I stand alone, weeping before her coffin, all I want is to will her back to life. I beg and implore God to bring her back. Shakespeare wrote that, "tears water our growth," but I cannot imagine what God expects me to learn from this monumental loss. The grief is choking me. Later I am told that my howling, sobbing and gut-wrenching cries sounded like a wounded animal and could be heard in the outer parking lot.

I have organized my mother's funeral, picked out the small wooden coffin and her plot. A few days before her death she was very specific, telling me to bury her in a spot that captured the afternoon sun. With her olive complexion, she was a sun worshipper. I had been asked about a double headstone when I went to pick out the granite marker, provide the inscription and other details but my father, still in his mid-forties, believed it would be a bad omen to have an empty plot waiting expectantly for him next to my mother. He would not even discuss it so, as always, I had to make all the decisions, all the arrangements, on my own.

My father, brother and sister take their seats beside me in the front row of the chapel. My father is as cold as ice, motionless, robotic, grief stricken. He is our father, I keep thinking. He is all we have now. We have no one but him, no one! But my mother had warned me. She feared that we would be left on our own to fend for ourselves and that I would be left to pick up the pieces and take on the role of mother, daughter and everything else.

The community pours into the funeral home. The parking lot is filled beyond capacity. My mother was loved. When the ceremony concludes, my father, my siblings and I silently follow the pallbearers to the hearse, get into the limousine and drive to the cemetery, the one where my mother expressly asked to be laid to rest.

It is November 6th. The day is blustery, bone chilling and overcast but as the coffin is lowered into the ground, the clouds suddenly part and the sun shines down to warm and illuminate her grave. I take some small comfort in the thought that my mother is being cradled in God's embrace and imparting a last blessing. People always said that she was the light, the sunshine. She always cared about others and saw the glass as half full. I pray that I can emulate her in character and substance.

The rabbi prods me with a hand to my shoulder, trying to move me away from her grave now that the service has concluded, but I remain rigid like a statue. "I won't leave you," I whisper. "You will not be abandoned and forgotten like you were as a child. I will show up. I will plant flowers on your grave and I will water them. I will talk to you and keep my promises." I drop the last shovel of earth on my mother's coffin and whisper, "Goodbye, mum. See you when I see you."

As I turn away, an old woman with salt-and-pepper hair, short and bent over, approaches and asks me if this is Rochelle's funeral. I nod. Then she hands me a pamphlet on the risks of contracting lung cancer. Is there no end to this hell, this nightmarish day? Angrily I toss the pamphlet into the trash can nearby, take my father's arm and steer him through the crowd of weeping friends back to the limousine. We drive home in total silence. I am numb.

My father sits in the mourner's chair in the living room while I take my place in the kitchen, arrange food on the dining table, check the coffee urns and wait for the crowds to arrive.

For the first seven days of *shiva*, the Jewish mourning period, I leave my newlywed husband and the tiny midtown apartment we share and move back into the family home to care for my devastated brother and sister and my grieving, non-functioning father.

On the seventh day of mourning, the rabbi walks us around the block to end the first period of *shiva*. This symbolic walk into the light of the outside world will be no match for the darkness that will soon enshroud the next three decades of my life.

Porcini, Prada, Puccini

I believe that I have finally escaped into the light after almost thirty years since my mother's death. As I grow accustomed to my temporary summer residence in Firenze after my move to Maui, I find myself getting into a new and pleasing rhythm. Like a Florentine, I begin to go to bed late into the night and sleep until the sun is shining brightly. I can gauge the time by the shadow on the buttercup-yellow and fuchsia-pink portulaca overflowing the flower boxes on my rooftop garden. When the sun illuminates these delicate blossoms, it must be close to noon. Time to shower and plan my adventure for the day. How I love to drink my first cup of cappuccino nestled into my little chaise above the vista of Florence's rooftops, the Duomo, one of the most important monuments in the city, in the distance. How delightful to turn my life and schedule topsy-turvy.

Once dressed, I decide that a second cappuccino is in order. I debate whether my motivation to walk to my favorite café is for the perfect cappuccino and a dolce, the admiring barista or the pleasure of practicing my much-improved Italian.

Lately, I have had a hankering for fresh porcini. You cannot pass a resto without noticing a large wooden crate of these fresh oversized *funghi* on display for all to salivate over. This prompts me to think that I have yet to use my well-equipped kitchen to prepare a single meal. I head to the Mercato Centrale in the San Lorenz neighborhood. Meandering through the narrow twisting cobblestoned streets, I make a mental note of the shops where I spot pretty hats, scarves and bobbles, should I return.

As I peek into an antique shop, I notice in the window's reflection that my fitted camisole is on inside out! I laugh aloud at myself and ponder a moment. What is a girl to do about this? My choices are to confidently wear my top this way and make a bold, new fashion-forward statement, or pop into a nearby shop, try on a few items and turn it right side out.

I enter a tiny shop bursting with vintage photos, shoes, bags, gowns and jewels stacked neatly in every nook and cranny—a true treasure trove. The owner emerges from the back of the shop, an older woman who, in her youth, must have driven young men mad with her radiant beauty and graceful, quiet elegance. Either she is too gracious to point out that I am wearing my top inside out or her eyesight is failing. Whatever the case, I am grateful.

She proudly and patiently explains that this is a vintage shop. Most of her merchandise dates from the '40s and '50s. Each piece has a history, a personality and a grand former owner. It is a treat to listen to her stories, which make each piece come alive.

I spot a small Prada evening bag in an unusual color: cranberry. When I ask about it, she scoffs. "It's too recent to be *importante* ... only ten years old or so ... never really been used. It's not something anyone would consider."

That was my cue. "Will you sell it to me?"

"Twenty euros for anyone who might find this unimportant little bag useful," she replies.

So my day begins with a Prada acquisition for the price of a very modest dinner and an opportunity to turn myself right side out!

Onward to the Mercato—a foodies' paradise, a cornucopia of the finest local ingredients and specialities. Porcini (also known as *cèpes* or boletus mushrooms) abound in every corner, perfuming the air of this remarkable market with their earthy mushroom odor. After perusing every aisle, I decide that all porcini look the same but, of course, I am a rank novice. In my less than *perfetto* Italian, I query a tall stocky merchant about the difference in the sizes and qualities of these precious fungi. Nonplussed at first, he begins to give me a lesson in porcini. Like an obedient student, I listen intently while he passionately explains all their subtleties, nuances and origin. I gain invaluable knowledge—and eight fresh porcini as a gift when the merchant learns that I have settled into an apartment in Florence for the summer. Of course, as with all Italian men, the gift comes wrapped in a very suggestive invitation to cook them for me in my apartment, which I graciously decline.

A few hours later, alone in my rented apartment, I whip up a simple but exquisite dish of pappardelle pasta with fresh porcini, cold pressed virgin olive oil tossed with fresh herbs, finished with a generous amount of freshly grated parmigiano reggiano and paired with a glass of Chianti. Perfection!

Not ready to retire now that I have acclimated to a European tempo, I remember that a few blocks away a local church hosts concerts most evenings. I dash down the block to pick up a few fresh golden peaches and, as luck would have it, run into a woman I met at a neighborhood concert. She insists that I join her and a few friends at the *chiesa* for tonight's performance by a violinist and pianist. Serendipity at work. This is precisely how I planned to spend my evening. Just twenty euros and *voilà*—two and a half hours of Puccini and Tosca that has me both smiling and weeping! Oh, the soul elevating power of music.

That is Firenze. On a modest forty euros, I acquired an Italian designer treasure, dined on handpicked fresh porcini and attended a superb concert. It was a day filled with meeting passionate, engaged and beautiful people who are living *la dolce vita*. This is a way of life I have managed to carve out for myself here in Italy, but it was not always this way.

Splayed Chicken

After "rising" from the first seven days of sitting *shiva* for my mother, I returned to the tiny one-bedroom midtown Toronto apartment I shared with my new husband. I resumed my teaching job and began a new routine. Each evening, after making dinner for my husband, I would drive the half hour to our family home to make dinner for my father and younger siblings, clean up the kitchen afterward, stay on until my father retired for the night, then slip out and head back to our apartment, drained and exhausted. I managed to keep up this routine for several months but the back and forth to look after the family combined with working and caring for my new husband, all the while ignoring my own unspeakable loss and profound grief, finally became untenable.

One day, I suggested to my father that they all come to dinner at our apartment instead. "Let's start with a traditional Friday night dinner," I proposed.

That Friday, after a full day of teaching and extra tutoring after school, I bought a large chicken from the kosher butcher near our apartment. My intention was to make the kind of *Shabbat* dinner my mother often served: herb and lemon chicken, roasted mixed vegetables, wild rice and a green salad, with homemade apple crisp for dessert. My mother used to tease me about my lack of interest in cooking although I did not mind doing the odd bit of baking with her. She often relegated me to peeling apples or rolling out cookie dough. This would be my first time roasting a whole chicken. How difficult could it be?

I carried home the heavy plastic bag with its butcher-paper wrapped chicken. When I arrived and stepped into my apartment, the bag slipped out of my hand and slid down our narrow hallway, spewing the chicken and giblets in front of our bathroom door. I shook my head and left it there, not wanting to touch the raw chicken or its slimy innards. I went into the kitchen, prepared and tossed a simple salad, roasted some vegetables, boiled a pot of wild rice and set out the fruit crisp I had baked the night before. By the time my husband and family arrived an hour or so later, our tiny square bamboo and glass dinner table was beautifully set, my paternal grandmother's tall antique silver *Shabbat* candlesticks taking a place of pride and prominence in the center. When mu family walked down the hall to wash their hands in the bathroom before dinner, they hesitated before the raw chicken splayed on the floor surrounded by giblets. "Ignore it," I instructed. "Just step over it because I am not touching it." I unwrapped the bakery bought sweet challah, poured a full glass of red wine to make kiddish. Then I began to serve dinner. So shocked were they by my pronouncement that no one dared mention "it."

Later that evening, as my father was about to leave with my brother and sister, he turned to me. "We will be coming every Friday for dinner, Heather, so you might want to learn how to cook; start with a chicken." Seething inside, all I could do was fantasize about next Friday's dinner which will feature eggplant disguised as breaded chicken! Retribution for my father's childish outbursts, cruel words and lack appreciation for my late mother's culinary efforts.

Pastry 101

Thank goodness for the cookbook store in the trendy neighborhood of Yorkville. Not only did they stock every type of cookbook but they also offered cooking classes at a restaurant supply company near my home. I signed up and after attending the first two classes, I learned that Michael Smith, host of the TV cooking show, *Chef at Home*, would be signing copies of his latest cookbook and giving a cooking demonstration of a complete dinner. His culinary point of view was simple: healthy home cooking using local ingredients. I can do that, I told myself, when I registered for his demo.

By the time I left his class, I knew this is easy—I could do what he taught but I was sure I could refine the presentation. I went home and tore my tiny galley kitchen apart, pulling out every bowl, a spatula and all the ingredients for a dark-chocolate molten cake. The chef had demonstrated how to bake this basic cake but I elevated it into an artful dessert with a dark-chocolate ganache, dusted with confectionary sugar, and served with raspberry coulis, a fresh mint garnish. My husband was a somewhat adventurous eater with a definite sweet tooth so I was sure to please him with my newfound culinary interest and skills.

This experience sparked my desire to enroll in a college-level culinary program. When we had to choose a specialty, I chose pastry over culinary arts because I thought it would be more creative, even though I personally preferred savory over sweet. I learned to bake cakes, pies, cookies, tortes, tarts, muffins, sweet buns, breads and all types of confections created from butter, sugar and flour.

At the end of this grueling program, I decided that I wanted to apprentice at Scaramouche, one of Toronto's most upscale and popular midtown restaurants. Their chef had made a name for himself as one of the best young culinary sensations in the city. The iconic restaurant, located in a very chic apartment complex, was famous for it's superb New Zealand rack of lamb. Scaramouche's signature desserts included coconut-cream pie garnished with white-chocolate shavings served with Chantilly cream and dark-chocolate sauce and homemade caramel ice cream.

One day in early August, I walked unannounced into their kitchen and suggested to the chef that he hire me to prepare their pastries. He started to laugh and asked me who I was. Thinking quickly, I mentioned that the previous pastry chef, who also happened to be the restaurant owner's daughter, suggested I apply for the job. Again, he just laughed. "I'll work for free until I prove myself," I blurted out, desperate to learn from the best. He sized me up and considered my offer. "Be here tomorrow by 3 p.m. Be prepared, you will work until late into the night."

The next day I arrived early and donned the oversized white chef's coat he threw at me. "See those baskets of Italian prune plums?" He pointed to several large bushel baskets. I nodded. "Peel and pit all of them." He must be joking! I thought. Those are impossible to peel let alone pit.

I started at three o'clock that afternoon and did nothing but peel and pit. My fingers ached and cramped. By 1 a.m., I was exhausted and happy to leave. The next day, this grueling punishment continued. "This is worse than potato-peeling duty in the military," I grumbled to myself. After the third night, I was certain that arthritis had set into my hands and fingers. I was done! I could not face another prune plum.

By the time I arrived for my fourth day, I had resolved to put an end to this misery. How long could a culinary-school graduate with a pastry speciality be expected to peel and pit? Local stone fruit was in season for another month so the chef could have me processing apricots next!

In the wee hours of the morning, I changed out of the chef's coat into my t-shirt and jeans. I crawled up the restaurant stairs, discouraged and determined to hand in my resignation the next day. As I waited, bone-tired, for the valet to retrieve my car, I mulled over how to word my resignation and at first did not hear the couple next to me in line ask if I had just dined at Scaramouche. "Sort of," I replied when they repeated the question. They ignored my cryptic response and excitedly recounted that they had just eaten "the best dessert" they had ever tasted. "An upside down plum tart, like *tarte tatin*, only better."

I suppose I could have confessed that it was I who had baked their dessert or even patted myself on the back for making my first sets of plum tarts after peeling and pitting thousands of those little fruit, but I did neither. Nor did I resign. My stint at Scaramouche launched my culinary career—but I vowed never to peel or pit again!

What's In a Name?

I have managed, somewhat, to master the Italian language—*scarpe* thanks to Ferragamo shoes, *borse* thanks to Furla handbags, *vestiti* thanks to every clothing shop in Florence, and the myriad flavors of gelato thanks to the De Neri *Gelateria*, an *acqua frizzante* bottle in hand everywhere I go!

Just when I am feeling empowered and proud of blending into this *bellisima città*, a local woman asks my name. After she tries five or six times to pronounce it, I finally agree that "Ether" is close enough.

"And your family name?" she asks. When she struggles with it, I know I will have to do something radical. I google the Italian equivalent of Heather and discover it is Erika. I may have disliked my given name since I was a young girl but Erika is out of the question! At that point, I dare not look up my surname.

At a Florentine paper shop, the shopkeeper considers my first name. *"Come Heather Parisi, sì Madame?"* she says finally, proud of recalling the popular Italo-American television star. I nod my head. *"Sì, d'vero."* One first name down, one surname to go.

The next morning, I walk into La Feltrinelli bookstore and order an English translation of Dante's *Inferno*. The man at the order desk asks for my phone number and name. After I pull out my European cell phone with the number pasted on the back and read him the long series of digits, I tell him, "Heather, like Heather Parisi, and Medici, as in 'Medici the first and most famous banking family that ruled Florence through the Renaissance'." He smiles and hugs me without blinking at my newly appropriated aristocratic surname. I think I will keep it!

Public Affection and Terms of Endearment

Traveling alone on *my viaggio da sola* has given me an opportunity to observe, reflect on and understand the world and how it works from a different vantage point.

I have noticed that those of us with a mainland North American mindset do not hold hands as a rule as we walk together. We tend not to engage in public displays of affection. We say very little to one another at the breakfast or the dinner table. For some cultural reason, we look for an occasion or reason to touch one another affectionately. We tend to express ourselves in a few curt words to make our meaning clear.

By contrast, Italians are expressive as a matter of course. They are physically connected to one another, not just to partners, lovers, husband and wives, but to children, parents, grandparents and friends, male and female alike. It is in the way Italians touch, in their hand gestures and in the expression in their eyes as they smile and share glances.

Caro, tesoro, carina, bella, back home, we would reserve such terms of endearment for a lover, a child, or perhaps a partner or spouse. We deliberate over whom to spoil with such terms. We carefully choose our superlatives, measure our words and limit our verbal expressions of affection. We hesitate to indulge one another with these terms of affection for fear of overstepping boundaries or creating too close a connection.

As a quiet observer, I have learned and loved hearing these beautiful words that bear witness to the connection they create. Listening, as the syllables roll off the tongues of these Europeans, so smoothly, sweet like honey, coating, caressing and exuding warmth with every breath. In Italy, it is natural and normal to address everyone this way, without embarrassment or reservation.

We often waste our words, too often using them to lash out and provoke, humiliate or cause pain. In fact, we do this far too well! And so I pray that the world will take a page from the loving and innate ability of Italians to connect and boldly display their affection for one another with terms of endearment!

Dimi

On my way from Maui to Florence in May, I stopped in Montreal to spend a day with Karen, my cousin and honorary older sister, a wise woman whom I adore. We hugged and kissed goodbye, knowing it might be a long time before we see each other again. She knows that my wanderlust, curious nature and love of exploring means that I could be anywhere, anytime.

Just before we parted, Karen turned to me. "Heather, promise me that you'll ask for what you need and want from all of us who love you. Tell me what you need." I am dumbfounded, not quite sure how to respond.

Although I heard her and understood the words, convinced that she was sincere, the concept was foreign to me. I agreed in order to satisfy her but she continued, despite my reply. "Heather, please let us care for you and love you the way you have always cared for and loved us. You must allow us to be there for you, the way you have always, unconditionally, been there for all of us." This was too much for me so I silently nodded, swallowing hard as I choked back a deluge of tears.

In Italy, there is a word I have come to use a lot: *dimi*. Literally meaning "tell me," *dimi* is used in a casual, colloquial way to say "ask me" or "tell me what you need" or "what can I do for you?" I have heard it hundreds of times here with friends, in shops and in markets. It is a tiny word with a huge, powerful meaning behind it. My handsome Italian tutor constantly reminds me at each study session that *dimi* is not just a word but an expectation.

To that end, as I celebrate my fifty-sixth birthday in the city I love most in the world, my beloved Firenze, I ask only that I hear from my family and friends in some way so that I can share my special day, my joy, with everyone I love and hold so dear. The journey this summer has been challenging, thrilling, freeing, frightening, delicious and stimulating but most of all, it has taught me to *dimi*, even though to *dimi* is *difficile per me*.

Questo è Normale

It is the end of August, time to leave my rented apartment in Florence and spend a week on the Amalfi Coast. I ask a friend to book me a hotel in the town of Amalfi, forgetting that Italians take their vacation after *ferragosto*, the Catholic mid-August Feast of the Assumption of Mary. The South will be packed with Europeans, Australians, Italians, of course, a sprinkling of Americans and ... me, the lone Canadian woman. I am grateful for any accommodation once I realize how difficult it is to find a room by the seaside. "It's a four star," warns my friend. No matter. I have spoiled myself all summer at five-star hotels and a luxurious rented apartment. Surely I can survive one less star, I tell myself, as I board the Naples-bound *treno* from Rome with eight large overstuffed suitcases (the concept of traveling light isn't something I can wrap my head around).

I am met on the Naples platform by a pre-arranged *"transfer,"* an Anglicized Italian term for a natty taxi driver who charges way more than a reasonable rate. The train arrives precisely on time; unusual in Italy. Antonio earns his outrageous fee as he struggles to load my bags into his large black Mercedes SUV, muttering obscenities in Italian, not realizing I understand him. I spend the next hour awestruck by the scenery along the coast. It is as if God has combined the best of Maui's beauty with Italy's majesty, grace and style. Antonio stops at a viewpoint so I can take in a vista more like a Monet canvas than an actual landscape. Large lemon trees laden with ripe fruit perfume the air; the figs are so large and overripe that they weigh down their branches; strings of multicolored peppers hang from the verandas of the terra cotta roof houses dotting the hills and are cantilevered over the azure sea below. I murmur *"Che bella, magica."* *"Grazie, Madame,"* Antonio responds proudly.

Arriving a bit disoriented at my quiet Amalfi hotel after the hustle and bustle of Rome, I check in, unaware of the huge change in store for me. I am given a key, a real key, oversized, burnished gold and slightly tarnished, and told to take the elevator down one floor to my room. As I step into the tiny elevator, I immediately smell mould. Eager to exit and find my room, I quickly discover that the elevator might be the better accommodation. The walls of my minuscule bathroom, blasted out of the sea-level rock wall, exude an algae-like odor. The blanket covering the double cot is stained, threadbare and damp. I am shocked given the exorbitant cost of the room but my friend from Rome did warn me about four stars in Amalfi in high season.

I hurry to the front desk and very respectfully request—more accurately, beg—to change my room for a less dank one. The front desk manager calls for Antonio, the bellman. He is ancient, older than my grandfather would be if he were still alive, and limps, so I insist on helping him carry my bags. It would be hard to imagine a more depressing sight but, sure enough, my replacement room is worse than the first. I sigh and resign myself to do a lot of exploring and return here only to sleep.

Slightly exasperated, I order a *cafe freddo* on the outdoor rooftop terrace. When I sit down, a gracious British woman who appears to be in her early forties greets me and introduces herself. Emily and I exchange a few words and I immediately sense that she is a special, warm soul. As we speak, I see that she is much like me, fiercely independent, compassionate, strong, creative, spiritual and on a journey of self-discovery and exploration.

We spend much of our time together on the coast—shopping, dinners and drinks, concerts but mainly talking and sharing our stories. Her story resonates with me as mine does with her. Our paths are so similar except for the timing that we connect on a deep emotional level; it feels as if we have known each forever. We both promise to keep in touch. At the end of her Amalfi stay, I wish her a *ci vediamo* rather than *arrivederci* because I know in my heart that we will definitely meet again.

It is such an extraordinary week of scrumptious white-peach Bellinis sipped at midnight; white, azure and *verde* grottos; outrageously large yachts; swimming at noon in the cool sea; breathtaking views; and cheeky drivers, waiters, shopkeepers and priests all named Antonio! So many Antonio's that I am forced to number them to keep them straight: Antonio #1, Antonio #2 ...

A highlight of my week is a day trip to Ravello, driven there by yet another Antonio #6 at this point. Ravello is an idyllic town perched on a hilltop more than 365 meters (1,200 feet) above the Tyrrhenian Sea. Its main *piazza* is lined with beautiful shops and a handful of outdoor *ristorante*—a gathering place for all who have the good fortune to live in this magical picture-postcard place. Thanks to its summer music festival, Ravello is known around the world as *la città della musica*, the city of music.

In the first shop I enter, I am greeted by an exceedingly handsome middle-aged man with an initial welcome hug and, in the Italian tradition, a kiss on both cheeks. How expertly and effortlessly Italian men manage to disarm a woman. I am slowly becoming accustomed to this gesture of warmth and wonder if I dare adopt this double kissing and bearlike hugging when I greet people back home.

The shop carries trendy high-end jewelry, elegantly displayed on glossy colored blocks. After many "*guarda bella, provare bella*," I succumb to his entreaties and begin trying on all the shiny pretty jewels, feeling like an Italian *principessa*. Within minutes, the proprietor has summoned his *padre* from the church to bless me in the store. He then proffers a small round perfectly polished silver tray bearing prosecco in champagne flutes and mini pistachio dusted ricotta filled cannoli and insists that I give him my personal coordinates so he can contact me. He invites me to join him in the *piazza* "after dark" for dinner, which is code, of course, for sex. I try my best to appear both flattered and gracious as I decline his overly friendly invitation. Moments later, his attractive wife arrives and he proudly introduces her to me. I mentally shrug and tell myself *questo è normale* in Italy.

After many frivolous purchases, I satisfy my passion for fine tableware at another shop offering beautiful hand-painted ceramics. I am so enthusiastic about each piece that the shopkeepers, a kind Ravello-born couple, forgive my less than perfect Italian. As we chat, it begins to rain, followed by lightning and a crack of thunder and then a torrential downpour. I peer outside as the shopkeepers scurry to lower their large awnings to protect their fine linens. They assure me that I am welcome to take refuge in their shop until the rain tapers off.

A man who had been inspecting a set of small hand-painted bowls approaches and offers me his umbrella. In a soft voice and distinguished British accent, he apologizes for bringing the inclement weather, explaining that he has just arrived from rainy London. We chat and he asks if I would be free to join him for dinner and a concert that he is part of this evening. "I may not perform brilliantly as I'm a bit fatigued from traveling, but I'll do my best," he says humbly.

Intrigued but non-committal, I explain that I am staying in Amalfi. "Perhaps, if I'm still here …"

He points out the small ticket kiosk in the *piazza* and asks for my name so he can leave a ticket there for me. Thank goodness he is a Brit so my name "Heather" requires no further explanation. Not long after we part ways, I find a ticket waiting for me, as promised, at the kiosk. I spend the rest of the afternoon perusing the shops around the piazza. Around six o'clock, I spot my new British acquaintance seated at an outdoor table at one of the little restos. He insists that I join him for an early dinner. It takes no more than a few moments to glean that he is a musician, intelligent, gentle natured and has a good sense of humor. At 7:30 p.m., he excuses himself "to practice for the little concert," as he calls it, due to start at nine o'clock.

As the sun sets, I wrap myself in a newly purchased shell-pink cashmere shawl against the night chill and enter the magnificent outdoor theater set in a garden overlooking the Amalfi coastline, the sea as backdrop. Awestruck, I follow a page who directs me to my front row centre seat at a sold-out performance of the London Philharmonic Orchestra.

A few moments later, a young blonde British woman seated to my left asks, "How long ago did you purchase your ticket? It was so difficult to get tickets for this concert. Thankfully, I purchased mine months ago when I confirmed my flight to Italy." I smile, knowing better than to admit my good fortune at having met one of the musicians and been "comped" a ticket at the very last moment.

The intensity of the chatter increases as the outdoor theater fills to capacity. When the stage lights dim, setting off the twinkling stars in the vast navy-blue dome, the crowd quiets as a handsome Italian man in a perfectly tailored tuxedo walks to centre stage. First in standardized Italian (Florentine Italian) and then in English, he introduces the music festival's illustrious guest performers and the program for this evening's *concerto*. He obviously has a key role in organizing the festival. The audience applauds as he walks off stage.

Once again, the buzz and chatter rise in volume, silenced only when the conductor walks to centre stage. He takes up his baton, bows—and winks at me! Without missing a beat, I jump up and curtsy gracefully, knowing this is one of the most memorable days of my journey thus far, one I will cherish forever. The miserable months spent practicing the curtsy at modeling school in my youth have finally paid off. I laugh to myself because I did not realize until that moment that the humble"musician" I had dined with only a few hours earlier was the famous British conductor.

The Amalfi Coast may be exceptional in its own right but what counts is what you make of each and every place, each and every day of your precious life.

What I Cannot Live Without

Being in Europe this summer has rekindled my passion for history, art, architecture, design, fashion, food and language. I have been seduced by the rich cultural layers that Italy offers. But as summer winds down here in Florence, I cannot help but think about the coming winter. Going "home" to Maui is something I have longed to do for so many years that I feel blessed to be able to do that in just a few weeks. I make my final return travel arrangements and begin confirming the dates when family and friends will fly over to Maui and stay with me.

Distance has been one of my greatest teachers. It has given me the opportunity to see things in a broader way, through a lens unfiltered by proximity. It has helped me compose a mental list of things I cannot live *without*. In the past, I always thought it so important to know what I needed to live *with*, but turning the concept upside down now makes more sense.

In correspondence with my friend the terrorist, who spends most of his time working far from home, I ask him what he cannot live without. In less than a minute, he responds with a four-point list. First for him is family, then love—he is a man, so he actually writes "making love." Music is next, followed by good food for the body and brain. Curiously, our shortlists are identical. I am a woman so I include love rather than making love but truthfully, we both mean the same thing.

What strikes me is how quickly and clearly he knew what he could not live without. When I offer him a chance to reconsider, he responds, "No *carissima*, no need, because distance and time are the greatest educators if you are willing to listen to their lessons. Most of us live in one place for our entire lives, which leads us to focus on what we need. But leaving that comfort, being uncomfortable, gives us the ability to see things with razor sharp clarity. That makes it easy to know what we cannot live without."

Thanks to Florence, my second home, and my dear peripatetic *amico*, I have compiled my cannot-live-without list, in no particular order: my son, love, black truffles, empathy, hugging, friends, gelato, music, good health, respect, art, Florence, words and acts of kindness, ocean, cappuccino, hope, papaya, kissing, faith, respect, a good hair salon, compassion, literature, books, personal freedom, dear friends, inner peace and memories. Florence is a place blessed with so many riches. It is a city where magic meets majesty to create a home for anyone who is clear on what they cannot live without.

Cruising on My Own

My summer sojourn in Europe is quickly drawing to a close. Back in my rented Florence apartment for a few last days, I decide on the spur of the moment to end my trip on a high note, with a luxury Mediterranean cruise, fondly recalling the cruise the year before with my aunt.

I call my long-time Toronto travel agent with my two prerequisites: that the duration of the cruise be no longer that ten days and that it is to begin and end in Rome . Since my return flight to Maui is already booked, there is no wiggle room on dates for the cruise. She sighs, knowing I never accept "can't be done" or "not available" for an answer. Within the hour, she calls back, surprised to have found one, and only one, spot available on a cruise that matches my exact criteria. "I should have known! You have the most extraordinary luck." I pay over the phone with my credit card and she emails me the ticket and voucher. The cruise itinerary includes some ports I visited the previous year but others are still on my "must see" list. I am thrilled.

A few days later, I am on an Oceania cruise ship in Civitavecchia, the port near Rome, spending the first day at the spa —and feeling some reservations about my last-minute whim to take a cruise on my own.

The first dinner is unsettling. Everyone onboard is in couples. Based on my first introductions, I discover that unlike the Regent cruise I took the year before, which was filled with Europeans, most of the guests are North American. The dining room is full as I enter dressed in Italian haute couture and request a table for one. I order a glass of Amarone, smile from deep within, enjoy three gourmet courses and linger over cappuccino and a sweet. Before I leave, an older couple, who turn out to have the stateroom next to mine, approach and ask if I have ever been to Florence, our next port. They want some sightseeing suggestions and I am more than happy to oblige. We return to my suite to chat about Florence over champagne. Naturally, we quickly become friends.

I continue to restore myself while living *la dolce vita* as this most beautifully appointed ship glides along the mediterranean — not alone but on my own.

One afternoon while enjoying the sunshine on the pool deck, I decide that I'm in need of an afternoon caffeine jolt; a cappuccino will not spoil my dinner. As I enter the poolside café clad only in an apple-green bikini and white Ferragamo flip-flops with a butterfly motif, I hear a familiar gravelly voice call out, "H, is that you?" I look up. Stunned and momentarily speechless, I see the terrorist standing before me. "What are you doing here?" we both blurt out simultaneously.

We order cappuccinos, both a little staggered and awkward. We have kept in touch over the past year via email and I called the terrorist to wish him well at Christmas and on his birthday. I have always ended my correspondence to him with "One day our paths will cross again, you will see!" He reminds me that I left a lasting impression last year when he shared his sadness over a failed relationship. I recall telling him that the world is full of girls, in an attempt to offer some comfort. Apparently, I hit a nerve and it helped alleviate his sorrow though I am surprised that my words had such an impact. We catch up on our news as the ship cruises down the Italian coast. He hugs me before excusing himself to practice for his next performance and gives me his schedule for the next few days.

Every evening on the cruise, I dress for dinner, glorying in the opportunity to wear my European finery, which I suspect will not leave my closet back in casual Maui. Predictably, as I enter the dining room, the maître d' asks me the same question. "Madame Heather, are you dining alone again? Is that a table for one?" As always, I respond, "No, I am dining on my own, thank you. Table for one, unless you are joining me." On the fourth night, I purposely wear my new Dolce & Gabbana strapless, floral brocade dress that I picked up earlier that month in Florence.

Haute Couture Pour Moi

When I spotted that embroidered floral strapless dress in the Dolce & Gabbana window, I fell in love with it, and asked if it was available in my size. I tried it on and it fit as if it had been custom-made for me. Then the salesman disappeared for a moment and was beaming when he returned with the matching shoes encrusted with tiny Swarovski crystal flowers. When I peeked at the price tag discretely tucked into the dress, I almost needed CPR to recover from sticker shock. Thank god I didn't tell him my shoe size and did not dare ask the price of the shoes. Thanking the salesmen, I told him that my birthday was in a few days; I would give the dress some thought and return if I decided to really, really, *really* treat myself and rob an Italian bank to pay for it. He laughed and suggested I walk down the designer retail lined cobblestone street to another boutique where they might have the same dress at a lower price.

As one does in Florence when needing to consider how to proceed, I stopped at Caffè Giacosa, a Roberto Cavalli café, and ordered a chocolate-infused cappuccino and a couple of *pastine di pistacchio*. A very attractive woman sitting at the next table spied the pistachio cookies and in British-accented Italian instructed the waiter to bring her "whatever that Italian redhead is having." *Finally*, I said to myself; I can now pass for *una donna Italiana*! Then she turned to me and asked, in English, "What are you doing in Florence?" Inflated to deflated in a matter of seconds. She clearly knew I was a foreigner but had played it up for the waiter.

She introduced herself and asked if she could join me. The benefit of traveling on your own is you tend to meet people. Bridget was one of those people and we connected instantly and with ease. She was a Londoner married to an Italian professor who taught at Oxford. They were holidaying in their villa south of Rome and Bridget had taken the rapid train to spend the day in Florence, a city she loves, to do the designer loop. We hit it off, sharing our love of fashion, food, art, architecture, opera, writing and all things Italian. She insisted we spend the afternoon shopping together—a perfect opportunity to get a second opinion about my ruinously expensive Dolce dress. When we happened upon the shop mentioned by the Dolce salesman, we headed inside where I found the identical dress on a rack near the back of the shop. After I poured myself into it and walked out of the fitting room, Bridget pronounced, "You absolutely must have it. You can wear it to Buckingham Palace for the event honoring my husband." I bought it—along with the matching shoes—at half price! It turned out to be a wonderful day: a designer frock and a lovely new friend and an invitation to a real live Palace!

The Terrorist Part II

So, as we sail toward Amalfi on the fourth evening, I walk proudly into the dining room in my new Dolce dress. As usual, the maître d' greets me with a kiss on both cheeks and repeats his question, "Are you alone, Madame Heather? Table for one?" Before I can fire back my usual response, I feel an arm wrap firmly around my waist. It is the terrorist, dressed in a trendy Italian suit. He walks me to a round table with a choice southern view, smiles and orders a bottle of Amarone Della Valpolicella. Impressive, he paid attention when I requested this wine last time we dined together over a year ago. He sits across from me, in silence, seemingly transfixed. I feel terribly uncomfortable and self-conscious and wonder if perhaps I have smeared my lipstick.

The waiter arrives at our table. He flourishes the bottle, opens it, pours a tasting portion and waits for the terrorist's approval. After the waiter decants the wine and pours us each a very generous glass, I swallow hard. I am very nervous, palms moist, not quite sure why the terrorist is still glaring at me. Finally, he breaks the uncomfortable silence. "H, that's quite the dress. Everyone is looking at you. You're stunning!"

That is the last thing I expect to hear. "It's just me in a pretty dress. It's really nothing special! I'm just an ordinary girl."

"H, you are anything **but** ordinary."

We chat through dinner, polish off the rest of the wine, order another bottle and eat like royalty. The terrorist is warm, effusive, animated and wonderful company. We banter and laugh and reminisce about our awkward first meeting in Valencia the year before. Although I am so full, I cannot pass up the tasting plate of three decadent desserts accompanied by a flambé of fruit and homemade gelato. We decide to enjoy a final drink on the outside top deck, some limoncello presented in miniature martini glasses. As the evening draws to a close, we arrange to meet the next morning and spend time walking around Positano together, then enjoying lunch. Abruptly, the terrorist gets up, walks towards me, bends down, kisses me passionately on the lips and sprints away. I am totally dumbfounded, prepared neither for his kiss nor for his unaccountably rapid departure.

A tad discombobulated, shaken, I have difficulty falling asleep trying to make sense of what just transpired, the terrorists unexpected display of passion and dash. Finally, the copious amounts of alcohol at dinner (unusual for me) take over and I drift off to sleep. The next morning, there is no terrorist in sight in the breakfast room so I grab a muffin and a banana and head back to my stateroom to collect my bag. When I call the terrorist to coordinate our meeting spot, there is no answer. I wait another half hour and dial his stateroom. Still no answer. Thinking that he must have left word for me onboard I head for the main reception desk. I learn that he left the ship very early that morning. He must be avoiding me! His odd behavior triggers my familiar rejection hot button.

Disappointed, hurt and confused, I refuse to let him ruin my day in Positano. Unwilling to squander my time in such a glorious place, I spend the morning on my own, revisiting treasured cultural hotspots, enjoy a delicious lunch with my friends the American couple from the neighboring stateroom and return to the ship late in the day. The mystery of the missing terrorist weighs on my mind but I know that I will see him later that evening in the ship's theater because he is the featured performer.

After ordering and enjoying a light dinner in my stateroom, I knock on my neighbors' door. They agree to accompany me to the concert since they know what has transpired with the terrorist (I brought them up to speed when we lunched earlier today in Positano) and understand that I am seeking safety in numbers. We ride the elevator down to a half-filled theatre and watch the terrorist perform haunting Spanish music against a backdrop of vintage photos of his family projected onto a stage curtain. A roar of applause, a bow, an encore, more applause and he disappears from the stage like Houdini.

When my friends and I walk to the lobby bar for a nightcap, we find the terrorist signing CD covers and making small talk with his admiring fans. After signing his last CD, he turns his attention to me but I do not acknowledge him. He taps me on the shoulder. "Can we talk?" I smile, agree reluctantly to join him on the outdoor deck, at a little café table, where we are now alone. On the surface I am collected but underneath I am seething and waiting for an explanation as to why he skipped out of our plans earlier today without so much as a word.

"H, I needed to think … but I had a marvelous time last night." Instead of challenging him, because I prefer to avoid confrontation at all costs. He tells me that this is last day on ship, so I hug him tightly, tenderly kiss his cheek and say goodbye. Despite his display of affection the night before, perhaps he has concluded that our timing is off because of his concert schedule and chaotic life. If there is to be another chapter to our story, it will be up to him to take the initiative. He assures me that next time he will come to Hawaii to see me.

Inclement weather forces the cruise ship to Genoa instead of porting again in Portofino. I am thrilled about this last-minute change since I have always wanted to visit Genoa. As we coast smoothly and effortlessly into the *porto antico*, I watch from my balcony, heart overflowing from the view of the multicolored landscape before me.

Genoa, an old city wrapped in an arch around its hills, is in Liguria and not a popular tourist destination. The port is not particularly pretty, gritty in fact and is filled with taxis competing for the few visitors going into town. My taxi driver's enthusiasm turns to disappointment when I ask him in Italian to take me to the *centro* of Genoa, just a short drive away which means pocketing a minimal fare but difficult to get to on foot. By now I know that "a wink and a blink," as my aunt jokingly calls it, and waving a twenty euro bill will smooth the way.

As I *grazie mille* the driver, then to discover that he has dropped me at the entrance to architectural heaven. Nothing could have prepared me for the extraordinary limestone and marble porticos, the carved ornamental details on every building, monument and street corner. Flanking the main street is a spectacular series of black-and-white marble arches faded to the color of ash that provide a regal frame and much needed shade. Shops galore, name brands interspersed with unique boutiques, but it is Sunday and everything is closed. I saunter along wide pedestrian promenades lined with treed boulevards, taking my cue from the inhabitants who are never in a rush, especially on a Sunday. This is the real Italy, steeped in history and cultural splendor, honoring the day of rest, unconcerned about keeping up with the times or making a fast euro or two.

All the cobblestone streets run in a serpentine pattern either steeply uphill or steeply downhill. Wherever I turn, I feel as if I have stepped back in time. I stop at a tiny pastry shop with a few round outdoor tables covered in traditional red-and-white checked cloths and order a latte macchiato. Two older men play chess on a faded coffee-stained board. While they drink their *doppio espresso*, they argue over whose move is next. Oh, the joy of finally understanding Italian and their colorful, animated gestures! Here is my reward for taking this journey.

My next stop is OVS, Italy's Macys, Bloomingdales and Saks rolled into one, and the only store to defy Genoa's' disdain and open on sacred Sunday. I head to housewares to look for a shower curtain to take back to Maui. When I find not a single one, I ask for assistance. "Madame, here in Genoa, we do not shower, so you will not find any." Stunned, I mumble *grazie* and leave. Then I began to think. Since my overly curious mind has gotten me into trouble in the past, I squelch my desire to go back and make further inquiries. By now, I have come to understand that taking words literally is folly. Culturally, things are just different here. Bathing is an old Roman custom; therefore, no need for shower curtains I realize.

I walk downstairs to the lingerie department, noticing that the offerings are far less alluring than in Rome. Long traditional heavy cotton nightgowns hang in a row, in white or off-white. Limited, conservative, almost a bastion of chastity compared to the Roman lingerie collections that scream passion and sensuality in shades of gold, crimson and black. My last stop is the food and culinary section which is located on the third and top floor of the department store. I stand astounded before an eight-foot wall of shelves lined entirely with jars of pesto—enough to dress all the pasta in the entire country.

Despite its claim to fame as the birthplace of Christopher Columbus, Genoa is also the biggest and most historic Italian port and home to the Acquario Di Genova, the largest aquarium in all of Europe—and I am probably among the few tourists to have ever visited it. Once again, I realize that somehow, someway, something always makes me veer slightly off the popular path of life, and how blessed I am to be in Genoa. My mother's words echo in my head: "Follow the yellow brick road, Heather, with all its twists and turns."

CHAPTER 3

MORE LIFE LESSONS

It is both daunting and exhilarating to rid yourself of all your worldly possessions collected over a lifetime and begin anew. This is the challenge now before me. With my history left behind in Canada, along with the most basic items required for a home, I am forced to start from the very beginning. Half the fun, I soon discover, is searching for, sourcing and choosing the things I need to create my simple, new tropical home.

I knew before I left for Europe that my new rental was an excellent choice. It fulfilled the wish list I had compiled over the twenty-five years of visiting this island: ocean view, mountain view, gated community, landscaped garden, cook's kitchen, bedroom suite for my son, private pool, safe and very nice neighborhood and privacy. Finding this house was a miracle, I told myself when I signed the rental agreement. It was the ideal place for entertaining, hosting family and guests and a perfect fit for me, a woman living on her own.

My dear friend and spiritual guru offered to bless the house Hawaiian-style by burning sage. It was a sweet and touching offer but having grown up Jewish, I explained that the first ritual would be to affix a *mezuzah* to the doorpost of my front door. As a young girl, I was taught that the *mezuzah* is a visible sign of our Jewish heritage. It is also a symbol that our home is a holy place and that we should act accordingly—when we enter and when we leave it to go out into the world. It is funny how traditions persist and evolve for thousands of years. In my studies, I learned that the word "tradition" is derived from the Latin *tradere*, "to transmit, to hand over, to give for safekeeping." Maybe it is the safekeeping notion that compels me to install a *mezuzah* in every place I live.

I call my longstanding friend, the rabbi. He graciously agrees to come for dinner and install my *mezuzah*. As arranged, he knocks at my new door at 5:30 p.m. We stand together as he recites the blessing and nails the tiny royal blue and white decorated box enclosing a Hebrew prayer scroll to my right doorframe in the proper position and angle. I feel elated and so light. I finally have a sanctified place to lay my head, brew my coffee and invite my son and friends to visit. This has been a difficult, unsettling, nomadic year, with its repeated moves, the packing and unpacking. This marks a new beginning—the new chapter I have waited years to write for myself.

As I relax into dinner and pleasant conversation with the rabbi over a glass of kosher red wine, vegetarian sushi and mango and mixed greens salad, we watch the sun set into the ocean from my second floor lanai with its spectacular one-hundred-and-eighty-degree view. Pure Maui magic, we agree. When I give him a tour of my new home, he tactfully refrains from commenting on its bareness, the lack of furniture and personal items. Our voices echo in the empty spaces and off the Crema Marfil marble floors.

We share news from our summers abroad. He talks about his spiritual journey while taking a course in Israel and his future career aspirations. I talk about being grateful for finally being able to move "home," and knowing what I want for my future. Two old friends sharing a religious ritual, a meal, our experiences and dreams: that is my perception of the situation. Until it all changes in a heartbeat.

The kitchen island is laden with dishes because part of my cultural upbringing is to prepare and serve a wide variety of dishes when entertaining. So I offer seconds and when we have both eaten our fill, I flit around my spacious kitchen and pack him a take-home container, turn on some music and quietly clear the table.

Kosher gelato is on the menu for dessert, in three flavors: salted caramel, vanilla bean and dark chocolate with almonds. Fresh fruit is cut and chilling in the refrigerator. Delighted that I have a new shiny fire-engine red cappuccino-espresso maker, I offer my guest his choice of specialty coffee but as we are both still nursing the bottle of kosher red wine he brought as a house-warming gift, he declines. We take our wine and dessert out to the lanai. The night is still and warm so I switch on the outdoor fans and set the outdoor lights to dim.

Before joining him on the lanai, I take my wine glass, still a quarter full, and walk to the double sink under the picture window overlooking the eleventh hole on the golf course and spill the contents into the sink. One glass is my limit if I want to keep my wits about me. and alcohol tends to make me drowsy.

I wash and dry the glass and as I turn around, I feel two hands on either side of my waist. "Dance with me," he says in a quiet confident voice. Shock and panic barely describe my alarm. I lean against the counter, frozen in disbelief. He moves me in time to the music, nuzzling my neck and murmuring something unintelligible. I am paralyzed, dumbstruck by this physical display of affection. He strokes my hair and softly kisses my cheek. I never imagined he was interested in more than a platonic relationship but this has always been my blind spot with men. I never look beyond the obvious, never wanting to see what lies just below the surface.

"You've changed," he says as he continues to dance me around the kitchen. "You came back from Europe with a very different sense of self. It's not only in your body language but in everything you say and do. You seem so happy, so comfortable in your own skin, so self-assured. Pretty girl, you are different … and I like it."

"Italy helped me see who and what I am," I reply.

He wraps his arms even tighter around me, glues his body against mine and kisses me with the kind of intention and passion reserved for a lover.

What now? How do I call him "rabbi" after this? Perhaps I will need to address him in a completely different way. *Shabbat shalom*, padre. Maybe that could work!

Really is that a Job?

"This cannot be a real job," says a visiting friend, her tone one of incredulity as I show her around the clothing store where I now work on Maui. "Explain to me again what you do here and how you manage to get paid for it."

"I chat with shoppers, try on and model all the new clothes and put fashionable pieces together for clients," I reply.

"So … you don't ring up your sales, don't fold, tidy or put things away, don't help in the stockroom …and you work in retail?" my friend continues.

"That's right."

"Unbelievable! Every girl would love to have this job." Little does she know that my in-shop modeling, my stylist and people skills have increased store sales exponentially, so the manager is very happy to let me to do what I do best.

One Friday afternoon, I am just about to try on a few new dresses when a tall, fit, fiftyish looking man walks in. He is dressed in an edgy upscale-casual but rugged way, and he smells divine. I give him the once over, assessing if I should offer my assistance. Before I have a chance to speak, he smiles and says, "You have the most beautiful hair. Your hair color is God given."

"You must be a hair stylist because everyone else assumes I color it," I quip.

He admits that he owns the largest hair salon chain in Aspen and suggests I thank whoever passed down the genes for my mass of long strawberry-blonde curls, as the color is rare and special. "Only two percent of the entire population on the globe can brag about having your hair color which makes you unique, not ordinary". I acknowledge his compliments and tell him that I am grateful to pop singer/songwriter Ed Sheeran and Prince Harry for making redheads cool. A source of shame and embarrassment for me as a child, my red hair—that has not a trace of grey well into my fifties—apparently has turned out to be my saving grace.

You are Unique

The principal is not smiling as she passes me in the narrow hallway outside her small dark office in our new elementary school. I am seven years old, in grade two. The elephant-grey resin chair with its curved back and shiny chrome legs on which I am instructed to sit and wait is hard and cold. It is obvious to everyone who walks past that I am in big trouble but I have no idea why. Yet here I sit, biting my nails, wondering what I have done and what the consequences of my mysterious crime will be.

I hear whispering from just inside the principal's office. I think it is the secretary, Miss Lamb, gossiping to the attendance monitor but the words are indecipherable. I wonder what Miss Lamb's first name is but I have been taught that it is rude for children to ask personal questions of adults. I imagine her to be a Frances or perhaps a Hazel, with her horn-rimmed glasses, white cotton shirt, straight navy-blue gabardine skirt and black oxford lace-up shoes. Her dark brown hair is always knotted at the nape of her neck. I secretly wonder if her head throbs from her bun being pinned so tightly in place. I strain to hear, picking up every other word through the slightly ajar office door. "Her mother is on her way," says Miss Lamb. My stomach grows queasy and I want to run into the girls' washroom and hide in one of the small stalls.

My mother is notorious in our neighborhood. She is the only parent who insists that all the children call her by her first name: Rochelle. She also has a well-earned reputation for being a nervous, terrible driver. I recall a frantic call one morning from neighbors across the street after my mother's car rolled onto their front lawn and destroyed their apple trees. She had forgotten to put her car into parking gear! My mother merely laughed it off.

But whenever the pavement is covered in even the lightest dusting of snow, she knows better than to endanger anyone by driving us to school. "Surely you don't expect me to drive in this weather?" she would exclaim. Funny how we children realized we were safer on foot, trudging through snowstorms in gale-force winds, than riding in the back seat of her sporty red car. On this blustery January morning, the snowdrifts are waist high, the temperatures, frigid. I know that I must be in a lot of trouble for my mother to agree to drive to my school in such conditions.

Classmates are laughing, teachers are smirking, the principal is gawking but no one asks me anything; no one talks to me. After what seems like an eternity, I see a familiar shape moving toward me down the hall. I cower as I recognize my mother although it is hard to be sure as she is bundled in so many layers of wool and fur. I feel my jaw tighten. I grip my hands together and brace myself, almost shaking. Biting my lip to stave off tears, I gaze at the ground to avoid making eye contact with her as she approaches. I dare not look up.

A leather-gloved hand touches my shoulder and then an ungloved hand firmly but gently lifts my chin. My mother's warm expressive dark-brown eyes exuding love meet mine. She is smiling, almost laughing, and my entire body slumps in relief. She asks me to stand and sits me on her lap as she positions herself on that uncomfortable grey chair.

"Heather, darling, you are unique and one day you will thank me for that," she says softly. "Today you decided that being like everyone else was important. Trust me, being different is a gift. It's what independent thinkers strive for. That's why they stand out. One day you will understand this and be rewarded for being different." She gently lifts the wig of long dark-brown hair off my head and puts it in her large purse.

My mother loves fashion trends and this year, a long "fall" is all the rage among women who want to sport a long, flowing hairstyle. But now, as she strokes my red curls, she whispers, "Your hair is your glowing mane, your crowning glory, my sweet little girl, a symbol of the fire that burns within you. This is what sets you apart from the rest of the pack. This will remind you each day when you look in the mirror that being different is an opportunity to make a difference in this world!"

She wraps me in one of her woolly layers and escorts me to her car and then home. The wig goes back into her closet to its rightful place on the Styrofoam form up high on a shelf.

Today was picture day, when we line up in the gym in descending order of height. I was tired of being the only redhead in the class, in the entire elementary school, in fact. While brushing my teeth this morning, I came up with what I thought was a clever plan. I quietly tiptoed into my mother's closet, took a chair and climbed up to reach her long dark-brown wig and shoved it into my schoolbag. Now I will look like everyone else, I told myself. No one will notice, or so I thought.

That day I learned two lessons: that being different, looking different, is special; and that my mother can drive in snowstorms after all!

Falling Off a Cliff

It is a Sunday in November and I am physically and metaphorically standing perfectly still at the edge of a precipice, the sweeping cliff overlooking Kapalua Bay. I take in the vast aquamarine ocean as the trade winds caress my bare shoulders, back and neck. This island of Maui is my safe place, where my heart is finally healing, where my spirit soars, where my body is returning to health, where I am embracing my freedom for the first time in my adult life. How I love this place I now call "home!"

In the brief moment when the marine biologist gently wraps his arms around me and kisses me softly but passionately, I have an epiphany: I am falling and my only options are to hope for a soft landing or back away from the edge.

I have lived my entire life safely away from the edge, grounded, my feet firmly rooted, fearful that if I fell, I would break and shatter into a million shards, the pain and vulnerability unbearable. This year, I vowed to overcome my fears, to be uncomfortable, if necessary, to seek love and completely open my heart.

This is my moment and I take it by returning his tender, passionate kisses. Standing at the edge of a cliff involves taking a risk, being brave and accepting that falling means falling in love. Strange that what seems so obvious is anything but to me. Friends immediately saw my deep feelings for this man but it is an overwhelming, surprising revelation to me.

I can recall every detail, every conversation, every silent moment that we have spent together exploring the island, his hand in mine as we walk in perfect harmony along the beach path; how he fusses over me every time he picks me up for a date, making sure I am happy and comfortable. He fawns over me, admires me with each glance and beams with pride at having me on his arm; he encourages me and praises my accomplishments. At each parting, he always thanks me, kisses me and murmurs his affection.

Over and over I repeat in my head, "I'm in love with this man," chanting it like a mantra to absorb and digest the reality that I've fallen in love with this incredibly kind, intelligent, secure and loving man.

Even though these words fill my head and my heart and permeate my entire being, all I feel is fear—fear of rejection, fear of loss, fear of missing him when he leaves, fear of losing myself in him, fear of wanting to lose myself in him.

Ten years my senior, this man, with his quirky laugh, his fractured English, his passion for the ocean and his commitment to his personal freedom, is a flashing red danger sign. What do I do now? He has knocked me off balance, made me crave his touch and his presence and given me reason to doubt my fierce independence. When I think of him, I hear him, I see him and feel warm and blessed to know I will be with him again. This complicated jumble of emotions awakens my vulnerability—my signal to shutdown, pull back and bolt.

But this time, I will not. I know that what I have been looking for is standing before me, to take for myself. Instead, I compose my usual terse, polite email thanking this man I adore for a lovely day, reading it aloud before deciding not to send it. "Fairy dust," my British friend, Bridget, calls this exchange of messages through cyberspace. When I rewrite the email, I sob, weep and weep some more until the phone rings, as if I have conjured his call. His number on my call display causes my heart to leap and my knees to weaken and I know I will be at a loss for words even though I am never, ever, at a loss for words!

Totally disarmed, I pick up the phone and step outside to sit under the twinkling stars, as if that will protect me from disappointment, and manage a demure "Hello." Detesting goodbyes, knowing that he is now almost finished his project here and will be leaving again, I make small talk, thank him, tell him to be safe and then, in an almost inaudible whisper, choke out, "Bye."

He, in turn, tells me the time spent together was wonderful and then he clinches my heart. "We will keep in touch. You will see."

Numb, I do not know when or if I hung up and put down the receiver. I crawl into bed, cocooned by my overstuffed feather pillows, hoping to fall into a deep sleep. But I wake repeatedly, nausea and overwhelming sadness washing over me. In the morning, I stumble up the marble stairs to the kitchen to make a *doppio espresso*, hoping to jumpstart my exhausted body and enthusiasm for the three-day staycation I have booked on the Big Island. It has no effect.

Nonetheless, I load my overstuffed suitcase into the car and check the house to ensure everything is securely locked. All I can think about is that I am leaving today when there is so much I have left unsaid to this man I have met on three separate occasions over the last six years.

As I drive along the highway in the early morning light, an outrageous idea pops into my head. It is barely seven o'clock and I cannot believe that I am seriously considering knocking on his door unannounced. If memory serves, he did say that I am welcome anytime. I know in my heart that it is now or never to demonstrate how I feel about him. As I draw near his house, reason and fear grab hold and I almost abort my turn into his driveway. Heart in mouth, terrified, I knock on his sliding glass door and stand back. No answer. I knock again. Still no response. Disappointed, I turn to walk back to my car. Oh, no! What if he has an overnight date sharing his bed? I panic and mentally admonish myself for acting so rashly.

As I press the key fob to open my car door, I see drapes suddenly open, then the sliding door. He is standing before me, dazed and half-asleep, in a black t-shirt and fitted black boxer shorts. He invites me in and puts his arms around me. I melt and mold myself into his warm, fit, inviting body. "What a wonderful surprise," he says and proceeds to kiss me softly and repeatedly.

I yearn to stay but I have a plane to catch for the Big Island. The terrorist is coming, the rabbi is waiting and the marine biologist is leaving the island. Talk about a puzzle—with all the centre pieces and no borders! Complicated is an understatement. I press my face into his neck so he cannot see the flood of tears. I whisper, "Come back, come back."

"I will," he says, "but we will vacation together. We will take a trip. You will see. I will call, email … you will see."

I have to leave now because in another minute I will not willingly walk out of that beach house. I am in love with him, of that I am certain. He promises to meet me in Europe next summer. I will miss him until then but time and destiny have reunited us before and will once again.

A Trip to the Big Island

The last time I saw the terrorist, he swore he would come to Hawaii to see me. Then, on one of his cruise-ship gigs, he met a couple from Maui. After his concert, they lavished him with praise, mentioning that many musicians had settled on their island and that he should come and check it out. "This chance meeting must be karma," he emails me in one of our many exchanges. I almost tell him that the world is a small place; even folks from Hawaii travel and it is the law of averages at work, not karma. Instead, I reply, "Wonderful. When are you coming?"

He tentatively asks if he can come in a couple of weeks at the end of his performance schedule. "I could fly directly from Mexico after my last gig to Miami and then on to Maui if that works for you. By the way, which airline flies into Hawaii?"

I am taken aback that someone who has travelled around the world three or four times over has no idea how to get here. Nevertheless, I send him flight schedules and a few days before his scheduled arrival, I get an apologetic message that he is not yet ready to come to Maui, whatever that means. Shake it off, I tell myself, though I am disappointed and somewhat confused. I vow to limit my texts and emails to him to holidays and special occasions only from now on.

The following September, the terrorist emails me an ad for a slack-key concert in Hawaii. "I'm coming," is his answer to my line of question marks. Laughing, I dismiss his message, considering it foolish to believe that the terrorist would travel halfway around the world to see a slack-key concert on this little island. A few weeks later, he asks if he can lodge at my house for a few days while on island. It is easy to agree to something that you know has no chance of happening so I write back, "With pleasure,of course." He thanks me and asks for my mobile number so he can call when he arrives. I am sure he will never step foot on Maui so I play along.

In his next email communication, the terrorist asks if I live closer to Kona or Hilo, it's only then I realize that he is serious about coming to Hawaii but has no idea of the state's geography. "I live on Maui. You are asking about the Big Island of Hawaii," I explain. When I probe further, I learn that he has negotiated to guest perform at a slack-key concert in Waimea on the Big Island. Dumbfounded but intrigued, I reply, "That's an island away. The only way to get there from Maui is by plane, so perhaps you could spend a few days on Maui afterward or before at my house." Despite my reflex to be hospitable, I feel a bit uneasy about having a man whom I barely know spend a few nights alone with me.

"Perhaps I could kill two birds with one stone," the terrorist writes back. "I'd be up for performing on Maui if you have contacts who could schedule a performance for me." My initial reaction is to call Fulton Tashombe, the top musician on island and my dearest friend here on island. Fiercely protective of me, Fulton takes matters into his own hands and asks for the terrorist's coordinates. "I think he should stay with me," Fulton states, on the pretext that the terrorist would have access to his music studio. I am grateful and relieved. After many email exchanges between Fulton and the terrorist, they decide the terrorist should stay for the entire visit on the Big Island. I consider flying over to see him perform but think better of it.

A week and a half before the terrorist's concert, I mention to my friend, the rabbi, over dinner that a talented classical guitarist I met in Europe is performing in the little theatre in Waimea. Boldly but never expecting an affirmative response I ask him, "Do you want to go to the Big Island for a couple of days?"

"I'd love to," the rabbi responds. A bit surprised by his enthusiasm but before I can reconsider, I book a suite in a Waikoloa hotel at a hugely discounted kama'aina rate and arrange for two tickets on the small prop plane with an inter-island airline. .The rabbi is thrilled but I insist that we are going as friends and that he must hold his romantic interest in me in check.

As I over pack my suitcase with beautiful sundresses, bathing suits and more shoes than I could possibly wear, I feel torn about the trip. I am heartbroken to leave for the Big Island knowing that the marine biologist is leaving Maui while I am away, yet I am looking forward to a few days of fun with my friend, the rabbi, while feeling anxious and unsure about seeing the terrorist.

On the way to the airport after my brief, tearful, impromptu visit to the marine biologist, I pick up the rabbi, who talks incessantly during the flight. I sit in silence, not sure if it is the choppy, turbulent flight or juggling three men that is causing my queasiness.

Upon arrival at Kona airport, we pick up our rental car and drive straight to the hotel to check in. The pomp and ceremony that greets me is embarrassing but I have earned a platinum status at this hotel chain by my repeated long-terms stays on Maui over the last decade. We are escorted to the "King's suite" on the top floor, with its million-dollar view of the ocean, a large bedroom, living room with a pull-out sofa bed, dining room, fully equipped kitchen and two bathrooms. We each have our own place to sleep, shower and change so all is well.

The terrorist's concert is scheduled for that afternoon so I quickly change into a long halter sundress, reapply my makeup and step into a pair of dress sandals. The rabbi puts on fresh jeans, a handsome dress shirt and a smart hat. We ask the concierge for directions and head off in search of the theater. As we drive toward Waimea, I am in awe. The Big Island is so, so big! I have forgotten the vastness of this place. We arrive at the beautiful little theater after a few wrong turns and find six iconic Hawaiian slack-key musicians already seated on stage. After a few pieces with an island vibe, the terrorist joins them. The musicians take a bow and walk off stage leaving the terrorist on stage to play a few Spanish classical pieces on his own. After much applause, an encore and a few *hui hous*, the musicians mingle with their audience in the lobby.

I head for the ladies' room after telling the rabbi that I will meet him back in the lobby. I am feeling slightly unnerved at seeing the terrorist again after our shipboard dinner two years earlier when he kissed me and fled. I do not know what to expect. I stall as long as possible in the washroom, making small talk with a few women who compliment me on my pale yellow and blush colored dress. Finally, it is time to face the music, so to speak.

I find the rabbi in the lobby perched in front of a ukulele display. "You should say hello," he tells me. I smile and walk toward the small admiring crowd surrounding the terrorist. I patiently wait my turn until at last we are face to face. It is a startling, stripped down moment. He stares at me. "Wow, H, you made it here and you look ... well ... you look incredible in that dress." "What is it with men; always so focused on the superficial?"

Tongue-tied, fidgeting I just stand there, struck by how out of place he looks in his dark heavy clothes more suitable for Europe than the tropics. For a man who travels the globe and is exposed to every imaginable culture, he seems stuck and isolated in a bubble of his own. I, on the other hand, prefer to adapt into the environment where I visit and live.

"Let's have dinner, shall we, H? Perhaps I can stay with you at your hotel because I don't have a car." As I desperately try to formulate a polite way to say "no, no, no," the rabbi arrives, wraps his arm tightly around me from behind, kisses me on the cheek and says, "Sweetie, it's time to go. We've got dinner reservations." He walks me out to the parking lot, holding me tightly. I smile, knowing that he not only has good instincts but my back as well. He showed up for me. There will be no encore performance for me and the terrorist.

As we drive off, the Andrea Bocelli song, "Time to Say Goodbye," plays in my head, reminding me that relationships are meant to teach us something. Sometimes they only last a season or two an with good reason.

The Wishing Stone

A few weeks before my departure to Europe in my second summer after moving to Maui, my special friend, the sage, reached out to me. We have known each other for many years. We share the same spiritual sensibilities and an optimistic glass-is-totally-full attitude to life. He has watched me and waited, sitting quietly with patience and Gandhi-like wisdom, always offering advice and encouragement as I work to realize my dreams. He had told me that I could manifest anything I set my heart and intention to, so when I called to announce that I had finally moved to Maui, to my "somewhere over the rainbow," he replied without a trace of surprise, "Of course you did, because you manifested it."

We get together from time to time to walk the beach path, to admire the inspiring beauty, to catch up or, as he likes to say, "talk story." Aside from being my spiritual guru of sorts, he is a gifted artisan, avid gardener and collector of artifacts, antiques and gemstones. One morning, ten days before I board my eastbound flight, we meet to wish each another a wonderful summer. His purpose for our meeting, I learn, is to give me a wishing stone. Worn and rubbed smooth over time, the triangular turquoise stone had been blessed by a Native American chief in Arizona held in high regard.

"Rub this stone, hold it and wish for what you really want," my friend instructs. He places an affectionate hand on my shoulder. "You have the capacity to get whatever you want—few can do that, but you are different. But be careful. There are two sides to getting what you want."

I hold the stone and study it, more intrigued with its history and geology than his message. That night and all the next day, I can think of nothing else. What can I possibly wish for? I already have everything my heart desires. I am finally living in the place I have yearned to be most of my adult life. I am healthy now. My son is safe and happy and finding his own way in adulthood. I have friends here who embrace me like *Ohana*. I have passions, career goals, aspirations and a strong sense of self, all of which give me peace and joy. For the first time, I can almost hear my late mother whispering in my ear each evening as I watch the sun set from the beach path, trade winds caressing my back. For the life of me, I cannot come up with a single wish or understand why my friend would give me the stone now.

I place the stone on my bedroom dresser beside a tiny silk travel pouch. I have a few last details to attend to before closing up the house for the next six weeks. After loading my many bags into the car, I drive, roof down, to Kahului airport. As I stop on South Kihei Road to take in the beautiful Maui sky twinkling with stars, I remind myself that I have still not formulated a wish.

My first stop on this summer sojourn is Toronto, where I spend a few days marked by warm embraces from my son and family friends and by teary, gut-wrenching goodbyes. On the flight to Italy, I have plenty of time to revisit my nagging preoccupation with the wishing stone but, try as I might, I am devoid of ideas. Finally, I push the blessed stone into the back corner of my carry-on and out of my mind.

In Rome, I am greeted by familiar faces and many old friends, as if no time has passed since my last visit eight months earlier. I join a close friend for dinner on my third evening in Roma, where we have often dined, walked and climbed the Spanish Steps together in the past. We stroll hand in hand and stop for a glass of wine. We talk for hours.

As we remind each other of the hopes, dreams and goals we set for ourselves a year ago, it suddenly hits me: I already made my wish the year before and it is the stone's intention that I be open to receive it. I wished for love to find me, a wish, I suddenly realize, that has come true on multiple occasions throughout the year but not in a way I could accept. I now understand the warning by my dear Gandhi-like friend: that a wish has two sides. It is not enough to wish for passionate all-encompassing love. You have to be ready to receive it by setting fear and vulnerability aside, by opening your heart a crack so that love can seep in.

The wishing stone is merely a symbol. It has no magic, no special power, no voodoo. *Wishing* is about asking but *receiving* is just as important.

Pasta a Casa Mia, Sì?

Roma is sticky and hot this summer, a Dante's inferno with the longest spell of record-breaking temperatures in over one hundred and fifty years. Tourists walk slowly, taking refuge in air-conditioned restaurants and museums, even in the less than spotless *bagnos*. Food is the last thing I want in this heat but, as my Roman *amica*, Sofia, says," We still have to eat, *è vero*?"

Before I left Maui, Sofia emailed to let me know that she had "put in reserve our lunch on Monday," which I understand to mean that we will have lunch on the Monday after I arrive. Rome has embraced technology, evident from the texting that I see on every street corner and roundabout. Instant messaging has replaced the elegant handwritten notes delivered in envelopes sealed with waxed family crests and presented on sterling silver trays. Or, so I thought.

When I return to my hotel laden with heavy shopping bags, I slip and fall when I enter my suite, scattering my neatly wrapped purchases all over the carpeted floor. The culprit: the wax seal on an envelope that had been slid under my door. It is a note from Sofia and very typically Italian. "Tomorrow will be the lunch at the best restaurant ... My mobile is ... See you at 13:30 ... Sofia."

The next day, I call Sofia for the location. She confirms that she knows every good resto in Rome—it is her job to know as the head of guest services at a six-star hotel—but she decides that the absolutely best place for lunch is at her home. I am touched by her gracious invitation. In Rome, this is a huge *gesta*. It means you are considered *famiglia*.

I make a quick stop at Eataly next door to my hotel to pick up a few *dolci* for my hostess and arrive just on time, pastries still right side up in their boxes, a miracle considering the harrowing taxi ride from the hotel.

The tall carved walnut door swings open when I ring the buzzer identified with Sofia's family name neatly scripted beside it. I walk into a courtyard the size of a small piazza filled with white wrought-iron furniture. A series of antique black-iron staircases lead up to each apartment. A young girl in a white linen dress is skipping rope. As I watch her proudly show off her technique, I hear my name being called. "Up here ... *guarda, bella*." Sofia is bending over the railing of the last set of stairs. "*Vie ne qui*." I ascend the fire-escape-like stairs to the top floor and am welcomed with a warm embrace and *baci* on both cheeks.

Quick introductions follow although there is no need, as I know the three other women, all employed at the same hotel as Sofia. I have stayed at her hotel often over the years and have become friendly with many of the long-time staff. I hand over the sweets, which Sofia places on the kitchen counter beside what appears to be every pot, pan, kitchen gadget, bowl and utensil she owns. She laughs, indifferent to the disorder, and announces that lunch is ready. "Everything else can wait, *cara*," she tells me. "The mess have no feet to walk away!" What a marvelous attitude, I think, since maintaining a spotless kitchen while cooking is one of my compulsions.

The priority in this Roman home is simply to enjoy a leisurely, delicious and copious meal with friends, while sharing stories of one another's loves and lives and offering encouragement. How liberating, how joyful, how exceptional!

Lunch consists of perfectly cooked pasta, *al dente* of course, topped with a rich homemade tomato sauce, a chiffonade of basil, a drizzle of golden olive oil and a cloud-like mass of freshly grated Parmigiana Reggiano. I could have licked my bowl clean if not in company, so delicious is this pasta. Our *secondo* is a small green salad served with sweet, aged balsamic vinegar and an excellent first-pressed olive oil. Espresso and the sweets I brought make up the finale to this incredibly simple but delectable and lovingly prepared meal.

Lunch turns out to be a gift, of being welcomed into a Roman sisterhood, a rarity for foreigners. I feel overwhelmed with gratitude to be included in this special club, one of the very best of its kind.

Cracking the Code on the Isola of Sicily

Isola means island, a cognate of *isolare*, to isolate, to seclude, to shut off. Even though I now live on the island of Maui, I never made the connection, so obvious in Italian. Perhaps that is why I feel such a deep sense of isolation on the island of Sicily where I feel so uncharacteristically like a foreigner. Unlike in the rest of Italy, where my much improved language skills, designer dresses and attitude fool many Italians into greeting me as a local, Sicily is proving to be a surprising challenge.

Despite its superficial welcome to tourists, Sicily remains a closed community, with its Greek influences and war-torn places. It is an island with its own personality, uniqueness, eccentricities and limitations, qualities that are becoming all too familiar on my own *isola* in the middle of the Pacific. Native Sicilians make sure that tourists understand who is in charge. Though every meal ends with an abundance of sweets, Sicilians themselves are anything but *dolce*. *Forte*, tenacious and unwavering, traditional, self-protective and stoic, they must be explored and treated with great respect. It requires care to gingerly peel back each layer and expose their vulnerable and tender, warm, kind center. Sicily is definitely not for the thin-skinned, for novice travelers or anyone looking for an easy vacation. It is an acquired taste; recognizing and appreciating its virtues can be a slow process.

Taormina is a bewitching town set high above the Ionian Sea but its southern latitude has temperatures climbing to 39° Celsius (102° Fahrenheit) during the day. Photographs do not do it justice or capture its inherent beauty. Like a fairy-tale village stuck in the 1940s, Taormina has not a single mobile-phone shop, chain store or any of the modern services you would expect in a town of its size. It is a place that forces you to stretch and grow, to learn and to understand.

My well-appointed stuccoed beach house sits at the edge of the sea, a stony beach away from the water, so unlike the soft sandy beaches of Maui. I see no evidence of other English-speaking North Americans. I am an anomaly at this luxury resort, its management not quite sure what to make of me. Sicilians tend to be rooted in older, traditional values so a confident, independent, middle-aged woman traveling alone is not easy for them to comprehend. Undaunted, I embrace the challenge. It merely reinforces my resolve to learn how Sicilians tick.

On my third day in Sicily, I pass a poster advertising a James Blunt concert at the Teatro Greco, an amphitheater built by the Greeks in the third century B.C., restored by the Romans and now used for summer concerts. I've always loved this British songwriter/singers pop music and know a concert in this venue will be memorable. The amphitheater is nestled into the hillside, with remarkable acoustics and spectacular, jaw-dropping views of the sea below and Mount Etna in the background.

When I ask the resort manager to please secure one ticket for the concert, she informs me that it is sold out to Sicilians and that there are no tickets available. Stunned, I assure her that I am prepared to pay a premium for a ticket. She is emphatic, telling me curtly not to ask about it again. I leave the lobby and head to my beach house, more determined than ever to attend this concert and overcome her calculated attempt to remind me that I am an outsider.

I deliberate all evening and resolve to find a way to attend that concert. Next morning, after a restless night, I take the funicular up to the *teatro* at the summit of Taormina to give it another try. As if to reinforce the resort manager's disdain, the ticket agent laughs mockingly, reiterating that there are no tickets left for sale. All the tickets have been sold out to residents the agent takes great satisfaction in telling me. I leave discouraged but undeterred.

A bit peckish, I decide to stop for coffee at the world-famous Belmond Grand Timeo Hotel, which faces the "Greek Theater" and the incomparable panorama of the Bay of Naxos and Mount Etna. After a tour of the hotel's spectacular gardens, I am escorted to a small table on the terrace. A waiter takes my order of a cappuccino and a *dolce*. By the time he returns, I have formulated a plan. After settling my bill, I request an eight o'clock dinner reservation for one for the next evening on the hotel's terrace. I ask the maître d' for a special favor—and to have a white-peach Bellini waiting for me upon my arrival.

The next day, I call the resort manager to order a taxi to drive me to the Grand Timeo Hotel. She goes dead silent. Who is speechless now? I laugh to myself. At a few minutes before eight o'clock, I walk into the lobby of my hotel wearing a white-and-black strappy silk butterfly print European-designed gown and high-heeled Ferragamo black and white sandals, and clutching a chartreuse Furla evening bag. After a quick *grazie mille* and *buona notte*, I climb into the taxi.

That evening at the Grand Timeo Hotel, I am greeted with a Bellini and enjoy one of the best meals I have eaten in Italy. I am served personally by the tuxedoed maître d', who dances with me between each course as James Blunt performs his greatest pop hits just a few feet away in the open amphitheater, granting my request the day before when I made my dinner reservation.

The morning after the concert, the resort manager rings my beach house and asks me to drop by the front desk "at your convenience madame, she says" After breakfast, I oblige. As I approach, she leaves her position behind the desk, greets me for the first time with a hug and kisses on both cheeks, and says, "You, *madame*, have a big head." I must have looked confused but it starts to make sense as she continues. "You, *madame*, must be Sicilian! When you did not get a 'yes,' you found another way, a better way, which means you have a big Sicilian head. *Bravissimo!*"

Back on my *isola* of Maui many months later, I head for the gym as I do most days. As I begin my workout, the James Blunt song, "You're Beautiful," comes over the sound system, instantly transporting me back to the terrace of the Grand Timeo Hotel in Taormina. Once again, I am infused with the sense of empowerment I felt that night, reminding me that I can handle whatever obstacles, big or small, life puts my way. That was the true gift of Taormina.

One Serving of Roma

When my plane landed on the tarmac in Rome yesterday, I sensed a shift. I have left behind the Sicilian *domani* attitude, the best *cannoli* I have ever tasted and the bright blue Sicilian skies for the realities of a major city: traffic and palpable stress, brusque taxi drivers and smoggy air. Rush hour in Rome at 19:00 is an experience! Drivers, cyclists, scooters, buses, tour buses, taxi drivers and pedestrians all vying for the same three lanes pass within rice-paper distance of one another. I dare not to put my hand out the window! This is *normale* for Romans. They grumble under their breath, light another cigarette while driving, and text, talk on their cell phones or read the newspaper while stalled in traffic. They all accept this chaos as part of the privilege of living in one of the most culturally and architecturally rich cities in the world.

Romans differentiate themselves very clearly from everyone else in Italy. As one of my Roman friends told me, they have everything—the Vatican, the Pope and the most important monuments and ruins in the country. I laugh to myself as she continues to expound on the particular excellence of Roman watermelon, Roman fried artichokes and the overabundance of fresh Roman water, as if Romans have an exclusive on these things. What I find most intriguing is that despite acknowledging the problems common to most major cities—the pollution, the economic strains, the noise, the congestion, the overcrowding—Romans still appreciate the extraordinary virtues of their city. They may suggest that you visit the stunning Amalfi Coast, the Venetian canals, the vineyards in Tuscany, the rolling hills of Umbria and the Duomo in Firenze, but they will always remind you that, of course, none of these places is as special as Roma! I now know that the only acceptable response to a Roman about this is *"certo, vero!"*

Positioned on the divide between the northern and southern parts of the country, Rome sets the tone for tourists who expect a mecca filled with everything their heart desires: world-class designer shopping on the Via del Corso and Via Condotti, people watching on the Spanish Steps, multi-cultural restaurants—and more eyewear shops than in all of North America. I suspect Romans wear eyeglasses even if they need no vision correction—purely as a fashion statement. Eyewear comes in every color, size, shape and material. Noteworthy is the number of people milling around these shops in white lab coats. Assuming they are optometrists or opticians at the very least, I hand one of them my prescription and select a pair of frames. Turns out everyone in these "optical" stores in Rome, even the clerks ringing up sales at the cash register, wears a white lab coast, no credentials required. When I question this, I am told with an incredulous look, "Because in Rome we do that. We are a city of style, fashion and artisans, Madame!"

So, today I treated myself to one serving of Roman traffic, one super sweet and juicy serving of Roman watermelon, and one serving of Roman fashion and style.

Roma is Steamy

As I walk through Rome's Borghese gardens, I can hardly articulate the magnitude, the beauty and the haunting spirit of this magnificent park. Oleander flowers in soft pink, white and bright purple grow prolifically in the semi-tropical climate. I have chills as I stroll along the promenades lined with trees laden with ripe figs and chestnuts.

I encounter an elderly gentleman with warm eyes and a sweet smile sitting on an old-fashioned carved olive wood park bench playing a vintage accordion. I ask him in Italian if I can honor his talent by taking a video. He stops playing, extends his weathered hand and gives mine a gentle squeeze, indicating that he is touched by my request. That is the magic and beauty of the human spirit—connecting with someone with a *gesta*, a warm touch. How I adore this country.

I take some time to walk through the Borghese Gallery to admire the great masters and the remarkable architecture of the regal *palazzo* housing the art collection. Oversized canvases hang wall-to-wall and as high as the crown moulding permits. I marvel at the life-sized marble sculptures.

The day flies by and I return to my hotel to shower and change for dinner—a chance to put on a really pretty dress and sexy high-heeled Italian shoes. I am meeting friends at a special outdoor *ristorante*. That is one the charms of Italy: little romantic restaurants abound. The *piazzas* are lit by old-fashioned black wrought-iron street lamps, the tables dressed in layers of crisp white cotton tablecloths and adorned with flowers in beautifully designed vases. Small flickering candles are placed strategically in outdoors restaurants to create ambiance. Details are everything here. Dinner is simple but delectable: warm, crusty rosemary and olive bread drizzled with extra virgin olive, grilled (sea bass) and steamed rapini and caprese salad served after the entree of course; after all this is customary in Italy. Lots of catching up with friends and then a lovely walk back to my hotel. Today I must have walked a dozen kilometers!

The next day is Sunday. Roma is sizzling hot, even steamy. Temperatures continue to climb to an unprecedented 37° Celsius (99° F) but the humidity makes it feel more like 42° (108°). Cobblestone streets, usually teeming with tourists, are almost deserted, as if Rome has closed down and locked the gates enclosing this ancient city. Traffic is eerily light. Of course, being a Sunday, most shops are closed. Even the bars and *gelateria*, which you would expect to profit from the high temperatures and the appeal of their air conditioning, are empty.

But this Maui girl, who thrives on heat, sets out on foot over the Tiber River to Travestere, a neighborhood with a chic come lately Soho/Noho- like vibe. A series of makeshift tables, protected from the beating sun by tattered dingy white canopies, are piled high with slippers (as opposed to "slip-pas," Hawaiian for flip-flops) and kitchenware, men's clothing, women's undergarments, books, toys and an overabundance of cell phone cases, covers, and every kind of electronic-gadget accessory! This outdoor market is run entirely by men, who seem not the least bit interested in selling much of anything. Their entire focus is on what each passing woman is wearing, her name and whether she is a local or a *tourista*, all in the service of their favorite sport: conquest!

I assume the heat is the cause of this hot pursuit by Roman men but perhaps not. A few hours later, dripping from the heat and humidity, my white linen dress a crumpled rag, I decide to return to my safe place, the hotel. After a quick change into something fresh,

I head next door to Eataly's shop and resto. After being seated on the *terrazzo*, I order a glass of Barolo.

Savoring the rich wine made from Nebbiolo grapes with aromas that include cherry, cranberry, blackberry and a hint of chocolate, I turn my attention to my electronic pen and paper: my iPad. As I begin to write, out of the corner of my eye I notice a very attractive man who appears to be in his late thirties pick up his glass of white wine and slowly get up from the next table. Interesting that in Italy you are allowed to walk around with alcohol in a resto, unlike in Canada, I note fleetingly to myself before turning my attention back to my writing.

It happens in a flash. So stunned that I cannot move or speak, I find the young man sitting next to me, his hand on my arm. "*L' Italiana bella, piacere sì?*" Dumbfounded by his offer of "pleasure," I stutter something unintelligible. He suggests dinner and "then we will see." So confident, so direct, so unconcerned that I might say "*niente*." I smile and tell him that my boyfriend is joining me but he is welcome to dine with us. His response is a classic. "And after your dinner with the boyfriend, then we will have a drink ... *sì?*" Men in Rome are steamy, that is for sure!

Pay it Forward

As I towel dried my hair, I laughed to myself. How I was going to miss the eccentricities of this luxury Roman hotel: the toiletries lined up in test tubes on the marble bathroom counter; the requested daily newspaper that was never delivered; the antique brass skeleton room key that never worked, forcing the front desk staff to unlock and re lock our door every time we went in or out. To any inconvenience the staff would nod and smile disarmingly, promising that everything would be dealt with—but nothing ever was. The dysfunction at this five star luxury hotel was almost endearing.

Julia and I were winding down a month's tour through Italy to celebrate our fiftieth birthdays. On the last morning of our trip, I woke up extra early, dressed and headed downstairs to the elegant breakfast salon. As usual, I greeted the front staff and was welcomed in turn by the stylish maître d' with a broad smile and the traditional *baci* on both cheeks. He escorted me to a table in the second of two rooms and brought me my usual cappuccino. When I told him it was our last day in Italy, he burst into song, an aria from *La Bohème*, knowing that I had fallen in love with the opera after seeing it in Florence. (Seven years later, I will see the opera again at the breathtaking Terme di Caracalla in Rome.) I thanked him with an *abbraccio forte*, ordered my breakfast, fresh squeezed orange juice, a combination of fluffy scrambled eggs, oven roasted plum tomato, pillowy bocconcini cheese rounds drizzled with orange blossom honey and picked up an Italian newspaper. As I struggled through it with my less than perfect Italian, reality was starting to set in that this our adventure in my beloved Italy was coming to an end.

Glancing up from my newspaper, I happened to catch the eye of a woman in a business suit seated at the next table. She smiled and wished me *bonjourno* with an American accent and when I returned the greeting, she asked me, in English, to please join her for breakfast. After she introduced herself, then she surprised me by asking, "Would you like to come with me and a couple of friends in Amalfi to meet the Dalai Lama?"

A bit taken aback by the question, I thanked her but explained that Julia and I had just returned from a week and a half on the Amalfi Coast. "And later today, we are flying back to Toronto."

"Can you postpone your departure?" she asked.

Not wanting to appear rude in response to this preposterous invitation, I thanked her again and explained that it was not possible. Relieved at the interruption of Julia's late arrival for breakfast, I turned and quietly summarized the conversation.

had worked as a waitress in a diner until she decided to "brave it" and start her own company. She partnered with a friend and set up what became one of the largest transport companies in the United States.

"I've been watching your friend interact with hotel guests and staff," she told Julia. "I can tell that she is a very kind person." She handed me her business card. "If you change your mind, you're welcome to join us in Amalfi."

Julia laughed. "I can just imagine it, Heather. You and the Dalai Lama sitting together on the floor in the lotus position chanting!"

After breakfast, we went upstairs to finish packing. I called down again to the front desk to remind them to call us a taxi for the airport. "*Certo*," they cheerily replied for the tenth time. *Naturalmente*, they had forgotten—again. As we waited in the lobby for the taxi, surrounded by our luggage, the woman we had just met at breakfast handed me a small pink envelope with the word "Believe" inscribed in silver script on the front and instructed me not to open it until I had left the hotel. "You'll know what to do with it," she told me mysteriously.

In the taxi, I opened the envelope and found five business-size cards with inspirational quotes from the Bible, Gandhi, Robert Schuler, Mark Twain, Henry Ford, Winston Churchill and others— along with a neatly folded crisp hundred dollar U.S. bill.

On the way to the airport, I asked the driver about his family. He recounted the difficulties of supporting his three children in Rome as a taxi driver. At the Rome airport, I paid the *tariffa*—and tipped the driver with the hundred-dollar bill.

The City of Lights

Three years later, Julia and I decided to celebrate our fifty-third birthdays with a weeklong trip to Paris, where I booked a hotel on the Champs Élysées. It was late August and we arranged for an airport limousine to pick each of us up at our homes. The flight was scheduled for an evening departure and once we arrived at Toronto International Airport, I did my usual dance of begging, pleading and negotiating for my extra suitcases. My bags, which were overstuffed and overweight, had to be repacked at the airport while Julia calmly checked her one small bag.

On the plane, we both took melatonin, hoping to sleep and hit the ground running in the morning. We forgot about getting stuck in the dreaded "holding cell" at immigration because our flight would land before the immigration officers arrived at their stations at Charles de Gaulle airport. In Paris, you learn how to wait. You may grumble and moan but wait you must. Paris, the city of perpetual strikes and bureaucratic disorganization, has little tolerance for demanding North American tourists.

Herded into a relatively small area along with the passengers from other flights, I struck up a conversation with a pilot standing in line behind me. He had just flown in from Tahiti. "Incredible!" he said in a thick French accent when I asked him about French Polynesia. I made a mental note to put Bora Bora back on my must-see list. Hot, sweaty and half-asleep, we could feel the crowd's mounting impatience. At long last, the immigration officers sauntered to their little glass booths. Movement, at last!

We collapsed into a taxi and inched our way into the City of Lights. It was exciting to see all the familiar markers: the long tunnel; twisting and turning down one way streets; the impossible traffic circles; the honking; the swerving to avoid cyclists and motorbikes; the Arc de Triomphe—and finally, our hotel.

After welcoming us in French, the hotel porter passed us over to a gentleman, too well dressed to be another porter, who told us that he had been waiting for my arrival. I felt slightly embarrassed. Surely the hotel chain was taking my platinum status a bit too far, especially when he told us that we were going to have a drink first and that our check in had already been taken care of. Curious, I thought, because he was not even French; in fact, he sounded American. He sat us in a quiet corner of the lobby and introduced himself as the general manager of the hotel.

"Ms. Samuel, we have an unusual situation. The Prince of Qatar has booked the entire hotel for the Royal Family, except for your pre-booked suite. We are happy to provide you and your friend with security on the property for your comfort. Or, if you'd prefer, we can arrange to move you to one of our sister properties."

Was he serious or was this some sort of practical joke? When I glanced around the lobby, I finally noticed that we were surrounded by white-robed men, women in black *abayas* dripping in gold and young children dressed in Prada and Burberry. A bit dumbstruck, I asked the GM if he would give us a moment to discuss and consider our options.

"I don't see any reason to leave," I told Julia. "I vote to stay." Julia agreed and we reconvened with the GM, who arranged for champagne and truffles to be sent to our suite. At our door we met our security detail and scoped out the security team at the other end of the hall where the Prince had his own suite. Surreal, I thought.

After a long first day of walking, lunch at Ladurée and more walking and window-shopping in the Marais, jet lag finally caught up to us and we retired early. Because of the time change, we both woke up in the middle of the night. When I opened the curtains to peer down into the round hotel lobby (our suite overlooked the hotel's interior courtyard), we could not believe our eyes. Every chair in the lobby was occupied by men in gold-sashed white robes. Children from two to eight years of age were running around, screaming and shooting toy guns at one another and at the front desk staff. We could make no sense of such a strange scene.

In the morning, we took the elevator down to breakfast. As we entered the breakfast room, we realized again that we were the anomaly. All the women were shrouded in black from head to toe, forking their fruit or eggs under the *niqabs* covering their lower faces. They ate in silence like black shadows while the robed men talked and ate freely and nannies chased after their young children.

Before we made it to our seats, the GM appeared to check if we were happy with our accommodations. He explained that he had recently been transferred from the chain's hotel in London "to improve staff morale and bridge the gap between the guests and staff." We understood exactly what he was insinuating so we merely nodded.

"We intend to visit Hermès today," I informed him. "I understand the newest shop is an architectural gem, converted from an indoor swimming pool." He gave us some background about the *piscine* and offered suggestions for lunch in the same area.

Everywhere we went, or so it seemed, we encountered the Royal Family's female entourage as they swarmed one luxury brand boutique after another. Their limousine driver stashed their purchases in the trunk, drove slowly down the street and dropped the women at the next shop a few doors away. We watched them point to entire walls of scarves, purses and dresses—all with the most expensive designer labels—and buy everything in sight. I, by contrast, purchased a single Hermès scarf after finding a way to justify the extravagance as my early birthday gift. We could only imagine how starved these woman must be for fashionable attire and wondered what exactly they were hiding under those black *abayas*.

When I looked at the women of the Royal Family, it struck me in such a profound way how important it was to have a voice. My entire life, I had remained silent when I should have spoken up. I had abdicated my volition to men and suffered in silence. But I had found a new purpose; not only to work, build a career and raise a son but also to speak a truth that every woman needed to hear. So, Julia and I spent the last few days purposefully laughing and speaking loudly in the breakfast room, addressing the women despite their lack of response.

On the last morning, I visited the opulent lobby washroom next to the breakfast room. Standing at the sink was a teenage girl, a member of the Royal Family. I asked her if she was enjoying her time in Paris. She did not answer me. I repeated the question and then did the unthinkable. I placed my hand gently on her shoulder and said, "It's okay. I'm a woman, I understand, but it's your right to have a voice." She smiled and that was enough.

The Transcendent Power of Music

When I was six years old, I was given a record player for my birthday, along with my one and only record, *The Sound of Music*.

I could not have been more excited. I played that slick vinyl LP until it wore thin, became scratched and started skipping. It was my introduction to music. I would sit for hours in my room, door closed, studying the lyrics that I had committed to memory. I sang each tune, convinced that I would entertain my parents with my rehearsed performance. But privately, in the dark, I wept, so affected was I by the heartwarming lyrics, rich notes and mood-altering melodies. It was a mystery to me, even shameful, how this spinning black vinyl disk could reduce me to tears.

As I grew into a teen, I rejoiced in singing and learning to play the viola. Convinced that music was going to be my destiny, I was stunned when my mother dashed my hopes. "Heather, dear, please stop! Even the dog hides under the bed when you sing because you are so tone deaf and off key." Hard to believe since I was so confident, thinking I sounded like an undiscovered combo of Itzhak Perlman and Barbra Streisand. That day my musical aspirations may have been arrested but I never stopped singing in private; in my room, in the shower, in the car—anywhere I would not intrude on someone else. Music has always brought me to tears. Its transcendent power has evoked feelings of love, joy, sorrow, elation, promise, hope, disappointment and beauty.

Italy celebrates and rewards its musicians by providing them with venues, promoting their talent and never squelching their artistic expression, whether it is a piccolo player in the *piazza*, a flutist accompanied by a piano forte at a neighborhood *chiesa*, an orchestra commanding a huge audience in an ancient colosseum overlooking the sea, or an accordion player on a simple park bench playing on a lazy Sunday for sheer pleasure under a leafy canopy. Thank you all for the pleasure and privilege of witnessing your gift of music. Kudos, *grazie* and *bravo* to you all. *Siete tutti i tesori*!

Somewhere Over That Damn Rainbow

"Can I sit with that man and play on his piano?" my five-year-old son asks as we walk into the lobby of the newly opened Kea Lani Hotel in Maui. "I don't think children are allowed to sit at that piano," I reply. Despite my warning, he runs towards the black Yamaha baby grand and climbs up on the piano bench next to the pianist whose hands are dancing effortlessly over the keys. When he realizes my son is sitting next to him, he takes one of his little hands and points to the ivory keys that my son should press. My little boy is thrilled, filled with glee and fascination.

That was the beginning of my son's love of music and my love for this kind, talented and brave soul who, over the next two decades, becomes my Maui brother, best friend, mentor and protector—a relationship that blossomed every winter from the day my son first joined him on his piano bench.

Fulton's life had always been about his love of music. An extraordinary child prodigy lucky to be born into a musical family, he was influenced by family friends the likes of Nat King Cole, Lena Horne and Jim Naybors. He would entertain them regularly on the piano at a young age. He continued studying music theory under the guidance of the head of the department of music at Stanford University. Nevertheless, his parents urged Fulton and his siblings to get professional degrees, a master's for its educational value and a doctorate for the distinction. In the midst of his studies in child psychology and his intention to attend medical school, Fulton's passion for music won over medicine. He mastered not only the piano but almost every other instrument he deigned to pick up. A musical genius, he also sang, conducted, directed, arranged and composed and taught classical and popular music.

Destiny and a pop musician friend lured him to Maui where he settled, married, raised his two youngest children—and became the most accomplished, versatile and beloved entertainer on the island. When the Maui Arts and Cultural Center (MACC) opened in Kahului, he became its musician-in-residence, a position that also required him to be on call to ensure that the baby grand and soundboards were in tune for visiting guest performers. He built a small music studio in his garage and invited visiting musicians to jam with him and record there.

His undergraduate years in child psychology held him in good stead; he had a gift in the way he dealt with children. I watched in awe as my shy little boy, ever reluctant to talk with strangers, opened up like a flower to this gentle soul. Fulton introduced my son to music, taught him piano and gave him his first guitar. They forged a close connection, mutual respect and a bond of trust.

In his late fifties, Fulton developed a serious lung disease that forced him to tote around a large oxygen tank wherever he went. When his condition worsened, he was advised that his only chance for survival was a double lung transplant. Miracles are few and far between but one day close to Easter holidays Fulton received the good news that hospital in Los Angeles had a lung donor and he was moved to the top of the transplant list. The surgery and recovery were incredibly difficult. Fulton fought like a lion to get back to his music. He triumphed and devoted the next few years before his death to perfecting his craft, spending hours late into the night practicing, recording, composing and making documentaries about music.

The summer after I moved to Maui, I left for Europe, promising Fulton that I would stay in close touch while away. He reveled in our talks and video calls, especially when I described the opera and classical performances I had attended. He told me it rekindled his desire to play Rachmaninov, Schubert, Chopin and Mozart and all the classical masters again. When he joked that my favorite piece of music, "Somewhere Over the Rainbow," was hardly classical piece, I retorted that it was, in fact, a classic.

A few days after my return, when I called Fulton to let him know I was back on island, he asked me to meet him at the Maui Arts and Community Center. Of course, I agreed immediately. When I arrived, he was waiting for me in front of the box office. "Follow me," he said. We walked to the back of the theater through a big steel door that led onto the stage from behind. The beautiful, familiar black Yamaha baby grand I had first seen Fulton play at the Kea Lani years before was waiting, centre stage.

"Imagine you're in Carnegie Hall just about to see a special sold-out performance. Choose any seat you like but make sure you feel it's the best in the house," he instructed. I sat down a few rows back from the stage in the center. He sat down on the piano bench, placed his long, agile fingers on the keys, closed his eyes and took a deep breath with his new lungs.

I was unsure why he had summoned me to the theater until he played the first chord of "Somewhere Over the Rainbow" in a classical style. A sea of emotion welled up in the deepest part of my heart. I wept as he repeated his rendition of my favorite song. Sobbing uncontrollably for minutes after he finished playing, I desperately tried to regain my composure. I stood up and walked toward the stage, climbed the few stairs and joined him on the piano bench. I wrapped my arms around him, still sobbing, lay my head gently on his shoulder and mouthed the words, "Thank you, thank you."

"I've been practicing this since you left for Europe, Heather. It's my little gift to you, my way of telling you what you mean to me. I, Fultissimo, love you and always have, girl! I will record this for you and one day, when I'm gone, you can play it and know that I am still with you—somewhere over that damn rainbow!" Weeks after he quietly slipped away, I gathered my nerves and turned on the keyboard he had gifted me. It was his first professional keyboard. By accident I pressed a button above the keys and to my surprise, Fulton was speaking to me. He had recorded a message and a song he had written for me, and then the most precious gift …he had kept his promise…"somewhere over the rainbow Heather, that's where we will meet again".

The Wedding Dress

Lace is the quintessential romantic fabric. To my delight, Italian designers are celebrating lace in their new summer and fall collections this year. The girly side of me is thrilled to see this feminine addition to structural and classic jackets, sweaters and dresses. Even this season's lingerie has stepped it up with lace upon lace.

Despite my love affair with fashion, living in Maui has limited my opportunities to wear all my beautiful clothes. Flip-flops and a cotton sundress seem to work best everywhere on the island. On occasion, I cannot resist donning a real dress or a pair of European shoes and heading for Safeway—the place, as everyone knows, to proudly show off the latest fashions, especially in the freezer isle where a shearling or puffy winter jacket helps stave off hypothermia!

On my third day in Firenze, strolling the main piazza, I spot a familiar shop with a sale sign in the window. It reads sixty to seventy percent off! Can't hurt to take a quick peek, although finding anything in my size is a bit of a challenge in the land of pasta and pizza, pistachio nuts and all things starting with the letter "p."

I am escorted to the lower level of the long, narrow shop where the discounted summer offerings are on display. Fall merchandise in tones of cranberry, charcoal and navy blue are being unpacked and featured on the main floor. When I descend the winding marble stairs to the bottom floor, I am surprised and delighted to see a full line of very pretty summer dresses, shirts and skirts. So much to choose from! As I peruse the racks, a salesgirl accompanies me.

In Italy, you only need two expressions when shopping: *guardo grazie* and *provare?* —"just looking, thanks" and "may I try it on?" As she assembles the garments I would like to *provare*, the salesgirl, in her broken English, tells me, "Madame, we have only a few dresses in your size as the season is over" so she will "control," which I assume means she will check the stock that always seems to be locked up in a back room.

Reappearing with five more beautiful dresses, she ushers me into a small well-appointed fitting room. A tightly nipped-in coral cotton sundress with white-lace trim at the waist, a baby blue sleeveless ruched dress suitable for dining out and a sophisticated formfitting black-lace evening cocktail dress all fit perfectly. Thrilled that these dresses are discounted an additional ten percent on top of the seventy because they are the last items in each style, I immediately tell the salesgirl I will take them all.

I dress quickly but then decide, given such reasonable prices for Italian-styled and manufactured goods, to have another quick look around to see if anything else catches my eye. In the distance, I spot a cream-lace dress so striking that I ask to see it. "Good news," says the salesgirl. "It's your size and the only one we have left. It's far too *zmall* for anyone to buy. Please try it on and note the dress is a special price." When she hands it to me, it is so beautiful that my heart almost stops. Once again, I undress and step gingerly into the long creamy lace dress fit for a princess.

The moment I walk out of the fitting room in the dress, I hear gasps. Not sure if this signals approval, admiration or dislike, I turn to see where the reaction is coming from. Three smiling Florentine women are standing before me and aloud are repeating the words *"Che bellisima."* I turn slowly to face the mirror and am admittedly overwhelmed by the image reflected back at me. "A minor adjustment in the shoulders is *facile*," says Carla, the salesgirl. Agreed, but given the limited services on Maui, I think it best that a local seamstress nip and tuck and press as only can be done in Italy. Reassured that the dress can be altered and ready within a few days, I agree to take it.

Carla disappears to contact the seamstress after accompanying me back to the main floor to pay for my purchases. "Madame, Stefania will take good care to 'control,'" which I assume this time means to handle the checkout. Smiling, Stefania ever so artfully wraps the three pretty dresses in tissue and packs them into a folding garment bag. She types all the pertinent tax-free information into the computer and runs my credit card. Good to go and ravenous for porcini pasta and an *insalata mista*, I thank both girls Florentine-style with warm hugs and kisses on both cheeks.

Just as I am about to leave, laden with my many purchases, Stefania wishes me *buona fortuna*. A curious choice of words or does this Italian expression have a *double entendre*, another meaning that eludes me? "*Qua?*" I reply, totally unprepared for her enthusiastic counter response. "*Buona fortuna, madame.* We are so '*appy* for your beach wedding!" I stop dead in my tracks. The look of horror, confusion and disbelief on my face prompts Stefania and Carla to quickly explain that the original cost of this designer bridal gown was twenty-seven hundred euros; that this special bridal collection was produced specifically for beach weddings, for casual, sophisticated brides; and that only one in each size was made, by hand. "You are so lucky to find the last one in your size, and for only two hundred euros!"

The irony is that the dress has found me, called out to me. Fear grips me when I realize that this extraordinarily beautiful gown is a wedding dress, and that it fits me as perfectly physically as it does in the deepest part of my vulnerable and finally open heart.

In the end, I leave the lace wedding dress in the shop. Despite my desire to own it and inhabit it, the symbolism and message are far too potent. Am I truly ready, open and destined to stand on the beach and commit my life and my love to someone? When I am, I will need to be sure that he is also dressed in something that fits, a suit of commitment, kindness, honesty, integrity, respect and, above all, love. And it will not even have to be made in Italy!

Not a Good Day to Get Married

How did May 31st get here so fast? It is too glorious and sunny a day to be inside being primped and coiffed. So here I am, twenty-two years old, sunning myself outdoors and trying to breathe normally. I feel as if I am suffocating. I hear my name being called and ignore it. It's when my mother calls out my full name I know she is not happy with me. She scolds me for sitting on the lawn of the synagogue in my outrageously expensive handmade designer wedding gown, a combination of lace, tulle and silk.

"Today is not a good day to get married," I flippantly say. "Another day might be better.

"Today is the day, Heather Joy! A couple hundred guests are arriving within the hour." She seems annoyed. I am thinking that they could all still come for the dinner and dance but I would rather skip the "I do part." Something does not feel right. When he asked me to marry him, I remember saying "okay," but he could have been asking me to take a trip, buy a sweater or test-drive a new car; my response and understanding of the ramifications would have been the same.

Since it is far too late to round up a horse and canter away from this situation, I do the only thing possible; I make my parents happy. After all, my mother has rallied, fought her way through chemo, radiation, multiple surgeries just see me say 'I do'. I walk up the aisle and stand under the *chuppah*, knowing I am marrying the wrong man—while the right one, or at least a better option, is standing nearby. It has been drilled into me until it has become second nature: do what is right, be obedient, do what is honorable; make your parents proud, be a good girl.

A week later, we depart on our honeymoon. I need a lot of persuading to leave my dying mother. She promises to hold on until I return and encourages me to enjoy a well-deserved respite. I have been teaching at a private school during the day, sleeping in a chair at her hospital bedside every night, planning a wedding and looking after my father and younger siblings for months in my mother's stead.

For years, I secretly harbored a dream of getting married in Bora Bora and honeymooning in Hawaii. Yet here I am, in a stinky humid crowded local bus on the way to Haifa. At the very least, I expected a taxi or an express bus from the Tel Aviv airport. It *is* our honeymoon, after all. Somehow my husband had talked me into going to Israel for two weeks because he wanted to see his elderly maternal grandmother. Not the romantic honeymoon most girls dream of but, as usual, I took the high road and acquiesced. Is that a goat in the seat behind me? Motion sickness from the bumpy stop-and-go ride sets in.

Because I am still jet lagged, reality does not hit until we arrive at our destination. No grand hotel, no doorman, no concierge, no guest suite, no pool; just Grandma's spartan apartment with its two bedrooms, a minuscule kitchenette and a single tiny bathroom. Grandma, who speaks only Hungarian and understands just a smattering of Hebrew, greets us each with a Dixie cup of vanilla ice cream, a serving suitable for a five year old. Night cannot come fast enough and all I want to do is phone home, like ET, for rescue.

Our bedroom has two single beds separated by an old wooden nightstand covered in crocheted doilies. That night and every other night of our "honeymoon" stay in Haifa, Grandma sleeps curled up in a little threadbare upholstered chair just beyond my husband's bed. Not the honeymoon I dreamt of …to Grandma's house we go!

Biscotti, Cantucci and Mandelbrot

Back home in Maui from Europe, a friend and I are talking on the phone, catching up with our news. In the middle of our conversation, we land on the subject of culinary delights. I mention my efforts in Italy to sample as many regional specialties as possible, unlike my normal fare in Maui, which I limit essentially to a few leafy greens, papaya, mango, a handful of seeds and nuts and ahi tuna.

Somehow we work our way around to the subject of *cantucci*. She has no idea what I am talking about. How best to describe these rock-hard, semi-sweet, nut-laced cookies? Instead of listing ingredients, I tell her that *cantucci* are much like Jewish *Mandelbrot* but harder and made with egg whites instead of whole eggs. Still does not ring a bell so I try again. "They are like *biscotti* but with less sugar."

Sometimes simple things can be profound if you spend a moment or two to consider them. *Cantucci* are much like people— essentially the same but with the recipe slightly altered in each of us. A little more sugar, a little less sugar; an egg white instead of a whole egg; lighter semolina instead of heavier cake flour; some laced with silky, dark chocolate, some with bittersweet cocoa. Stirred or whipped instead of gently blended; under baked, over-baked or twice-baked to perfection. Subtle differences affect the outcome.

These Italian cookies, I explain, are never eaten on their own. They are meant to accompany a good strong velvety espresso, a creamy rich cappuccino or a golden *vin santo* dessert wine. They work as a pair, making the combination sweeter, softer, tastier and smoother. They complete each other. Together they are better than on their own. In tandem, they form a perfect union!

Aha! At that moment, I realize that it is time for me to find love!

La Bohème—*A Lesson in Love*

Where better to experience opera than in Rome? I have a burning desire to see opera at the Terme di Caracalla and turn to a Roman friend to get me a ticket for Saturday night, regardless of the opera being staged. In Italy, a phone call that begins with *ciao* followed by a few *dimi*, a *certo*, *grazie lei* and a *va bene* always works like magic and gets you anything at all. Being Italian and having the inside track means you never pay what is asked but only what you feel is fair. So when tourists and foreigners moan and lament about things not working in Italy, Italians just shrug because they know that their chaotic system *does* work, but only for them.

I make a quick run to the opera house around the corner from my hotel to pick up my ticket for tonight's performance. Predictably, a five-minute jaunt turns into an hour-long ordeal. There is no ticket waiting for me under my name. After checking for the name of my friend (the hotel's guest relations manager who arranged for my ticket), we try every Italian surname in the greater Rome phone directory. We eventually find it—under the surname of the boyfriend of the guest relations manager. How *stupida* of me not to have guessed that at the outset, but never mind. The box office manager and I are now very well acquainted and he is planning a trip to Maui as a result—because we are now *famiglia*. I *grazie mille* my new *amico* at the theater and finally notice that my ticket is for *La Bohème*.

I dash home to lay out my best dress, shoes, bag and all things Italian for tonight's special event. I quickly check the ticket and realize that the opera starts way past my Maui bedtime, at 9:30

p.m. I decide a quick nap is in order. When I call the concierge for an eight o'clock wake up call, he laughs, "Have a *gooda nappe*. We will wake you at twenty hours or you will *missa di opera*. Eight will be morning!" See, Italy does work, just not the way we foreigners expect.

My best Prada silk chartreuse dress with a coordinating wrap, a kiss on both cheeks to everyone at the hotel's front desk (a ritual by now) and the taxi is waiting.

Set high above the center of Roma in a park-like property, the open-air theatre is nestled between majestic ruins flanked by tall cypress pines. I could never have imagined such a remarkable setting. The Teatro dell'Opera's open-air theater was created in 1937 on the site of the Terme di Caracalla, the third-century Roman baths bearing the name of their founder, the Emperor Caracalla. The open-air theatre began as an experiment but soon became popular with Romans and spectators from around the world. When in Rome, opera at the Terme di Caracalla is a must. By chance and a stroke of luck, I feel like I am simultaneously living in the present, experiencing the past and getting a hint of a possible future. It feels as though the Terme di Caracalla is enchanted,

As the seats fill and the lights dim, performers and orchestra members make their way to the stage. Projected onto the thirty-foot-high ruins are giant images of paintings by the French masters —Monet, Renoir, Degas and others—that change with every scene. *La Bohème* is a classic star-crossed love story: the opera tells the story of the love affair between a poor poet and an equally poor seamstress in nineteen thirties Paris. Their love story is juxtaposed against a concurrent love story of a wealthy young socialite in love with a humble, starving painter. The message, so clear, seems to elude us today—it is all about love. The rest, the social pressures and minutiae that get in the way, cripples our chance for what is most important and precious in life.

I had not planned on seeing *La Bohème* but I did not plan to fall in love, either. I suppose that is part of the lesson; that we need to let go of the pretense that we can plan and control every aspect of our life, and just live it. And when love finds you, grab hold of it and love back!

CHAPTER 4

TAKING THE LEAP NAME

I fly home from Rome in a flutter, eager to pursue the unexpected romance kindled just weeks before I left Maui. Our constant communication during the summer months apart has won me over. Primed for a relationship of substance, I may have fallen in love so suddenly that my excitement is fraught with trepidation.

How did this happen? A meeting with my yoga instructor to discuss my idea for a private health and wellness business targeting woman in my age group set it all in motion.

After a year of settling into island life, I finally relented and began attending yoga classes. Everyone on Maui preaches the benefits of yoga for overall health and balance. I must admit I was skeptical, so I did what I usually do when things seem sketchy to me: I dive in.

The yoga *shala* was only a few blocks from my house and offered classes in the morning and at sunset. Attending the first few classes, I felt awkard, especially when lying perfectly still in *shavasana*, the corpse pose that ends of the practice. My mind kept buzzing and my body wanted to get up and move. As everyone around me breathed deeply, letting go of their identities, thoughts, tensions and intentions, I wondered how they did that and had difficulty grasping the concept. Trying to let go and surrender unnerved me.

By the end of the second week, I had become more familiar with the yoga flow and could even manage the poses without falling over and loosing my balance. A month or so later, I fell into a light sleep during *shavasana*. When the yoga instructor gently roused us with a light touch of essential oil to our temples, I realized that there was a point to this whole yoga thing after all. Finally able to quiet my mind, I also learned to quiet my body, recognizing that this was a healthy, mindful way to find my internal balance and keep my auto immune condition in check.

I did not realize that my triweekly yoga practice had also changed my body shape until I dressed to join friends for dinner one evening and slipped on a tight, fitted dress. Could those impossible poses be elongating my muscles? A nice bonus but the main benefit was how a "type-A" personality like mine could find inner peace and quiet through yoga. If it works for me, I wondered how many other women in their fifties on the island would benefit from yoga as an alternative to yo-yo dieting, crazy workout programs and weight-loss pills.

I arrange to meet my yoga instructor at the coffee bar of an organic supermarket to discuss my idea. Having arrived a few minutes early, I walk inside the market. An attractive younger man in jeans and a black t-shirt approaches and asks me if I am looking for the coffee. I assume he is another customer as he directs me to the self-serve coffee station. I thank him but ask about specialty coffee. He points to the back, where I place my order with a friendly woman who I assume is the manager.

When my yoga instructor arrives, we embrace Maui-style and sit down at an outdoor table. As we begin to talk, we are interrupted by the same man, who places my cappuccino, spoon, sugar and napkin on the table before me. Vaguely baffled, I pay no attention. We barely have a chance to exchange our ideas when he turns up again at our table, grinning, with a large bowl of purple grapes. "Since you work out so much, I thought you'd like something healthy." Perplexed, I look at him, look at my instructor, and say, "Okay, thanks."

"He is crushing on you, Heather," says my instructor.

"What? Who is he? I thought he was a customer. And he is *not* crushing, whatever that means!"

"He is the manager here and clearly has a thing for you."

I totally ignore her comment and we continue our discussion about offering private yoga sessions and designing a nutritional program. I'm now totally convinced that the benefits from yoga practice are underestimated. Regular practice works to decrease stress, reduce inflammation, promote sleep quality, foster heart health and provide over all mind and body balance. We put a tentative plan and timeline in place for the fall when I return from Europe and bid each other goodbye.

I carry our coffee cups inside and as I am about to leave, the manager calls out to me by name. Stunned, I turn and ask him how he knows me. "I've been watching you go to yoga for a while. I also asked one of the girls here for your name and number. I wanted to call and ask you out. You shop here sometimes, don't you?" "Do you ever walk the beach at sunset?" I just nod yes.

"Thanks for the coffee and grapes. Nice meeting you." Before I make it to the door, he calls my name again and asks for my phone number. I usually choose one of three options in this situation. I give a false number, say that I do not have a mobile phone or ask for their number, promising to be in touch. It all means the same thing: I am not interested. The manager catches me so off guard that I blurt out my landline number before I can think better of it. No harm done, my landline is still listed under the owner's name. I reassure myself on my way home; he won't call. I walk into the house and drop my purse on the kitchen counter, then notice the red light flashing on the answering machine. The message is from the manager, wondering if he had the correct number and asking me to call him back. Not sure why but I jot down his number. He sent me a text which bounced back and did not realize I gave him my home number which is not set up to receive text messages. So when I returned his call, he was thrilled. "I could meet you after work today and walk the beach with you, if that's okay?"

" I guess, but I speed walk."

"Great, see you later around 5:30 in the parking lot across from the beach."

Can't hurt to go for a walk, I tell myself. I am leaving for Europe in ten days so there is nothing to worry about. We meet as planned. Unaccountably, I feel completely unhinged. He unnerves me and I do not know why. We walk, make small talk, exchanging basic information about ourselves. He talks about his passion for food and cooking and his love of surfing and Maui. Guarded and shy, I offer very little about myself. After the sky turns to shades of pink and crimson and the sun sinks like a fireball into the ocean, we walk back to the parking lot. I thank him for joining me on my sunset beach walk. His smile is dazzling. He embraces me with a typical Maui hug.

"See you," I quip as I get into my car.

"Tomorrow, same time?" he asks. I nod.

The next day he calls and asks me how I feel about dogs. "I love them," I tell him.

"I could pick up my dog and bring him with us, if that's okay with you? He's a big dog but everyone loves him."

In the parking lot before sunset, I watch the manager get out of his Tacoma pickup truck and open the back door. A dog the size of a small pony leaps out and runs toward me. I cower, unprepared for such a large rambunctious animal. The manager attaches him to a leash until we get to the beach where he lets his dog run free to bob and weave among the last beachgoers. I tell myself not to worry about entanglements, about dogs or anything else. I will soon be on a plane to Europe.

"Another beautiful sunset," I say as we approach the parking lot after our walk. "See you." I am in my car with the engine running before he has a chance to say goodbye.

He wraps on my window. "Could you please get out of the car?" When I step out, he moves toward me and wraps me up in a Maui embrace, then softly, tenderly kisses me. I say nothing, get back into my car and drive home.

An hour later, sitting on my lanai, I am treated to a spectacular fireworks display courtesy of a corporate event at one of the large five-star beachside hotels. The phone rings. It is the manager. "Are you watching the the display? Ironic that there are fireworks tonight of all nights. Amazing, isn't it? That is exactly how I felt when I kissed you. I saw fireworks. Can I see you tomorrow?" I'm at a loss for words!

The next two evenings confirm that there is definitely chemistry, a potential for more if only I were staying, but I am not. The next week is filled with more exchanges of personal history. I learn that he is younger than I am but he seems to consider us contemporaries. Since he never asks my age, I never volunteer it. Each time we are together, he asks when he can see me again. I mention that I am leaving for Europe but it is only on the day before my departure that he realizes that I will be gone for several months. He insists that he will wait for me and that we must stay in touch. In truth, I have grown more than fond of him. The manager is endearing, boyishly handsome, educated and seems to have career aspirations beyond his current job at the market. On my last day on Maui, we both know that the seed of a relationship has been firmly planted.

Thanks to FaceTime and Messenger, we speak every day while I am in Europe. Despite the twelve-hour time difference, we develop a deeper connection. He counts down the days until my return to Maui, but at the same time encourages me to make my time abroad exciting and memorable. I return home early on the morning of my birthday to surprise him. I drop my half-dozen suitcases in both the family room and spare room and drag myself into the shower. After a quick espresso, I put on a summer dress and call the manager. After all the texts, emails, FaceTime and his excitement about my return, I am terribly disappointed that he does not answer my call.

A few minutes later I am unpacking my cosmetic bag and the phone rings. "Are you really back?" Before I can make a second espresso, he is standing at my front door, carrying a bag of groceries in one hand and a pretty little white bag with small celadon box with a matching bow inside. "It's your birthday, baby, so I am making you a special birthday dinner. And I have a present for you!" he says, beaming. "But the best present for me, Heather, is that you are home and we are together." Words I have longed to hear but have only imagined.

The manager cooks me a scrumptious birthday dinner and we enjoy a romantic evening, dining on the lanai. After a homemade dessert, he hands me the little green box with a card. I open the card first and am overwhelmed by his warm and effusive message, thanking me for coming home to spend my birthday with him. That is enough for me, no present necessary, but he urges me to open his gift. I am secretly grateful that the box is not turquoise, since little turquoise boxes will forever be negatively associated with my ex-husband.

While I was away, the manager had asked me what my favorite color was and had obviously paid close attention. When I open the box, I turn away to avoid him seeing me so emotionally affected by this beautiful gesture and gift. He had picked out a delicate gold necklace with a cluster of hearts in peridot, my birthstone. No one has ever given me something like this. How can I accept it? But what I find most endearing—and incredible—is how thrilled the manager is to give me something he thought I would love. "On the day before you left for Europe, you were wearing the most beautiful lime-green dress. You were extraordinarily beautiful in it. I thought this necklace would look good with that."

That was the beginning of something I had yearned for but never believed I would find: a love affair with a man who wanted to see me happy. A month and a half later, the three of us were living together in my house—me, the manager and "our" dog!

The Iconic Turquoise Box

My mother never had loving parents to celebrate her birthdays so she always made a big fuss over her children's birthdays. In turn, I worked to create a special day for my son, from his very first birthday. I always looked forward to August, my birthday month, but after losing my mother, my special day was never quite that again.

My husband thought that celebrating birthdays was banal, the custom of gift giving annoying and overrated. When I made the mistake of organizing a surprise thirtieth birthday bash for him, he was not overly pleased. Although I never dared ask for anything of substance, I secretly hoped that one year my husband, or my father would acknowledge my birthday, perhaps by organizing a gathering of everyone I loved. But it never happened, so I stopped hoping, stopped expecting.

On my thirty-ninth birthday, my eternal optimism was sparked. When my husband informed me that he had made a dinner reservation for the two of us at a new bistro, I was touched and excited. Our son was seven years old so he was bathed and in his pajamas by the time we were ready to leave for our evening out. When I hugged and kissed him before we left, he wished me a happy, happy birthday, nudging his father in some kind of secret code.

At the bistro, we ordered a bottle of sparkling mineral water and a glass of cabernet each and discussed what we might like to order for appetizers. When my husband pulled out a bag from behind his chair, I could not believe it. It was the iconic turquoise bag from Tiffany's, the one every girl recognizes instantly. The turquoise box tucked inside seemed too perfectly wrapped for me to even attempt to open it but when I did, I found a tiny pair of silver open-heart earrings. They were more appropriate for a young girl but I gushed over them nonetheless, thanking my husband over and over, trying them on in appreciation.

Stone-faced, as usual, he admitted that our son had reminded and pestered him to buy something for my birthday. "I took him to the store with me and he picked out these earrings. He told me how much you love hearts. I really wanted to buy myself new golf clubs instead." His words pierced my heart like a knife. I could feel his hand turn it, the blood spurting everywhere, causing my slow, painful death.

I took off the earrings, put them back in the little turquoise box, placed the box back in the bag and murmured, "You can take them back and buy golf clubs." I pushed the bag over to him across the table.

"Okay," he replied.

I put on a brave face, smiling through dinner, but I was devastated and desperately hurt. My disappointment was with myself, that I had been fooled again into believing that my husband valued and appreciated me, even if only for the duration of my birthday. We drove home in silence. I never saw the earrings or the turquoise box again and I never asked about his golf clubs. One day, I vowed, I would be worth something to someone.

A Princess Phone

What fourteen-year-old girl would not be thrilled to get a pink Princess phone for her bedroom? My mother had an ulterior motive. After several years of jockeying for phone time while I spent endless hours chatting with girlfriends and giggling with boys, she ordered me my own phone line from Bell Canada and finagled my father into buying me a pink princess telephone of my own. I memorized my phone number and have never forgotten it, even though I can now barely remember what I had for breakfast.

By the time I was fifteen, my father had finally stopped grumbling about the cost of my telephone line. Always suspicious when he switched positions from con to pro, I suspected he had a hidden agenda. He rarely gave me anything without strings attached.

Around that time, my father and a partner had launched a new business to acquire the patents, purchase the machinery and set up a large plant to manufacture boxes—pizza boxes, cake boxes, take out boxes and a variety of industrial paper products for commercial use in the hospitality industry. My mother supported my father's transition to his new career and company, a move long overdue. Until then, he had been earning a modest wage working long hours for his mother at the variety stores that she and my grandfather owned for a couple of decades.

Although my grandparents had worked hard to create a comfortable living with a number of businesses and some prime real estate investments, my grandmother held tight to the purse strings. Much like my father, she was cold, controlling, distant and lacking in empathy. She ruled by fear and demanded respect; she was rarely demonstrative and detested public displays of affection.

The new business took off and my father's income grew exponentially. This suited him because he had a taste for luxury and the finer things in life, probably because his parents had spoiled him as a child. He became more generous with my mother, surprising her with jewelry, dinners out and short vacations—an attempt to overcompensate for his random outbursts of temper, indifference and moodiness. As a young girl I judged my mother, disappointed that she would foolishly settle for material things over respect, kindness and attention from my father. She deserved so much more than he gave her, she deserved love.

Nevertheless, my mother reveled in the gifts and perks since she had grown up so poor, abandoned and orphaned. And I benefited, too. Every weekend, she would take me out for a treat: a manicure, a lunch or to the salon to have our hair washed and styled. Despite my mixed feelings about my father, I could see that our home life had become more peaceful with our rising affluence, and I felt more hopeful.

On Saturdays and Sundays, my little pink Princess phone would ring off the hook but almost every time I answered, the caller would hang up. I was sure someone was playing a prank and found it disturbing. "We should call the phone company and lodge a complaint or call the police and report it. Let's at least change my number," I implored my parents.

My father laughed it off. "Leave it be. Don't answer it. *I'll* answer your phone on the weekends." Curious response, I thought at the time. He found it bothersome to answer the phone at anytime.

A few weeks later, the police barged into our house, rushed straight upstairs and into my bedroom. I was arrested, taken to the police station and fingerprinted. They informed me that my phone line was being used to place and take gambling bets. I was in shock. My father had been running a bookmaking operation through my pink Princess phone! How could he do that to me?

He promised to meet me at the police station. "Don't worry, you're still a minor. I'll hire the best criminal lawyer in the city to have this unfortunate situation taken care of, don't be concerned Heather. There will be no record of this."

No words can describe my shame, mortification and disappointment that my own father knowingly and willingly set me up, his own daughter for his illegal dealings. It was no consolation that he didn't commit some heinous crime., just gambling as he called it.

At our high school, the public address system broadcasted a local radio station after lunch. I cringed when the station chimed the news for I was the top story of the day. No charges were laid in the end but the emotional damage was done.

My mother was heartsick for me, apologetic, forced once again to pick up the broken pieces that my father always left behind. Then our lives simply returned to normal, or what passed for "normal" in our family.

Namesake

It is a bitterly cold February day and no matter what I do, I cannot shake this stomach flu. I have tried to rest and have been drinking copious amounts of fluids but after nine days, nothing seems to be working. I am tired of waking up feeling as if I have been run over by a freight train. I drag myself to the bathroom and look at the hot mess reflected back at me. Maybe if I have my hair done I will feel better. I make an appointment and dress in a cozy black cashmere turtleneck and pulled on a pair of faded blue jeans. It takes all my stamina to drive to the hair salon while fighting off the bone-throbbing aches, nausea and vertigo.

Maria, my hair stylist, is the one of the busiest in town. We all love her ability to transform the rattiest nest into a coiffed masterpiece fit for *Vogue* magazine. Maria also fancies herself a psychic medium, a channeler of spirits. When I arrive, she is conjuring a client's deceased husband to ask permission for his very much alive wife to marry his best friend. To hasten his response from the spirit world, Maria is also burning incense and chanting. The stench infiltrating the salon's waiting area and her voodoo-like incantations are exasperating my already overwhelming nausea.

The last time my stomach was this upset I was pregnant with my son. I cannot be pregnant, I tell myself; my hormone levels are too low. "There is no way you can ever get pregnant," my doctor informed me last year. "That portal is closed."

Finally an update after waiting for my appointment; the receptionist reports that the dead husband is finally responding but he is not keen on his wife's wedding plans. More waiting is in store. "I will come back," I tell the receptionist, who is now preoccupied with polishing her nails. I head to the pharmacy across the street. Maybe some mints and a little club soda will help deal with my nausea. As I round the last aisle, the pregnancy tests catch my eye. No, no, that's ridiculous, I tell myself, but something forces my hand and *voilà*, the box appears in my little wire basket, makes it to the cash register and into my bag. I trudge across the street, annoyed by the giant wet snowflakes falling like mush from the sky.

Since Maria is still busy negotiating the terms of her client's prenuptial agreement with the afterlife, I figure I have time to pee on a stick. A blue line appears in less than a minute. Shock, disbelief, confusion and a hint of relief all converge in my head and heart. At least this explains why I have been feeling ill for so long. I immediately call my obstetrician, who scoffs. "No way Heather, it is not possible."

"The stick says so," I protest. She insists that I take a taxi to the emergency department of the downtown hospital where she is treating a pregnant mother. "Before or after I get my hair styled?" She pauses, then says in a very stern doctor-like voice, "Now, Heather. Right now!" Too bad about my hair but at least I am wearing clean underpants.

I ask the receptionist to call me a taxi and telephone a friend to pick up my parked car from the lot across down the street. In what seems like a mere minute later, I have been admitted and am immediately surrounded by equipment, nurses and a team of physicians in my small cubicle. Why all the fuss? Surely I am not the only woman who is almost forty and pregnant! It is only when I catch sight of the name tag of the last doctor examining me that I begin to understand the gravity of the situation and the cause for concern. Below his name is his title: oncologist. "Call your husband," my doctor says. "We need to talk."

Two and a half months later, after biweekly ultrasounds, weekly physical examinations and frequent blood tests, I am being induced into labour. In the operating room, my doctor comforts me, again explaining the necessity of delivering my baby now. "A cancerous tumor in the fetal sac has compromised your baby's lung capacity. If we wait any longer, the tumor will burst, the cancer will spread and kill you and the baby."

I deliver a baby girl, who does not survive, an outcome I had been forewarned to expect. My sympathetic doctor encourages me to name baby girl. She knows it will give me solace. "Rachel Madeleine" is named, wrapped and placed on my chest and I hold and kiss her before she is taken away. I am alone. My husband had a very important business meeting that day. "After all," he reminded me just before the procedure, "There won't be a baby so why do I need to be there?" I suppose I could have insisted he be at the hospital but I have more pressing things to deal with now — chemotherapy infusions, a seven-year-old son waiting for me at home and a busy catering business.

There is no time to cry or grieve. Now it is my daughter's time to move on and connect somewhere else, perhaps to join the soul of my mother, her grandmother and namesake. When I come home from hospital a few days later, I go straight back to work and never speak of my daughter again.

Nurture versus nature

The end of summer is fast approaching and I am counting the days until I sell my retail hosiery business in Hazleton Lanes. My son's sixth birthday and the beginning of his school year are just around the corner. I am thrilled at the prospect of being a full-time mom for a while before venturing back into the workforce.

With more free time, I am able to volunteer on Friday afternoons at my son's private day school in our synagogue. I bake *challah* with the children in his class and help them with their reading and art projects.

I also sign up to work on various hospital fundraising projects and join a group of school mothers keen to affiliate with the new "Out of the Cold" program that has begun offering the homeless a hot meal and a warm place to sleep at a few midtown Toronto churches.

A girlfriend and I approach the rabbi to discuss the possibility of implementing the "Out of the Cold" program in our synagogue. We see it as great opportunity to get the school aged children involved in community service. The board of directors approves our proposal to open the synagogue to the homeless one night a week, leaving us with the daunting task of bringing our vision to fruition. We convince a congregant, whose family owns a supermarket consortium, to donate all the staples. A well-known baker in the community agrees to lead a team to bake all the cookies, cakes, muffins and confectionaries in the synagogue's commercial kitchen. We organize a group of volunteers to pick up the groceries each week. Another group is assembled to prep and cook the hot dinners ,breakfasts and prepare the takeaway bag lunches.

The students are given the task of setting the dining tables as their last activity of their school day—a way for them to learn about *tikkun olam*, the Jewish concept of performing acts of kindness and giving to others.

Every week, a few of my girlfriends and I pick up enough groceries to feed thirty or so homeless people and spend the better part of the afternoon in the synagogue's commercial kitchen cooking and baking. Most of our husbands pitch in to set up mattresses and blankets and pillows at the end of their workday.

Once word gets out about our delicious and nutritious menu—crudités, freshly baked bread, soup, salad, main course, side dishes and dessert—the crowd at our door grows quickly. With our limited space and capacity for approximately thirty guests, we soon have to send the overflow to other churches. We refer to the clients as "guests" in an attempt to restore their dignity. Everyone, guests and volunteers alike wear a name tag so we can call people by their name as a token of respect.

Within a few months our program is lauded by the synagogue board and congregants and the community at large. I am fortunate to be a part of it and thrilled that my six-year-old son, who has never known cold or hunger, is learning the virtue of giving to others without expectation. That is the lesson the program is teaching him, I tell my husband. He commends my efforts but has no interest in participating, being far too busy with work.

One evening in late spring, as my husband and I leave an upscale Yorkville restaurant where we had been entertaining business associates, a scruffy looking man approaches us. He thanks me wholeheartedly for providing a safe shelter, wonderful meals and a caring environment at our synagogue. My husband is incensed and embarrassed. "I cannot believe that you talked to that homeless man! He knew your name and, what's worse, you knew his." Completely dumbfounded by his reaction, I say nothing as we drive home in silence.

That night I decide to make it my mission to teach my son about empathy, praying fervently that nurture will prevail over nature.

My Fraught Forty

It is August. My fortieth birthday is coming up at the end of the month and my son will turn eight in early September. Our beautiful English Tudor home is no longer ours. This is not the birthday present we expect or deserve. "Where are we going to live now?" my son asks me.

A few months earlier, my husband asked me to put our house up for sale—the house I have so lovingly and painstakingly redesigned and decorated for months after moving in. He wants to make a sideways move to a house with a flat backyard where our son can run and play and he can have a pool. Ironically, our "backyard" is the main draw for me—all ravine with a natural stream lined with ferns and century-old trees. Despite our home's location in the middle of a busy city, it feels like the country from the back deck. I sip my morning coffee in the kitchen solarium and watch baby red foxes frolicking beside the brook below.

With a heavy heart, I agree to the sale. I want to make my husband happy and realize there will be no peace at home until I agree to listing it for sale. Since I was the one who had chosen this particular house, I must bend, now that I accept that it is not his dream home after all., Our home is expensive to maintain and this becomes an additional source of resentment for my husband. It takes some time but we finally find another house that he deems worthy and more suitable, in the same neighborhood. Because he is a real estate lawyer and investment banker, he negotiates a private deal with the owner. After parading our son, my father, my in-laws and a few of his close friends through our prospective new home, we sign the listing agreement to sell our house.

Not surprisingly, we receive an offer to purchase on the first day the house is listed for sale. The official offer is presented to us two days later and my husband implores me to sign it back, to close the deal. I pack alone and I clean alone to accommodate the forty five day closing date. I let go of most of the furniture and the decorative touches I worked so hard to create in our four-story home on the assurance that everything will be even better in our next home. "I'll buy you all new things," my husband promises, "so give the new owners anything and everything they want."

But a few days ago, all those expectations are dashed. "I'm leaving," my husband announces just two days after his return from a business trip out west. Confused, I ask him where he is going so soon after his last trip. "I'm leaving *you*, Heather. I love our son but I'm just not into this family thing." He pauses for a moment. "What are you going to tell him?" he asks.

Not sure if it is shock, disbelief or just raw maternal instinct but, for the first time ever, my steely conviction kicks in. "*You* will tell him what you are doing and that I will be there to comfort him, because I am his mother."

He calls our son to the den/library on the second floor and sits him down on the leather love seat. "I love you, buddy, and your mom, but I don't want to live with you both anymore. I'll see you but now I have to leave."

Our son begins to cry as we watch, through leaded-glass windows, his father drive away. I can barely think straight but there is no option but to hug, cuddle and reassure my son that everything will be okay, that we will be okay.

I walk down the stairs to the kitchen. On the counter, I find a cheque for three hundred dollars and a note. "This is for both of you. It should help you get what you need for a while." I tear up the cheque and call our listing agent. I ask her to find us a rental condo or townhouse in the area, not quite sure how I will pay for the deposit, let alone the rent.

My husband has taken it all. He has locked me out of our bank accounts, cancelled our joint credit cards, stopped payment on our son's summer camp and school tuition and arranged for the proceeds from the sale of our house to go directly to him. He has even changed the beneficiary of his life insurance policy.

I know that I must rise from the pyre like the phoenix, spread my wings and soar. I sell the only thing that I have of my mother's, her diamond stud earrings.

On August 15th we stand, homeless, by the curb of our house as a moving truck loads the last of our possessions. I turn to my son and take his hand. "Don't worry, my sweet boy, everything will be just fine. I can fix this!"

Ask Quietly

Early on Wednesday morning not long after my move to Maui, I awake to a swell of anxiety, still haunted by my fall off a horse some years before. I must be crazy to get back on a horse. Then I open the box of black Massimo Dutti riding boots and am reminded of the day, the place, and what I was thinking when I bought all the riding equipment, I needed to get back to dressage. I can vividly recall coaching myself aloud to dive into what I feared in order to create my own happiness.

I load my little white convertible with riding gear and head upcountry. Minutes later, as I zigzag up the mountain highway, I am awestruck by the beauty unfolding before me—cane stalks as high as my shoulders, pineapple fields wafting a sweet, almost acrid scent, and the green, green mountains straight ahead. I catch site of a double rainbow stretching across the horizon creating a multicolored canopy. This is my Wednesday morning, my life now on Maui.

My trepidation dissipates as I get closer to the horse academy. It feels right, as familiar as returning home after years of wandering. I park, slip on my fitted boots, grab my black velvet riding helmet and leather riding gloves. Without even realizing it, am smiling a mile wide.

I fetch Mr. Bud from the upper field, groom him and tack up at once. My instructor, Liz, cues me to walk toward the mounting block where I carefully grab a fistful of Bud's mane, climb up, swing my leg over his wide girth and ease myself into the small English saddle. I am passionately connected to this horse. My fear earlier this morning has now been replaced by excitement and a bond of trust. I can feel a wave of calm wash over my entire body. I take a moment to adjust my feet in the stirrups and sit up square and tall, a reign in each hand. Liz waits and then quietly says, "Walk ahead."

With laser focus and maximum effort, I work to move Bud forward. He does not respond despite my insistence. Liz seems agitated. "Do less, let him carry you ... get quiet, release the tension." We enter the indoor arena where I move Bud to the outside of the mud track. He is sluggish so I step him forward by giving him a nudge but he does not react. I squeeze him firmly with my inner calves as his rib cage expands against me. When his energy picks up for a couple of paces, I slide my sit bones back and forth in rhythm. His momentum is short lived. As I round the corner of the arena, I bite my lip, wince and give Bud a sharp kick with both feet to get him to move. "This is what I want," I say to myself aloud. Liz walks away, shaking her head, no longer calling out three-word instructional cues like "feel his mouth," "sense his energy," "doing too much!" Ugh, I think. What ... what does she want? I am focusing. Why is nothing working? Why is Bud resisting?

I am now determined to move Bud along the rail and have him do perfect dressage circles in the far end of the arena, as Liz instructs me to do. I have done this countless times. I've got this! The more I press, tighten and shorten the reigns, the more he pulls in the opposite direction.

"You won't win," Liz calls out. "He's stronger, Heather. He will win. You will not. Be quiet. Listen."

I am so frustrated and bewildered by what she wants me to do, I shout back, "I *am* listening to you!"

Liz smiles as she walks towards us, holding a long lunge line. She clips the line to Bud's halter, tells me that she is going to set the pace and direction and that I must simply tie up my reigns, stand in my stirrups and post. "Place your arms over your head and lightly squeeze Bud with your inner thighs. Then wait to see what you get."

Bud and I are now so totally in sync, it is as if we are talking. This time when he slows down, I gently rub one of my feet against his hindquarter. It works. Liz signals that we are done. We slow to a walk, then a halt. I untie the reigns, jump down and hold onto Bud, stroking him with praise. We walk back to the stables and Liz congratulates me on my success in the last part of the lesson.

"When you get on a horse, you and he are having a conversation. It's important to understand that if you keep talking and don't get quiet, wait and listen, you will never give him a chance to give you what you are asking for. Don't work so hard. Bud is your riding partner so he needs to try to comply. But if you don't give him the time and opportunity to do the work, you'll be stressed, he'll resist and a fight will surely be the outcome. Figure out what you want, ask once with conviction and strength, then get quiet. Nudge Bud gently if he takes too long to respond and then, when he cooperates, sit back and enjoy the intimate relationship you've just worked to create."

As I untack, curry brush Bud's coat and lead him out to the field, I am teary-eyed. Head down, lump in my throat, I remove my gloves and helmet, wash my hands and walk toward the arena looking for Liz. She rounds the corner and I am certain I am taking her by surprise when I grab hold of her and blurt, "Thanks Liz, amazing lesson, l just love you, see you next week." She nods.

As I walk toward my car, I wonder if she realizes that I was referring to her wise relationship advice and not the riding lesson.

Pony's Do Not Belong in Backyards

"You *cannot* keep a horse in your backyard!" scolds our curmudgeonly neighbor. He is standing at our front door, glaring at my mother as he pushes his horn-rimmed glasses back up the bridge of his nose, a bead of perspiration dripping down his face.

He is dressed in a wrinkled long-sleeved white cotton dress shirt and a too-short pair of trousers that reveal his woolly argyle socks. An odd way to dress on the weekend I reflect, when all the other fathers are casually attired. He is not a bit like the other fathers, with his aristocratic British accent and eccentric appearance. As I consider his strangeness, I sense an escalation in the tone of their exchange.

My father emerges from his sacred man cave (otherwise known as the den) and that signals trouble. I hide in the kitchen at the end of the soft pink leather bench in our breakfast nook where I can listen to the conversation without being seen from the front door. At six years of age, I get frightened when adult voices grow loud but I am forced to emerge when my father bellows out my name, demanding that I come to the front door. I dutifully walk over.

My father places his large hand on my tiny shoulder. "You want a pony for your birthday, don't you, Heather?" "That would be fun," I answer innocently. My mother looks confused.

"You cannot keep a pony in a suburban backyard, especially when there is no fence between our properties," the disgruntled neighbor repeats, scowling at my father.

My mother turns to my father. "What is he talking about?"

"I got Heather a pony for her birthday. He is on loan for a while. He's tied up in the backyard. It was meant to be a surprise." Looking smug, my father continues. "I know how crazy she is about horses. The only thing she has ever asked for is a pony."

My mother walks through the house to the backdoor. I hear the screen door slam behind her. Moments later she returns, shaking her head in disbelief and wearing a half smile. "If you would be kind enough to put up with the pony until tomorrow," she says to the neighbor, "I promise you that it will be gone. I give you my word." She squeezes my father's arm to restrain him, I suppose, from creating a scene. The neighbor leaves in a huff but seems to have accepted my mother's assurances.

My father grins. He takes me to the backyard where I saddle up and ride around and around on the pony until dark. My mother explains that there are zoning regulations; the pony must leave in the morning. I lay my body flat over the saddle and try to wrap my arms around the pony's neck as a gesture of affection. I inhale its intoxicating scent, which smells like perfume to me. After my last circuit, I sadly kiss the pony goodbye.

When my father tucks me in that night, he explains things in a slightly different way. "I know that ever since I put you on one of my race horses at three years of age, you have always loved horses. So why not have one? Rules are meant to be broken, Heather. Never follow the crowd. Dare to be different."

I am not quite sure which of my parents' perspectives to believe. Even at that young age, I already understand what will become a pervasive theme in their marriage: that my father will do whatever he wants and my mother will try to make him do what is right.

Bora Bora … At Last

Bora Bora has always been my dream destination, my imagination sparked in my youth by the romance of James Michener's novel, *Hawaii*, and by one of my all-time favorite movies, *South Pacific*. I have always planned to sail, fly or swim there if necessary (ambitious, I admit, given my fear of deep water) but somehow the decades have passed without this dream coming to fruition.

Now that I am living in Maui, Tahiti is a mere five-hour plane ride away. I contemplate going there on my own but friends and travel agents advise against it, insisting that it is a romantic couples' destination. So I bide my time and one year after first considering a Polynesian cruise, I book a cruise with the manager. The Paul Gaugin Cruise Line offered a special discounted fare for Hawaiian residents which made the ten day cruise in French Polynesia even more enticing and very affordable.

The day I moved to Maui, I pasted some pictures of Bora Bora on an empty jar and labelled the top, "Heather's Bora Bora Fund." Once we book our trip, I add the manager's name to the label. We have two months to drop in all our loose change and small bills and make weekly contributions to our spending-money fund, a symbol that we are working in tandem as a couple. We spend days shopping for bug spray, swimsuits, water shoes and an underwater camera, and before we can blink twice, we are standing in the impossibly long TSA line at Kahului airport.

Because of delays getting through immigration, we miss our first flight to Honolulu, throwing the manager into a tailspin. Since I am the more seasoned traveller, I am able to calm him down. We catch the next flight and line up at the gate in Honolulu's international terminal for our flight to Papeete. When I hand the flight attendant our boarding passes, she looks at them and tells me to return to the Hawaiian Airline desk. Our seats have been double booked! Once again, I have to temper the manager's anxiety. I sort everything out and we are on our way. No need to be perturbed over the seating glitch, easy to resolve especially after a lifetime of being the fixer.

We arrive in Papeete, clear customs, get our passports stamped and collect our luggage. Our shuttle driver is holding up a sign with our names just outside of the airport terminal. The chaos in this humid, very French overcrowded airport is not what I expected. The port is not far from the airport and we are almost the last of the two hundred and twenty passengers to board the luxury Paul Gauguin cruise ship that evening. We watch from out balcony the lights of the port's restaurants, bars, dozens of food trucks flicker and disappear as we sail off toward Bora Bora, our first destination.

Early the next morning, we can see linear colored bands ranging from light blue to azure in the distance. How can the Pacific Ocean look so different here? At the cappuccino/juice bar, the manager remarks, "*Pain au chocolat* and coffee taste so much better on the top deck with Bora Bora on the horizon." Hand in hand, we watch the ship glide into the lagoon surrounding the island. The next two days are sublime. We swim and paddle board in the tepid lagoon, lunch on *poisson cru* at five-star beachside resorts and shop for Tahitian pearls.

On the tender to the island of Huahine, our next stop, an attractive older woman begins chatting with me. Within minutes, she boldly asks, "Are you Jewish?" Caught off guard but wanting to be polite, I reply in the affirmative. She asks if I would join her for the Friday evening *Shabbat* service in the captain's lounge, which she noticed on the daily event calendar placed in each stateroom. I agree to be there.

The following day we drop anchor close to Moorea. After the manager polishes off what he calls as "a light breakfast"—freshly squeezed orange juice, scrambled eggs, crispy bacon, Belgian waffles with maple syrup, croissant with assorted jams, several cappuccinos and fresh fruit—we pack our beach bags and take the tender into the port where we find long banquet tables on which local artisans are displaying their jewelry and crafts.

We purchase an insane amount of vanilla in every form—bean paste, oil, cream and room spray—rationalizing that it is all for gifts. We strike up a conversation with a local vendor who directs us to her cousin who drives us to another family member's motor bike rental office, where we rent a scooter for the day. Everyone on this island is related, it appears. We are soon driving along the coastal road through quaint villages bordered by the glistening ocean.

Despite being in the middle of the South Pacific, we are constantly reminded that these islands belong to France. We wave to locals carrying baguettes, wine and fresh produce tucked into cotton bread sacks slung over their shoulders. Half way around the island, we pull over to take in the breathtaking view of Bali Hai, its massive carved tikis and picturesque little churches. The manager snaps photos with his newly acquired camera. He fancies himself a photographer and I do not have the heart to tell him that some of the photos he proudly shot on Bora Bora were blank because he forgot to turn on the camera!

We stop at a recommended lunch spot, a tiny pizza place with an open-air counter, eight stools and a blackboard menu hanging below the thatched overhang. A gruff looking man who turns out to be the owner tells us that he emigrated from France years ago. We listen attentively as he extols the virtues of the superior, sweeter pineapple grown on Moorea versus the mediocre pineapple from Hawaii. Now we feel obliged, but almost fearful, to order the pineapple cream pizza.

The owner points and mumbles something to a frail-looking older woman eating lunch on the furthest barstool. She gets up posthaste and carries her half-eaten meal into a makeshift kitchen at the back of the open-air structure. She prepares our pizza and places it on a gigantic wooden pizza paddle as the owner recounts his tale of woe: too much work; too few tourists. The woman is standing in front of an open wood-burning oven in the 35° Celsius (95° Fahrenheit) heat of the day. How can she stand it? She rotates the pizza on the paddle and in six or seven minutes serves us a sizzling hot, slightly charred pizza, which she cuts into wedges with a large metal pizza wheel. She resumes her position on the bar stool until the owner orders her to fetch us two plates. "That's my wife," he explains with a shrug. I whisper to my partner, "If *he* is complaining, imagine what her life must be like! The manager reaches for my hand and gives it a loving squeeze. He wants me to know that he appreciates me unlike the owner with his wife. We dive into the delicious pizza, wash it down with a gallon of mineral water, pay for our lunch with French francs, thank the owner and his overworked wife, jump on our scooter and head back to port.

Despite the scorching mid-afternoon sun, our daily ritual is to partake of four o'clock high tea on the top deck. We have never seen tea being offered or served, (must be upon request only) and we never order it, but we cannot pass up the daily baked warm scones, clotted cream, the array of freshly baked French pastries, jams, miniature tea sandwiches and flambé fruit with homemade ice cream. The manager has a serious sweet tooth, unlike me despite my training as a pastry chef. He gorges on enough sweets for the both of us.

Back in our stateroom, he is wired from the sugar high but I am ready for a nap after exploring Moorea in the heat and from loading up his plate of sweets from the buffet table more times than I can count. "Come on, Heath, just one more scone," he begged. Come on Heath, get me one more cookie." Naturally, I obliged.

Just as my head hits the pillow, he reminds me that the Sabbath service is about to begin. I groan and force myself into my sandals, splash water on my face, apply some lipstick and head to the captain's lounge, conveniently located at the end of the corridor on our deck. When I walk into the oversized suite, I am pleasantly surprised to see a very long dining table dressed in a simple white cloth. There is a stack of prayer books at one end, electric *Shabbat* candles in the center of the table, two bottles of kosher wine, one white, one red, wine glasses and a freshly baked braided *challah* with a bread knife on a silver tray.

I am still taking stock of the effort made to recreate a Jewish Sabbath table when the woman I met on the tender to Huahine appears in the lounge. She greets me warmly and we decide to wait a few minutes to see if anyone else turns up for the service. She asks me if I can read Hebrew, conduct an abridged service, as this is meant to be a self-led Shabbat service. At 6:15 p.m., I open a prayer book, hand one to her and began reciting the prayer over the *Shabbat* candles. I go through the service in Hebrew and translate some of the key prayers into English for her benefit (This reminds me that I can recite the entire prayer book in Hebrew, a legacy of thirteen years of religious school). I conclude with the *Kiddush*, the prayer over the wine, and the *Hamotzi* prayer over the *challah* before tearing off a piece for each of us.

She thanks me with a warm, tight hug and then asks if I would help her recite *Kaddish*, the mourner's prayer, as this the first anniversary of her husband's death. I am happy to oblige sensing her sadness. The prayer comforts her but she obviously needs to talk about her late husband and her profound sense of loss. I listen as she tells me about her life as a little girl growing up in New York City. In her twenties, she dreamed of traveling the world and became a flight attendant. She met her future husband, a celebrated Dutch journalist/news correspondent, on one of her flights bound for Europe. It was heartwarming to hear her recount how they fell in love, married, had three beautiful daughters and an on-going love affair for their entire marriage. Her husband's ill health, suffering and rapid decline in his last year devastated her.

After he passed away, she grew depressed and found it difficult to leave her home. Her eldest daughter, worried about her mother, suggested that she take a trip to cheer herself up but she could not face traveling alone. Then her daughter forwarded her an email from a friend in New York. It was an excerpt from a series of short pieces written by a woman traveling on her own in Europe for the summer.

"I was so inspired by her courage that I immediately booked a Polynesian cruise. Bora Bora was our preferred spot in the whole world." Then she adds, "I think this woman plans to write a book about her life, perhaps a memoir. She picked up and moved to Maui from the East Coast." I can barely make eye contact as tears well up. " And by the way, where do you live, Heather?" she asks, trying to make small talk in response to my now obvious distress.

"Maui," I murmur as I try to hold back tears, overwhelmed by how my writing had affected her.

She studies me for a moment. "You are that girl! You are that brave girl," she cries as she embraces me. "Thank you, thank you!"

By telling my story, I had hoped that one day it would make a difference to someone. I knew then that it already had.

Try It On ... But Keep the Receipt

As I approach an age when many women consider tying the proverbial knot for a second or third time, I begin to question the merits of remarriage. Long gone are those youthful fantasies—of walking down the aisle in a flowing white gown and a pretty tulle veil; the perfect Tiffany heart-shaped diamond engagement ring and matching wedding band; the entourage of family, friends, acquaintances, colleagues, friends of friends and friends of friends of friends all celebrating you on your special day. Gone, too, is the fairy-tale notion of marriage promoted by the media and society as a whole.

After years of an unhappy marriage, separation and divorce, many women find themselves reeling, alone in midlife. Although I find myself in a similar place, I see it differently. While it has taken much soul searching and some self-coaching, I have come to realize that I am "on my own," not alone. I have the freedom to choose what is right for me, to own my life.

And so I spend a summer and the following fall and winter after moving to Maui putting this realization into practice: traveling, preparing dinners for one, yoga by the ocean at sunset and chick flicks with my gal pals.

Then, without even trying, I meet the manager. We take long beach walks, meet for espresso, text and text some more. Despite my negative attitude to dating, I have to admit that we have a connection. He is as eager to leap into a relationship as I am to put on the brakes and head for the upcountry to the mountain. To ease my anxiety, he tells me not to think of it as a long-term commitment. "We are just spending the day together, and then the next, and the next ..." Persistent and patient, he has somehow managed to sustain an ongoing relationship with me day after day, week after week, month after month.

We often go to the beach together where I have watched, fascinated, as bridal consultants arrange Hawaiian flowers into a giant lei on the sand, the unbroken circle a Hawaiian symbol for eternal commitment and devotion (the couple stands inside the circle for the ceremony). I have witnessed brides in long gowns with trains sweeping up sand like dust brooms, brides in short white sundresses with fragrant gardenias woven into their hair, and brides in white bikinis, flip-flops and short veils, their makeup melting in the hot sun, march onto the beach to say, "I do."

As I ponder the prospect of marriage, my "warden" (as I jokingly refer to the manager to friends) asks me to accompany him to the Tommy Bahama shop. When he loads a fitting room with armfuls of shirts, shorts and t-shirts, I tell myself to prepare for a long try on session. Fortunately, there are comfortable upholstered bench seats—a much better spot than the beach, I think, for a couple to make important decisions. After a twenty-minute fashion show, the store clerk takes pity on me and offers me a glass of lemonade in a crystal Tommy Bahama glass and a pineapple-shaped Honolulu Cookie Company cookie. More shirts, more shorts and my opinion solicited before any article makes it to the yes pile.

After more than two hours of this, something begins to occur to me. Why buy something when all the fun is in trying it on? And why worry if the purchase does not work out? Simply return it. It is so uncomplicated that way. At Tommy Bahama, you can return an item for credit, money back or a trade-in for something else. What a novel concept that would be in a second or third marriage!

I am not necessarily against the whole "I do" redux, but it might be more fun to just try it on. But if I do buy it, I will certainly make sure to keep the receipt!

A Sister From Another Mother

It is almost dinnertime. My mother is in the kitchen, my father at the outdoor grill, while I sit on the sofa in our den watching the CBC News, the station our TV is always tuned to as my parents are fanatical about watching the daily local and national news. Suddenly, the news turns tragic. There has been a car crash on a highway outside of Toronto. "A woman in the vehicle was pronounced dead at the scene," intones the newscaster. When I hear the victim's name, chills run down my spine and I scream for my parents. "We need to find Karen. Her mother has just been killed. She is alone and doesn't know!"

Karen's father, my paternal grandmother's much younger brother, died years ago, leaving his wife to raise her only child, my cousin Karen, on her own. Her mother is unconventional, glamorous and very bohemian; what our traditional, judgmental family considers unstable and flighty. Although she and I as young girls spent little time together over the years but I have always longed to be closer to her. To me, she is a free spirit, a wild child with extraordinary peacock-blue eyes and a mischievous smile.

My father promises to do his best to find my cousin but that is not good enough for me. I beg, badger and guilt him into agreeing to let her move in with us. I remind my dad that his uncle, Karen's father, when diagnosed with cancer, asked him to look out for her if something happened to him. I track Karen down to an address outside the city and write her a letter telling her how much we love her.

At nineteen, Karen is about to embark on her adult life without parents, which is unthinkable to me. I am fourteen years old and cannot imagine growing up without my mother. I hope and pray my letter will convince her that she has a safe and loving place to live. I can fix this, I tell myself. I finally get the big sister I always craved when Karen comes and lives with our family for just over a year.

Now, more than forty years later, I find myself doing the exact opposite—retracting a welcome—something that is entirely foreign to my nature and so very difficult. I hear my big sister/cousin encouraging voice in my head: "Ask for what you need."

The manager and I have been living together in my rented Maui house for almost nine months and I could not be happier. At a very fundamental level, our relationship works because he "shows up," a sine qua non for me that he absolutely gets. He is there for me, lavishing me with more love and attention than I could ever imagine. This is a new experience for me and I sometimes wonder if it is too good to be true.

Still, all is not perfect in our island idyll. A number of very tough conversations about sharing expenses lead nowhere in an otherwise warm and committed relationship. I pay for almost everything; he contributes only his devotion and presence. He argues that he buys groceries but the quantities are minuscule compared to what he consumes.

I am beginning to feel the emotional strain created by my resentment. I contemplate giving him a final ultimatum that requires a more equitable financial arrangement between us. After all, he is working and earning a decent wage; I am not. Obtaining my green card has become a tortuous and surprisingly lengthy affair. (I eventually prevail but not for another year.)

One day, the rental agent calls. She has learned that a dog is living here—a breach of the terms of the lease, she tells me. I counter that the dog lives outside on the lanai which specifically in not a breach as pets are allowed on the exterior of the house as per the lease, but she is adamant: the dog must go. I pass on this disturbing news to the manager and ask him how we should resolve this situation.

"Don't worry, Heather. Invite her over so she can see how spotless you keep the house. The dog is not making a mess or disturbing anyone. Besides he lives outside and never barks. All the neighbors love him. We will offer the owner a pet security deposit to cover any damage though I'm sure there will never be any."

I am thrilled. For the first time in my life, a partner is stepping up and taking responsibility for his own problem! At our next meeting with the agent, the manager suggests pet security deposit as the best a way to give the homeowner some security and peace of mind. He shows the agent around the house and introduces her to his beautiful gentle dog. Impressed with the spotlessness of the house, with no sign of a dog living in it, she agrees to speak to the owner.

A few days later, I almost faint when I hear from the rental agent. The owner will allow the dog to stay but only if we pay him a pet security deposit of five thousand dollars. To add insult to injury the owner has asked for an additional three hundred dollars a month for the manager to live in the house. I consult with an attorney who reconfirms my suspicions that this is a greedy cash grab and illegal to charge per person given I have a pre signed lease and it is a five bedroom home with only two adult residents.

The manager is unperturbed. "Pay it, Heather. You'll get it back when you move out." Floored, I choke back angry words.

A few days later, I delicately broach the pet security deposit issue again to the manager. "I simply don't have the cash," he snaps in exasperation. "Why are you making such a big deal about this?"

Time goes by and my relationship with the rental agent grows acrimonious as she continues to push and threaten. I love the dog and his owner but, for the first time in this relationship, I take control. "You have one week to come up with the pet security deposit or please find somewhere else to live as the dog cannot stay here," I tell the manager.

A week to the day, I find him somewhere else to live that accepts pets (as he is unable to find a place on his own). I pay for his security deposit and help him move out. I am heartbroken to have to take this step but hope that this jarring separation will force this almost fifty-year-old man to take responsibility for himself so that we can continue our relationship on a more mature, equitable and financially collaborative footing.

Unfortunately, the next time I hear from him, he asks me to meet him in town—to buy him a bicycle! He reminds me of my handsome fifty-year-old Florentine barista who still lives with his mother. One day, he invited me to ride home with him along the Arno on his vintage bicycle, for a dinner prepared by his *mamma*. Perhaps I was hasty to have rebuffed his offer. She might have done my laundry, too!

I cry myself to sleep for months but there is to be no reconciliation with the manager. A year and a half later, I learn that he has moved in with another woman and that she is footing his bills which is no surprise.

Autumn Colors

Autumn in Toronto is glorious. The trees in shades of red, amber and gold lining the city streets; the clear crisp air; people walking at a slightly brisker pace, clad in shades of grey, camel and black, their cashmere scarves wrapped tightly around their necks; food shops bursting with displays of pumpkins, squash, pomegranates, pears and apples; picking Macintosh apples at a favorite orchard to take home for baking pies.

Despite my love affair with the magical island of Maui, there are times when I miss all that. When I lived in Canada, I used to start my day with a strong cup of coffee and a crisp apple cut into wedges. Since moving to Maui, I have made a steady diet of strawberry papaya for breakfast. Considered to be the sweetest, most flavorful of all papayas, this salmon-red fruit is a great source of vitamin C and A. But an unchanging diet of anything, no matter how delicious, can become monotonous, and recently I have felt something lacking.

Still reeling from my breakup with the manager months earlier, I am suffering from a lethal combination of overwhelming sadness and guilt. Despite its beauty, spiritual energy and tropical clime, Maui has proven to be challenging and heartbreak happens, even here. Julia, who speaks to me almost every day from Toronto, has grown impatient with my chronic melancholy and urges me to take a quick trip to the mainland to shake off my temporary and uncharacteristic blues. Resetting one's life involves being bold and trying new things so I half-heartedly agree to book a ticket to the East coast to revisit my fond fall memories. And what better place to take in the autumn colors, fall fashions, culture, art and theater than the "Big Apple"?

I pack, pulling out all my cashmere sweaters from their plastic bags, my beautiful leather-and-suede camel-colored boots that have been so carefully tucked away in the back of the closet and the soft leather gloves I purchased in Italy. I used to be known as the girl who kept a packed oversized bag under her bed, ready to pick up and roam the world whenever the fancy struck, but I am now feeling conflicted. After booking my roundtrip ticket with a stop in Toronto to visit my son, an anxious feeling settles in the pit of my stomach.

A few days later, I am still procrastinating about booking a hotel, unable to commit to the trip. "Stop over-thinking. Just do it!" Julia admonishes. To counter my resistance, she books a hotel for me. "Just get on the damn plane."

I finally head for the airport with enough luggage to make a permanent move, my bags weighing in at three times my bodyweight. The moment I board the first leg of my overnight flight, to Dallas, I find I can breathe again. At the Dallas airport, what strikes me, even in my groggy state, is the sheer volume of stuff for sale in this artificial retail space—the overabundance of food, clothing, electronics and sundries. It is my first aha moment of the trip: I have been living on an island and islands come with limitations. I walk over to Starbucks, order a coffee and grab an apple for breakfast. I board the second flight a couple hours later bound for La Guardia Airport in New York. After dozing on and off, reading a few magazines, the flight attendant announces that we are beginning our decent.

Walking through the jet way in New York, I am hit with a blast of cold air. I zip up my black leather jacket, wrap my heavy grey pashmina tightly around my neck and shoulders and brace for the cold. I drag my bags, tagged "Heavy," outside to the taxi queue.

Dazed, sleep-deprived and shivering, I yearn to be back in my warm Maui cocoon.

I arrive at my boutique hotel with barely an hour to shower—in cold water, as they seem to have run out of hot—and change in time to join a friend in a trendy new upscale Madison Avenue resto. I quickly dress in Paris-purchased black from head to toe, tousle my unruly red-gold mane, put on ruby red lipstick and run out the door to hail a cab. As I walk into the restaurant, my phone pings with a text from my friend, letting me know he is seated at the end of the bar. Why does he need to send me his location when we are in the same place? Then I look up. Right! This is the Upper East Side of Manhattan, where people line up at the bar a dozen deep and wait for an hour or more for a table, even with a reservation. My friend greets me and we catch up over a scrumptious dinner. As I look around, I take in the energetic, kinetic vibe. The evening ends with a hug and a thank you. I feel reborn, alive and excited to see what tomorrow brings.

Returning later to my hotel, I discover that there is no closet and lack of hot water I encountered earlier, is a permanent condition. I also glean that the hotel is not located in the best part of town, the clue being the sound of gunshots reverberating through the hotel all night long.

The next morning, I pack up and check in at The Plaza on Fifth Avenue. Being at The Plaza takes me back to my late twenties when I was learning about fashion and business and that anything is possible if you set your mind to it. I was about to open a Fogal of Switzerland hosiery shop in Toronto and the licensee agreement I negotiated included luxury accommodation in Manhattan while I trained in their product line. The Plaza became my home-away-from-home for a couple months.

Fogal of Switzerland

In his second year of working for a European-based real-estate development company, my husband finally agreed to take a vacation. Normally, I had to fight to get him to take even a few days off so when he informed me that we were going to Europe, I assumed there had to be a catch. Fortunately, all my husband was required to do there was meet with a few prospective European investors; the rest of the time was ours to freely explore the continent. The company's president generously lent us his sporty little BMW, which let us roam from Zurich to Interlaken, Paris, Provence, Florence, Siena, Venice, Innsbruck. We picked up the the car southwest part of Germany. In our first week, we visited Grindelwald in the Swiss Alps. Unprepared for the *cold* so late in May, I walked into a hosiery shop looking for warm tights and was immediately captivated by a very cleverly designed round display tights in every shade of the rainbow. I ran my hand over the different tights, some in nylon, others in cotton, silk, even cashmere. The discreet red label announced "FOGAL of Switzerland." Everything was so neatly organized and perfectly displayed in this tiny Swiss shop. I purchased a pair of cotton tights and tucked a business card into my bag.

At the hotel that evening, I looked up Fogal's history, learning that it was a legacy brand dating from the 1920s when founder Leon Fogal, the son of a stocking weaver, opened the first store in Zurich. By the late 1980s, when we were there, this luxury brand was expanding to major European cities and to New York.

I wore my new tights for the next few days and hand washed and wore them again. In Paris, I located the Fogal shop, noting that it was identical to the one in Zurich. By the time we returned the car in Germany, I was determined to bring this brand to Canada.

Back in Toronto, I tried to contact Fogal's president in Switzerland. After a few months of futile calling, I finally got a call from Fogal's representative for North American business ventures, who suggested we meet in New York at their shop on Madison Avenue near 59th Street.

Fast Forward to New York

So here I am, back again at The Plaza, forever associated with the start of my retail career thirty years earlier. I check in, take the elevator to the sixth floor and wheel my carry-on bag down a wide beautifully decorated hallway. My key card bears an etching of Eloise, the beloved fictional child who has been "living" at The Plaza for more than half a century. As a Fairmont Club member, I was automatically upgraded and the suite is palatial. The king-size bed dressed in white hand-stitched European linens is flanked by two antique nightstands. The bathroom, fit for royalty, is covered in miniature gold-and-white mosaic tile in a floral and vine pattern.

Up next is lunch at Bergdorf Goodman with Emily, with whom I have become fast friends since our chance meeting two years before in Amalfi. She has temporarily moved from Britain to New York to take master classes with Seymour Bernstein, a famous concert pianist, composer and mentor to world-class musicians. There is something inexplicable when you meet someone in midlife and instantly connect on a warm, intimate level —a friendship that defies time and distance. When we met the year before in Florence, we vowed to meet every year for lunch or coffee in some part of the world. Serendipitously, we both find ourselves in New York at the same time.

Walking into Bergdorf Goodman after so many years is a girl's fantasy come true. The beautifully appointed store is like a fine gallery of all things fashion and beauty. In every department, the attention to detail—in the displays, the merchandising and the svelte, perfectly groomed sales staff—speaks of quality and luxury.

We take the elevator to the restaurant on the top floor, which also houses the children's department, housewares, antiques and estate jewelry. The elegant hostess suggests champagne at the bar or a look around. Despite our reservation and timely arrival, our table is not quite ready.

We use the time to peruse the estate jewelry. An elderly shopper, clearly a Manhattan socialite dressed to the nines, pointing to a pair of vintage opalescent and rose-gold earrings priced at the equivalent of a new Mercedes, asks me, "Are these not the most darling little earrings you've ever seen? Are you buying them?"

I laugh and answer "Yes and No." She compliments me on my silver and mock-diamond bow necklace. "That's vintage Van Cleef & Arpels." Again, I thank her and laugh to myself. When I bought this knockoff at the Jewelry Mart in downtown Miami, I recall getting change back from a twenty-dollar bill. As we browse the fine china and silver flatware, I feel a pang of nostalgia for my exquisite tableware that I used for dinner parties and holiday occasions, now languishing in a sealed crate in a storage container in Toronto.

Lunch is divine, coffee served in fine bone china, salads so well executed and plated they look like works of fine art, service with finesse and sophistication, girl talk for hours. The delicious finale is individual creamy pumpkin cheesecakes accompanied by champagne in cut-crystal flutes. The perfect New York afternoon for two friends who love fashion, fragrance and finery. When another New York friend joins us for coffee, I can almost hear the song "The Ladies who Lunch" by Stephen Sondheim playing as our soundtrack in the background. Two and a half hours later, Emily and I walk across the street to my hotel and linger for hours more over cappuccinos in a gourmet food and wine emporium on the hotel's lower level. How stimulating to connect with someone who shares the same interests: politics, music and the arts, travel and higher education. This is what I have been missing on Maui.

The next day, I attend an "Entrepreneurs in Transition" luncheon at the invitation of the convener/moderator, a close friend and successful New York businessman. The boardroom on the 40th floor is almost full when I arrive. My friend greets me warmly and compliments me on how professional I look in my perfectly tailored Massimo Dutti black-watch cashmere suit. I take a seat next to a man munching a cookie with his coffee. He appears to be in his mid-sixties. Then it hits me: I am the only woman thus far at a think tank with two dozen men—all entrepreneurs, all successful, all looking for their next opportunity, all captains of industry, all veterans in their fields. I am filled with excitement. I listen, fascinated, to three men who speak about their last businesses and their prospective plans for new ventures.

My friend then announces that he would like to interject a personal story into the discussion. Odd, I think, but what do I know? He is the "network king" so he must have a good reason to share a personal anecdote with the group. It is only when he says, "Do you see that woman at the end of the boardroom table?" while gesturing toward me that I realize he intends to talk about me, my career path and our friendship.

After showering me with more praise than I deserve, he asks me to address the room. Having had no advance warning and with no time to formulate a single coherent thought, I simply begin to speak. I share my business plan for a new venture in Maui which includes publishing a travel book and my forecast for the hospitality industry in Hawaii, in general. It is the first time in a long while that I feel truly empowered and in my element.

The next hour or so passes with more discussion, introductions, business plans, forecasts and questions and answers. I revel in the stimulating exchange of ideas. The final half hour is set aside for mingling and networking. As I am about to leave, several of the attendees approach me. They all want to discuss their businesses and my potential new venture, exchange ideas, business cards and to meet for coffee or a drink.

This is the boost I desperately needed. This is where I feel comfortable and happy, where I get my adrenalin rush, where I feel my self-esteem being renewed and restored. This trip is a reminder of who and what I am.

Launching Fogal

By the late 1980s, Toronto was becoming more sophisticated in terms of luxury fashion. I was convinced that a Fogal shop, with its unique marketing approach to selling luxury hose, leggings and tights in decadent fabrics and vibrant colors, would be a hit since there was nothing comparable in the city. My husband, who recognized my fashion sense, work ethic and networking skills, encouraged me do the groundwork to determine if this could be a viable business venture. When I walked into the Fogal shop on Madison Avenue for an initial meeting, it took but a nanosecond to see that this was a business that I could manage and build successfully in Toronto.

Knocking down one roadblock after another, I was determined to open a Fogal of Switzerland shop by the spring of 1988. Fogal insisted on a location on Bloor Street, known as the "Mink Mile" for its concentration of high-end designers and luxury department stores like Holt Renfrew, but the rents had become prohibitive. After days of negotiating for an alternate location, I finally convinced Fogal to locate in Hazleton Lanes. Unlike Bloor Street, it had the advantage of being an indoor mall, a convenience much appreciated by its wealthy patrons, especially during the long cold winter months. Fogal would also be in the right retail company. Ralph Lauren's flagship store, Hermès, Yves St. Laurent, Valentino, Sonia Rykiel, Versace and other European luxury brands were already located there.

My next challenge was to prepare a business plan, budget and sales forecast so that I could approach a bank for a line of credit. I put it all together: the capital expenses for building out the store; the cost of Fogal's patented fixtures that had to be built exactly to spec; the cost of the initial inventory, salaries, rent, advertising, window displays and associated operating costs. My husband suggested taking on a partner as this was a fairly ambitious project to tackle alone. Two business associates that invested with my husbands' real estate ventures together had wives who were looking for part-time jobs to keep them busy, but not too busy. We struck a three-way partnership deal. I agreed to put in a little cash, take a modest salary and operate and build the business. In exchange, their husbands agreed to co-sign the line of credit at the bank and the wives agreed to work in the shop once a week for a few hours.

Emboldened with cash, a corporate license agreement with Fogal and the hottest, most talked about design team ready to build the shop, I made an appointment to meet with Hazleton Lanes' director, Ron Salcer, a former chief executive of one of America's iconic department store chains and known to be a very tough negotiator.

With the benefit of youth and inexperience, I fearlessly walked off the elevator on the third floor of Hazleton Lanes and down the hall to a set of large double carved wooden doors that opened into an old mansion-style office, fitted out with Ralph Lauren furnishings and fabrics. (Salcer was credited with helping Ralph Lauren early in his career and later became a partner in many of Lauren's ventures) Slightly intimidated, I approached the large desk and told the women behind it that I was here to see Mr. Salcer. She immediately picked up the phone and buzzed his office to announce my arrival. Another set of double wooden doors just beyond a credenza swung open and out came a large balding man dressed entirely in Ralph Lauren finery, including a silk pastel paisley tie. In his deep, gravely voice, he ushered me into his office furnished with large overstuffed tufted leather chairs and a massive wooden English-style desk with leather insets. This was someone who obviously reigned supreme.

Cutting to the chase, Salcer asked me why I was there, what I wanted and to access my retail experience. I felt like cowering behind my chair but opted for bold. "I've got something you are going to want." I handed him a copy of my Fogal license agreement, my quarter-million-dollar line of credit and a letter I had written about my experience and commitment to perform.

After a brief glance at my documents, he looked straight at me. "You will fail, little girl. You just told me you have no retail experience to speak of. This is hard work. It takes grit and more commitment than you realize and long grueling hours every day."

"I know. I'm prepared for that," I replied, trying to sound more confident than I felt.

He took a moment to size me up and then opened the top drawer of his desk. He pulled out a lease, scribbled something on a few different pages and handed it to me. "Take this, read it, sign it and you will have a location here once you bring it back."

"Thank you, Mr. Salcer, but I want a specific location, the best location here."

His face flushed a deep red. "You will take what I give you!" I simply smiled. "We are done. Bring the signed lease back this week." He then turned his attention to the papers piled on his desk and did not look up as I walked out of his office.

Elated, I took the lease home to our tiny midtown apartment and showed it to my husband. He gave it a quick review, called my business partners and instructed me to sign it. But I never take the easy road. I poured over the lease, researched all the lease terms and crunched the numbers. With a red pen, I made all my desired changes. I cut the rent and the rental percentage, adjusted the mandated hours, wrote an addendum and more.

The next day, before dropping off the lease, I checked out the specified six hundred and four square-foot space on the first floor. It was located between the best-known women's designer clothing boutique in the complex and an exclusive French restaurant. I was very pleased. The location was ideal.

Riding the elevator to drop off my lease, I imagined coming to work every day and already felt a huge sense of personal accomplishment, convinced that Mr. Salcer would be impressed by my diligence with the lease. I could not have been more mistaken.

After looking over my work, he began to seethe. He threw the lease on the Persian carpet next to his desk. "Get out!" he screamed. I was too stunned to move. "How dare you redline my lease after I gave you a plum location! Who do you think you are? Get out!"

He was still screaming when I turned around, desperate to hold back my tears until I was out of his office. I sprinted down the hall to the elevator and pushed the elevator button. As I waited for the door to open, I stopped and considered. I want this shop, I told myself. I can do this. I can create a successful business. I *will not* let him bully me!

I ran back down the hall, barged back into the office and brushed past his assistant. "You can't go in there! Mr. Salcer's on a call," she protested.

I stood in front of his desk with my arms crossed in front of my chest in an attempt to communicate my steely resolve. After he finished his call, he told me that I had chutzpah to mark up his lease. I apologized and promised it would not happen again. He glared at me as he handed me a clean copy of the lease. "Hope I still have the best location," I could not resist adding.

"Don't push your luck, little girl. Work hard, be the last to leave at night. I will know because I know everything that goes on around here." I signed the lease, handed it back to him the following day and the work to build and fixture the store began. It took approximately six weeks until the shop was ready to be opened. I then started working ten to twelve hours a day, seven days a week.

A year later, I happened to bump into him at the Toronto airport on the way to the gate for a flight to New York City. Unsolicited, Ron Salcer upgraded my ticket so I could sit next to him in first class. Then he took off the same pastel paisley Ralph Lauren tie he had been wearing at our very first meeting and handed it to me. "You've earned this, little girl. I'm proud of you."

Ron Salcer was always encouraging and gave me a hug every evening on his walk through the mall before leaving. He was the first man to be a positive, supportive influence that under his tough and commanding exterior was a teacher, a true mentor and that I am and always will be grateful.

The parent company of Fogal of Switzerland was thrilled when I sent them the press releases for the opening of their first Canadian shop. I had contacted the media and been interviewed, photographed and quoted in the fashion pages. The publicity was extensive: Fogal appeared in newspapers and magazines, on the newswire and radio stations. I also sent Fogal the schematics for the three window displays, designed by the talented visual merchandiser I had hired.

On opening day, the shop gleamed, all its surfaces polished. Large posters of European supermodels sporting Fogal leg-wear in bold colors were displayed in key spots around the shop. By seven that evening, the champagne flutes were filled and ready to be passed around on round silver trays. Dark chocolate truffles and mini sweets were arranged on pretty trays for the taking. A few prospective clients were ushered in from the designer ladies-wear shop next door. Ron Salcer, my mentor and director of Hazleton Lanes, arrived next with his entourage, followed by other shop owners eager to check out the new boutique. I had sent out invitations to a top-tier prospect list and the boutique was soon abuzz with an affluent fashion-savvy crowd of predominantly women.

The months leading up to the official launch had been draining but the opening was a success and I felt proud that I had achieved my initial goals. My two partners, who came to the opening to introduce themselves to clients and familiarize themselves with the merchandise, both left at eight o'clock, singing my praises, but excusing themselves to put their young children to bed. I still had work to do before I could leave. I cleared the counter of champagne flutes, organized the business cards scattered around the shop, balanced the cash from the evening's sales and prepared my first bank deposit.

Just as I was about to lock the double entrance doors at 9:30 p.m., I heard a deep voice say, "Congrats, Heather. You should be proud. You managed to steal this away from my mother."

Can't be! I thought. Grinning at me was a tall thin man in finely tailored pants, a perfectly pressed ultra fine cotton shirt and Italian shoes, his thick black hair slightly salted with grey. He was staring at me and, as always, I was unbearably uncomfortable in his presence. I wanted to run, lock myself in my minuscule office in the back of the shop but it was too small for even a door so I stood before him and glared back.

"My mother had an exclusive agreement to carry Fogal in her shop until you managed to get the license. Bravo."

"Really," I replied, hoping he would hear the sarcasm and the satisfaction, noting but declining to mention the incorrect gender agreement of his accolade.

"The shop is beautiful. I'm impressed. You did good." He moved closer in an attempt to unnerve me, as he loved to do. I backed away. He continued to step forward, closer, like a cat with a mouse. I continued to retreat but could smell his cologne, which conjured memories from the past. He backed me against the cash counter and lifted my chin to make eye contact. He drew my face closer to his and despite my resolute intention to resist his attempt to seduce me, I was completely disarmed. The attraction had always been strong ever since meeting at nineteen years of age. He had been a guest at our wedding; he was my husband's friend and that automatically prohibited anything other than a platonic relationship.

Why had he come here tonight? It had been a year since he had kissed me at a ski lodge while my husband was on a ski run. I had told him then that that he must never do that again. He removed his hand from my chin, placed both hands on either side of my cheeks and drew me closer. I was paralyzed. I could feel his mouth graze my lips. Despite my urge to fall into his arms, I turned my head away.

Gathering all my resolve, I slithered out from his embrace and thanked him politely for coming to the shop, for supporting my new venture and wishing me well. "I need to close up now," I said, indicating that he should leave. I gave him a quick hug, praying and hoping that the decade-long attraction would suddenly evaporate. I knew better. I was only fooling myself.

My mother had known about our mutual attraction; she had told me so on her deathbed seven years earlier. She kept my leather-bound wedding album beside her hospital bed. Together, we would pour over the photographs when she awoke in the middle of the night. It was a good way to distract her from the pain. In so many photos, she pointed out, I was dancing with him, laughing with him, talking with him or standing next to him, and he was beaming back at me. "Remember, Heather, you don't have to live with a mistake for the rest of your life." But it was too late. I had made a promise, a vow, a pledge, on my wedding day, to love, honor and obey. Well, at least I could honor and obey. Love? Maybe one day it would find me.

The Tuxedo

A few months after my son was born, my obstetrician scheduled an appointment for a thorough checkup due to my extreme exhaustion. I was not especially concerned. I assumed my fatigue was entirely normal given ten-hour days at the Fogal shop and interrupted nights feeding my infant son. I was also busy decorating our modest three-bedroom starter home. So, when my doctor tells me there is a problem, I am surprised, though I should not have been given my medical history—a series of miscarriages followed by toxemia and a growing mass in my uterus that caused issues especially towards the end of the pregnancy.

"A mass in your uterus is causing bleeding and your exhaustion," the doctor explains. "We need to remove it now."

"But I have a three-and-a-half-month-old baby who needs me and a store to run," I protest. "Five couples are coming over for a very special dinner on New Year's Eve. I've even hired a visiting chef from Paris for the occasion. Can't surgery wait?"

My doctor knows how single-minded and fierce I am when I make up my mind so she schedules surgery for the New Year but cautions that she will be out of the country over the holidays and unavailable if an emergency arises. "If the mass grows any larger and bursts, it could kill you," she warns. "Head straight for the hospital if you feel any numbness in your legs. One of my colleagues on duty will take good care of you."

I thank and hug her. Before I leave the examining room. I mention that I just bought an Yves Saint Laurent tuxedo from his haute couture line designed for his Paris runway show. We share our plans for New Years Eve." I can't wait to wear it on New Year's!" She chuckles. She and I share a love of all things fashion! My doctor on the other hand, will be clad in a swimsuit and cover up as she is going to be celebrating in the Caribbean with family on New Year's Eve. I wish her a wonderful vacation and all the best in the new year and she once again reiterates her concern and preference to do surgery immediately.

New Year's Even nineteen ninety is going to be at my house this year. I invited four couple to enjoy a festive French inspired menu and hired a chef who was just due to arrive from France. One of our friends had sponsored him to work at her family's lake side resort but he was not to begin working for a couple of weeks so was available.

A few days later, Jacques, the Parisian chef, lands in Toronto. He is free for a few weeks before starting a six-month *stage* at a five-star resort north-east of Toronto to improve his English and is happy to make some extra money. When we meet at my house to finalize the menu, I instantly like his jovial animated manner, his mustache and mop of dark unruly hair and his crooked smile. His thick French accent makes his few English words sound like a foreign language but I am thrilled to practice my rusty French. We soon find common ground in the language of food as we plan the menu and shop together for ingredients.

The next afternoon, I put my son in his swing chair and join Jacques in my small galley kitchen to make pasta. He started earlier and is already elbow deep in flour. I grab both our chefs' aprons, offer to tie one around his waist and fasten mine. The kitchen is a disaster. Bowls, utensils and a dusting of flour cover the limited counter space. I take a deep breath, reminding myself that this is my happy place, my creative outlet, and what could be better than creating a meal with a French chef? Then I realize that executive chefs are messy because they have staff to clean up after them so I am relegated to cleaning and sous-chef duties.

After we finish the pasta dough and roll it out by hand, Jacques turns to me. "Do you ave wire angers, Ether?" When he sees the blank look on my face, he grabs a few wire hangers from the front-hall closet and wraps them in cellophane. Then he cuts the pasta into long strands and carefully places them over the hangers. My son has not made a peep in all this time. He is transfixed by the chef, whose antics he seems to find highly entertaining.

Next up is dessert, a dark chocolate molten cake with chocolate ganache, garnished with raspberry coulis and fresh berries. "Let's make it into art," the chef suggests. "We will bake them round and cut them to form." Once again my face tells him that I am not following. He draws a heart on a piece of paper and I nod in agreement.

After three joy filled days of prep, cooking and baking together, we are ready for my New Year's Eve party the next day. Confident that my guests will be impressed by the meal and its presentation, I set the table with my best china and glassware and handwrite the place cards and menus. Before I go to bed, I pull my brand new Yves Saint Laurent tuxedo out of the closet, hang it on a hook in my bedroom, line up my matching black silk shoes and choose the jewelry to complete my designer ensemble.

Exhausted, I fall into bed close to midnight. When I try to turn over onto my side, I cannot move. My brain is signaling my body but my legs feel numb, as if they are encased in cement. I nudge my sleeping husband awake and tell him that I need to get to the hospital. He wakes the nanny to tell her we are leaving and carries me into the car. At the hospital, I am immediately admitted and prepped for surgery. As I lie on the gurney waiting to be wheeled into the operating room, my mind is whirring. All I can think about are the strands of homemade pasta dangling from hangers in my kitchen and that my untimely medical emergency is ruining everyone's New Year's plans. Maybe they can still come for dinner. The chef can finish the meal and serve without me. I will suggest that!

That is the last thing I remember. When I next open my eyes, I see my Yves Saint Laurent tuxedo hanging on the closet door. Like Dorothy in the *Wizard of Oz*, I wake up to find my all-powerful doctor sitting by my hospital bed surrounded by my friends. I am not quite sure if this is real or an anesthetic-induced hallucination.

"I was worried that you might get into trouble, Heather, so I didn't leave on my vacation, after all," says my doctor. "We managed to remove the mass—fortunately, it was benign—but we had to remove an ovary and the opposite fallopian tube. I'm afraid having more children is probably not likely."

All my dinner guests come to the hospital to ring in the New Year with me and my husband. The doctor had sent my husband home to pick up my designer outfit, hoping it would make me feel more festive. How kind and clever of her! New Year's Eve may not have turned out as planned but I had so much to be thankful for.

Dumpster Diving

After I sold my designer hosiery business, I took some time off before committing to my next career. Most mornings, after we dropped our children off at school, Amelia, a close friend, would drop over to my Toronto home for her first cup of coffee so we could plan our day. It did not take us long to decide that we wanted to devote some of our energies to community service. Together, we volunteered for the Mount Sinai Hospital Auxiliary. Most of the other volunteers were socialites, the wives of Toronto's financial elite. Amelia and I knew that we would be the worker bees.

Our first charity event was a "Marketplace" bazaar to be held in the lobby of the hospital, all proceeds earmarked for the neonatal care unit. This fundraising event was just up my alley. It required soliciting fashion wholesalers and retailers for donations of clothes and accessories, and I had solid connections in the fashion world after owning and operating Fogal of Switzerland for almost eight years. Like the dynamic duo, Thelma and Louise (before they went off a cliff!), Amelia and I made up a list of all the businesses in the downtown core to hit up for goods. After our initial contact calls, we fixed dates and times to make the rounds and pick up the donated items for the bazaar.

Wanting to make a good impression as a representative of the hospital's Auxiliary, I made a special effort to dress professionally. Clad in a grey Armani suit accessorized with pearls, graphite-grey cashmere-and-silk tights and Stuart Weitzman charcoal-grey suede boots, I put on my cashmere coat and gloves and climbed into the van whose horn had been tooting outside my front door.

Parking in downtown Toronto can be a challenge, especially in the fashion district, so I had asked the Auxiliary's administrative assistant the day before to print and laminate an official-looking sign that read "On delivery for Mount Sinai Hospital." Who would question that? Much better than borrowing my aunt's dangling "handicap" sign which would necessitate one of us feigning a limp or a heart condition. Being somewhat superstitious, I also did not want to risk creating bad karma for crossing the line into dishonesty. That is not how I operate.

We spent the day loading bag after bag of donated goods and clothing into the back of the van, our mock parking permit working like a charm. As we were about to drive away from a loading dock, I noticed a large metal trash bin. "Wait. I think I see something," I told Amelia ." I jumped out of the van, walked over to the bin and squealed in delight. "Someone has dumped a huge pile of brand new wool and flannel designer scarves! They even have the original tags. I'm going to grab them for the bazaar."

When I leaned in, forgetting that at five feet, two inches I was not nearly tall enough to reach, I fell into the bin head first, legs waving straight up in the air. Undeterred by my undignified pose, I continued to dig for the scarves. "Only you would dumpster dive in designer clothes," Amelia said mocking me.

The scarves were a hit at Marketplace, selling out and at good price, but our real reward came a month later at the Auxiliary board meeting. We realized as all the other board members that paraded into the boardroom were wearing these scavenged scarves with their fanciest furs and expensive cashmere coats. Amelia and I smiled throughout the entire meeting thinking about the "not so glamorous" dumpster where they came from!

What Grandmother?

A year later, I was sitting in my makeshift Auxiliary office in the basement of Mount Sinai hospital, preparing for the upcoming gala fundraiser I was chairing, when my assistant hollered from her office next door that I had a phone call. Perfect, I thought. The corporate sponsors are finally returning my calls.

This black-tie event was the city's most prestigious fundraiser of the year. I was expecting over a thousand guests and to raise several million dollars to buy a new MRI machine. I had gone to

Los Angeles to negotiate for the evening's talent and had interviewed and hired all the outside vendors after securing the ballroom at the downtown Toronto Sheraton Hotel. My son, now seven years old, was eager to be my junior assistant on the day of the big event.

I walked to my administrative assistant's office, grabbed a yellow lined pad and a pen and advised her that I would take the call in the conference room. Anticipating the sale of a corporate table to a bank or law firm, I confidently stated, "Heather, speaking. Thanks for the return call. Hope you are calling about a corporate table for our gala." There was silence on the line so I repeated, "Heather, speaking."

A voice finally said, " Ms. Samuel, I am your grandmother's doctor at Toronto Western Hospital. She needs immediate surgery." It took a minutes for the words to sink in and to process what he was saying. I informed him that I did not have a grandmother; he had contacted the wrong person. But he persisted, reiterating that he needed me to come to the hospital right away. "Your grandmother fell and broke her hip. I need you to fill out the paperwork to authorize her surgical procedure." Again, I explained that my only grandmother had died three years ago, that he had the wrong person, and hung up.

A minute later, my assistant called out that I had another call. With pen in hand, I answered with the same sales pitch. Unbelievable! It was the doctor again. "You need to come to the hospital right away or your grandmother won't pull through. Pneumonia will set in and kill her. How soon can you get here?"

There was no point in repeating that I did not have a grandmother so I asked him the name of the woman he referred to as my grandmother. When I heard her name, I felt all the blood rush out of my head and had to put the receiver down on the table. It took me a few moments to regain some semblance of composure. I picked up the phone and, in a flat emotionless voice, asked the doctor where I should meet him. Her name was familiar; I remembered only too well my mother speaking of her.

Holding back a flood of tears, I grabbed my purse and neatly arranged my files for my assistant. She was waiting in her office and I could see the concern on her face. "See you tomorrow," I mumbled. "I will be back in the morning." She hugged me, sensing that I was shaken. "Let me know if there is anything I can do."

"Apparently, I have a grandmother." I mumbled.

Numb, I walked to my car in the underground parking lot and drove home while trying to process the situation, not quite sure what to make of it. When I got home, I greeted my son and checked that he had completed his homework, discussed dinner with the nanny and looked upstairs for my husband. Before discussing this with him, I called my father, begging him to come to the hospital with me to sign the papers, but he was unequivocal. "She is dead to me. Your mother had nothing but heartache from her." A predictable response from my disengaged father. Hoping that my husband, at least, would accompany me, I headed upstairs to find him watching the news. When I told him about my newfound grandmother, he looked at me as if I were speaking in a foreign language. "Just ignore it," he advised.

"How can I? She will die and it will be on my conscience." When he looked up at me impassively, I continued my appeal. "My mother would have gone. She would have done whatever it took to ensure that this woman got the right medical attention despite how she felt about her. So, will you come with me?" "No," he replied categorically Disappointed but not surprised, I changed my clothes and called Julia.

In the emergency department, the doctor informed us that my grandmother had fallen and broken her hip in her retirement home, which ironically turned out to be only a few blocks from my home. Her primary caregiver, searching her room for next of kin, had found my name written on one of her papers and a few photos of me as a baby and young girl, the word "granddaughter" scribbled on the back of one of them. "That's how we managed to find you," he explained. "Your housekeeper gave us your phone number at Mount Sinai Hospital."

This woman had abandoned my mother as a baby. This had been so deep a source of pain and sadness for my mother that we rarely spoke of my grandmother especially once I was a teen and adult. How a mother could abandon an infant and walk away was inconceivable to me but that is what my grandmother had done. I knew that my mother had tried to make contact with her, reach out after I was born but her efforts were thwarted. She continued to make overtures to her mother during my childhood but things always ended badly. I vaguely recollected meeting my grandmother when I was very little and being carried out when she began flogging me with a slipper. Contact with her after that was sporadic and always ended the same…my mother sobbing. In my head, I was screaming, "I don't want to be here. I don't know this woman. I didn't even know she was still alive!" After I signed the papers authorizing her surgery, the doctor directed us to my grandmother's room, where she was being prepped for surgery. Bracing myself, holding back tears, anger and a mix of other emotions, I walked into her room.

When I saw her, I realized that she was the strange elderly woman who had approached me at the cemetery at my mother's funeral. She had handed me a pamphlet about cancer. A little late for cancer education, I remembered thinking at the time. I had been so grief-stricken that I never wondered who she was or how she came to be there.

I nudged myself back to the present, taking in her tiny shrunken body. I noticed her hands, the same hands as my mother's. She was sedated and as I gingerly approached her bed, she mumbled something I could not decipher. Enough, I said to myself. I have to leave. She will have a chance to live, to survive, thanks to me, which is more than she did for my mother, her daughter.

At home later that night, I felt utterly broken. All I wanted to do was flee—to take my son and run away to a place where I could find some peace, somewhere I did not have to deal with, care for or fix someone else. I had a husband who was totally disinterested and a disconnected self-absorbed father. My siblings, who were still struggling with the loss of our mother and our father's subsequent abandonment more than a decade and a half earlier, wanted nothing to do with this grandmother. They had refused to help when I called them on the way home from the hospital.

The next morning, I did the right thing. I called the doctor to see if this stranger, my grandmother, had made it through surgery. The next evening, I secretly returned to sit vigil by her bedside. She awoke and looked at me, bewildered, unsure of who I was and then dozed off. The following week when I called the retirement home, I was told that she was back in her room, recovering well and on the mend.

A month later, a different doctor from the retirement home called to report that my grandmother had passed away. By then, it was late November. The days were short and dark so I waited until the following morning before going to the retirement home. When I walked into my grandmother's room, I found a family friend there. Confused, I asked him what he was doing there. "I am the physician on call for this facility," he said. "Why are *you* here?" Before I could answer, he scratched his head, walked over to the night table beside the single bed and opened the drawer. "Of course! You are the little redheaded ballerina in the red costume. I should have put it together with the name scribbled on a piece of paper but I've always known you by your married name and didn't make the connection. I am sorry for your loss. She was your grandmother. Now I understand. I was her general practitioner."

I was stunned. This woman, my grandmother, had lived only a few blocks away, had my friend as her doctor, yet never had the desire to contact me. She had been the only connection to my mother. How tragic. I left, crestfallen.

I spent the rest of that afternoon making calls to secure a plot in a Jewish cemetery and arranging for a private graveside service. Sixteen years after burying my mother, I buried my mother's biological mother, my grandmother, but ensured she was as far away as possible from my mother's grave. My father and siblings begrudgingly attended, then vanished the moment the rabbi finished reciting the mourner's *Kaddish*. I paused and took a few moments to speak aloud, forgiving her for abandoning my mother. It was all I could do. I knew in my heart that my mother would have done exactly the same.

Following the Yellow Brick Road

With great resolve and tenacity, I have worked to fulfill my dream of living in the rainbow state of Hawaii. As a child, my mother would sing me her favorite song, "Somewhere Over the Rainbow," and wake me in the middle of the night to watch *The Wizard of Oz* with her when it played on TV.

As the child of a mother who had been abandoned at birth and shunted from one foster home to another, I was acutely aware of how this film affected her. She always longed to live somewhere over the rainbow. Married at seventeen, not even of legal age to sign the marriage license, she was wise beyond her years, with a generous kind-hearted old soul. She was intelligent and had a great sense of fun and an infectious laugh.

Everyone recognized the bright light that shone within her. She had an innate ability to attract people to her like a magnet. She was humble yet confident, stable yet fearless, curious and questioning, and a remarkable role model, though as a child I did not appreciate it. Everything she touched became beautiful. She had a gift for painting, a talent for music, an aptitude for languages, a desire to understand cultures and an insatiable appetite for higher education. Often, when she was not looking, I would stare at her, assessing, trying to understand where all her goodness came from despite her miserable childhood.

Then, at an age when most adults are just hitting their stride, her life was taken. Selfishly, I felt my loss was the most profound but also believed that I was the luckiest because she imparted her wisdom to me as I stood by her bedside on her last night.

"Heather, follow the yellow brick road over the rainbow, like I taught you. That, my brave girl, is where you are meant to be. Seek joy in both big and small ways. I chose "Joy" as your middle name so you would never forget. Find your life—no matter the path you have to take to get there, even if it seems unconventional, unpopular and lonely—and I will know."

I chalked these words up to the morphine dripping into her veins to help manage the excruciating pain and to her desperation because she knew she was slipping away. I held her hand as she labored over her last breaths. That day was the saddest and most significant day of my life.

I have finally followed the yellow brick road, with its twists and turns, the incredible people who have crossed my winding path, the life lessons learned, the hopes and dreams realized as I take each step. I suppose there is no need to say "thank you" or "look at me now" because, as you told me on your last night, you will know.

CHAPTER 5

LOVE , LOSS AND LIGHT

Thirty-six years ago today, my mother passed away—most of my life lived without her. Sitting on my Tommy Bahama beach chair on my favorite beach, I am thinking about her, what her life would have been, my life and everyone's life that she touched, had she lived to old age.

The one thing I have learned living on this island in the middle of the Pacific is how small each of us is in the universe. The majesty of the grass-covered West Maui Mountains, the expanse of the ocean and the dense abundant vegetation all remind us of our insignificance.

So, why would my mother, a petite woman who lived a relatively ordinary life, make any difference at all? Why, when I have access to so many people with whom to forge and nurture meaningful, deep relationships, do I feel such a sense of loss and longing for her? Strange, that after all these years I still feel this way.

I stare out to the ocean and watch the waves roll in gently in sets of three, with the sun creating a large glistening pool of light on the water off in the distance. Intrigued by an arrangement of tiny shells at the edge of the sand where the water breaks, I walk down to take a closer look. A family of crabs are intermingled with the shells. The water washes over the sand. A flock of feral chickens led by a rooster run past, almost colliding with the crabs. I am mesmerized.

A blonde curly haired girl who looks about five years old is building a sandcastle village with her father next to the shells and the crabs. A golden retriever runs after a yellow tennis ball thrown by his master. Before I can track the dog's path along the beach, a man holding a large shell and two leis marks a spot only inches from the shells, the crabs, the little girl digging in the sand, the running dog. A petite woman joins the man with the shell and begins taking flowers out of a bag and placing them in a circle on the beach. A photographer and a flutist arrive followed by a young man in a light-colored suit who walks to the floral circle on the beach. A few more people dressed aloha-style, smiling and chatting, join the young man in the suit. I watch intently and moments later a pretty young woman in a strapless white-lace gown, hair curled and tightly pinned on top of her head, sweeps the sand with her long train. A beautiful, simple beach wedding ensues, its backdrop the all-encompassing beauty of Maui.

In that moment, I see how one ordinary person can change the lives of so many by her absence. All things are connected and happening simultaneously to create meaning and balance. Today, two people pledge their love and their commitment to each other while the living things around them bear witness—the shells, the crabs, the running dog, the chickens, the little girl, the wedding guests and the participants in the ceremony. Everything and every single life is important, relevant and integral to someone else's. That is what I am missing: my mother bearing witness to my life. Perhaps it is time, absent my mother, to let someone special in, someone to bear witness to my life going forward.

Cognitive Dissonance

My heartache over the breakup with the manager continued despite a trip back to Toronto and New York at the insistence of my Toronto girlfriends, whose counsel can be reduced to the maxim: "The cure for losing one man is to find another." The idea of dating was still unthinkable, even abhorrent—admittedly an acute case of cognitive dissonance on my part, since I still longed for a loving, respectful, kind partner with whom to share my life, while rebuffing all overtures. The late psychologist, Leon Festinger, would have had a field day with my conflicted emotions.

I push away all this white noise in my head and resume my normal routine on Maui. New York has given me my mojo back and reminded me of who I am. After the private forum with twenty-five highly successful businessmen and the exchange of cards, I begin to get follow-up emails. Then, a few days later, my email account explodes with addresses and names I do not recognize. I click on the first and read, "Beautiful pic, beautiful girl, beautiful setting." I dismiss it as junk mail and open the next. "Stunning dress, pretty girl, love to meet you." Now I am totally bewildered. I know that my Mac rarely get viruses but my technological expertise only goes so far. I call my son, a Millennial, certain that he will be able to figure it out. Mystery is solved; someone has signed me up to an online dating site and used my Facebook picture. I suspect my Toronto girlfriends and one confesses but persuades me to go on a few dates using the rating system she and my other gal pals have developed. I am irritated but after her badgering finally agree. "I'll consider it research for my monthly magazine column."

Over the next few days, hundreds of emails flood in. I grow weary of hitting "Delete" so hit delete in batches. I imagine my girlfriends, who have access to my account, sitting together sipping wine, scrutinizing and giggling over every picture and message from the hopefuls. This must be so entertaining for them, better than reality TV! I am equal parts amused and annoyed.

One morning, I brew an extra strong cup of Kona coffee, sit down at my computer and take a closer look at the glut of messages clogging my inbox—strictly for research purposes, I tell myself. The first message is from a man who appears to have stepped out of the wilds of the jungle. He is shirtless, unshaven, covered from head to toe in tattoos and holding a primitive looking walking stick. I laugh aloud and click on his profile: profession, it reads "entrepreneur" [sic]; education, "life." What shall I do first—delete or refill my coffee cup? The next message, from a man on the other side of the island, reads, "Beautiful dress but would love to see you without it." Double delete! Scary *and* disturbing! This is going to be a long morning. I will need to brew a second pot of java.

The next email is almost endearing, from a retired lawyer on a neighboring island who may have been handsome in his younger days. He admits to seventy-nine but I suspect he may be misrepresenting his real age when I click on recent pictures of him. His message is respectful, gentle and kind: "You look like a lovely young woman, let's chat sometime."

This message reminds me of an earlier dating fiasco the year before I moved to Maui. It was just before Passover and I had stopped by the synagogue to see my old friend, the rabbi. During our conversation, an elderly man hobbled into the building and introduced himself. A fellow Canadian, he usually spent three months every winter in Maui. That year was particularly difficult for him, he explained, as he had just lost his wife after sixty years of marriage. I sympathized with him as he spoke lovingly about his wife and politely excused myself shortly thereafter.

The next morning the elderly Canadian rang my hotel room. "I would like to take you out for dinner tonight. You are a very attractive young woman ... so ... so ... wait...could you please hold for a moment?" I waited, and waited, until he returned to the phone, thanking me for holding. "I had to put in my hearing aids. That's better. Now I can hear you. What time should I pick you up? I don't like to drive after dark though." I caught myself before giggling or saying something inappropriate but I was secretly seething, plotting a way to repay the rabbi for giving this eighty-plus-year-old man my phone number. Before I had a chance to reply, he said, "See you tonight, Heather," and hung up, leaving me holding the receiver in disbelief. A few minutes later, he called back, realizing that he had forgotten to specify a time, so I was able to graciously decline his invitation with the excuse that I already had dinner plans. "How about tomorrow or Friday?" he persisted.

"I'm terribly sorry. I have plans all week but it was so kind of you to think of me," I said in an attempt to make him feel less rejected.

"I am leaving on Saturday but can change my flight if you can go out then," he mumbled. I was stunned but again declined with grace. Undaunted, he concluded the conversation with, "How about giving me your Toronto number so we can hook up when you are back home." I almost fell over at his chutzpah. Talk about an inflated sense of self! But I had to give him credit for trying for someone clearly thirty years younger. I wondered if he knew the real meaning of "hook up"!

As I recounted the story to friends that night at dinner, they teased me about my date with grandpa—helping him with his walker, speaking loudly enough to compensate for his hearing loss and keeping him out past his bedtime.

Chuckling to myself at the recollection, I move on to the next email, a promising prospect despite the twelve-year age difference. His photo looks reasonably recent; he appears handsome, in relatively good shape, fitter than most and, eureka, the message is grammatically correct, in complete sentences, with proper punctuation and no spelling errors. I may have hit the motherlode! A retired attorney, lives on the island, looking to meet someone for a long-term relationship. His message is very direct. "I'd love to meet you for coffee. I am from the same tribe as you." Interesting. I brace myself, take a deep breath and place my hands on the keyboard to type a reply. "Coffee sounds good, thanks for your message." Enough for today! I walk away from my computer after verifying that the message has left my outbox.

In the evening when I next open my email, I find, as expected, a message from the attorney. "Please meet me at 9 a.m. for coffee this Saturday at Sorento's." Oh my! That's the day after tomorrow and I am in the midst of packing my belongings and moving back into the hotel because the house I have been living in for more than three years is going up for sale. I have every reason to refuse yet I type, "See you then."

On Saturday morning, with more than half my closet packed and ready to move everything into a temporary storage unit, I quickly shower, air-dry my hair, apply a little makeup and slip on a long blush-colored cotton dress ,a pair of sandals and grab my bag. I have perfected the three-minute get-ready-and-out-the-door technique. In the restaurant parking lot, I reapply my lipstick and make my way to the entrance of Sorento's, where a handsome grey-haired gentleman is waiting for me.

As I approach, he moves quickly toward me, smiles, hugs me and says, "You look exactly like your picture, Wailea Girl." How does he know the tag line of my column, I wonder. "Shall we have breakfast?" he asks. "You don't eat, do you?" I am taken aback by his bold assumptions, unsure if he means to be insulting. "You have an amazing figure so you must watch everything you put in your mouth." Okay, he has just redeemed himself after his socially inappropriate but well-intended comment.

We order coffee, breakfast and exchange our moving-to-Maui stories. A second cup of coffee and more small talk, then discover that we live in the same gated community. "Are you the girl who does yoga on her lanai? How can you be moving? All this time I missed out on the opportunity to date you when you were living only a few houses away." I laugh at the coincidence. We finish breakfast and walk outside where he gives me a traditional Hawaiian hug that feels more testosterone than culture-driven. "I should warn you," he says, "I'm aggressive." I am rattled by his choice of words. My expression must be what prompts him to say, "I mean … demonstrative. I'd like to take you to dinner tomorrow night to Spago okay?"

What is it with these men who think that a five-star restaurant meal at a luxury hotel will automatically lead to … what? … sex, an instant relationship or worse, a commitment? It is just dinner, I want to forewarn him.

"No thank you, perhaps next week or the week after," I say. As I walk to my car, I hear him yell in the distance, "I'll call you." True to his word, in less than twenty-four hours, he calls and insists on a second date. I put him off a week. When he asks where

I am living while looking for another house, I tell him that I am staying at the hotel.

The following day, I walk back to the hotel after work at the clothing store, do my regular rounds of greeting the hotel staff and stop at the valet desk to admire a beautiful tropical floral arrangement. "Some girl must be special; she is going to love those flowers," I tell the valet. By the time I walk into my hotel suite, I find the floral arrangement on my desk. The card says, "You are fabulous, Scarlet. Here's to tomorrow, your Rhett."

A bit overwhelmed, mostly flattered and slightly frightened by the intensity of this gesture and his persistence, I try to not to overthink it too much. He spends our next dinner at Spago trying to impress me, find out who I am, what makes me tick, and then ends it with his desire to see me again the same week.

"Too much, way too soon. I'm known as the runaway bride. Don't push or pressure me," I warn him, so he backs off somewhat. A few days later, another floral arrangement arrives in my room. It is bigger, more dramatic and more expensive than the one before, with a card that reads, "Tomorrow, Scarlet."

A few more dates—a drive and coffee stop upcountry, an afternoon watching the windsurfing on the north shore, another dinner out—and before we have finished our hors d'oeuvres, he is pressuring me to stay over at his house. Even as a little girl I hated sleepovers, I think to myself.

I decide to turn the tables and invite him instead to an outdoor film festival. I purchase the tickets so that I am in control. He is not pleased with my independent spirit. "I wish you were needier and not so intelligent," he complains.

Despite taking me to the best restaurants and his desire that I dress up each time, he becomes annoyed if anyone pays me any attention or comes over to talk to me. I begin to question his irrational possessiveness and jealousy. I am sure he would install a tracking device on me if he could! Talk about a red flag!

A month later, he invites me to go to Europe with him but I refuse to commit, much to his frustration, even though he offers to pay for the trip. The floral arrangements become more elaborate and ostentatious as the weeks go by. I fear that a full sized palm tree will be delivered next!

One Sunday, six weeks after our initial date, I invite him to spend the day with me at the hotel, first at the pool and then lunch. That afternoon, our final date plays out like a scene from a Virginia Wolf play. In the lobby, where we are sitting and chatting with our cappuccinos, he gives me strict instructions never to speak to my male friends in his presence. As luck, or karma, would have it, a few minutes later, one of my closest male friends walks by on his way to the coffee shop. Naturally, I get up to greet him—and then all hell breaks loose. The attorney begins cursing, spewing obscenities and screaming that I have defied him. Horrified but silent, I turn on my heel, leave him sputtering and walk back to my suite to shower away the unpleasantness. From then on, I respond to his emails with the most potent message of all: silence.

After that scene, I decide that dating is much too scary, but a few days later I get an email from a man inviting me for a drink asking to meet at the Four Seasons Hotel to celebrate the New Year. Before I agree, I check with a girlfriend who knows who he is to confirm that he is not a lunatic or a mass murderer. Once again, I dress up and as I pull up to valet parking, I see an old Tacoma pickup truck drive past the valet area toward the self-parking section. I squint to get a closer look, wondering if there is a surfboard and a mattress in back on the Tacoma.

The bar area is full save for one seat beside a very handsome, dirty-blonde, well-built man in a trendy short-sleeve shirt, faded jeans and slip-pas. He introduces himself and asks me what I would like to drink. So far so good. Our conversation is flirty and easy until he explains that he is an engineer who works hard but plays hard too. "I live to surf the big waves," he says proudly. "In fact, I went to Fiji on a surf trip recently. All I need is a board and a bed in the back of my truck and I'm good." Oh no, I can't believe it. He is a replica of the surfer-boy manager I ousted six months ago! I refrain from asking him whether he wears underwear or goes commando like the rest of the surfer dudes on Maui because I already know the answer. He is a type I am determined to avoid. I inhale my Cabernet, give him a kiss on the cheek, thank him for the drink and run away as fast as I can.

The next man I bravely agree to meet for coffee and brunch is a welcome departure from the usual offerings. Incredibly handsome, a Canadian investment banker, intelligent, sophisticated, funny, well travelled, tall, super fit and oozing with charm; he gets my attention. We meet at a venue set amidst fruit trees below the grass-covered mountains. After hours of conversation, numerous pots of French-press coffee and an intense physical attraction, he tells me is leaving Maui in a few days but promises to be in touch when he returns in a few months. Potential, attraction, and for the first time in ages, I can see the merit in dating again. I am disappointed when I do not hear from him again but I understand that geographic distance has worked against us.

My next date is the following week, in the same venue, this time a dentist and the quintessential opposite of the investment banker. So small I could fit him in my pocket, he is even shorter than my five-foot-two stature and is holding out two large avocados as a gift. Unattractive and very intense, he seems to have no sense of humor, especially about himself. When the waitress arrives to take our order, he orders his lunch without even asking if I plan to eat. When his meal arrives, he begins eating long before mine turns up. I am anxious to end this painful encounter as quickly as possible but work hard to remain gracious and appear interested. He walks me out to the parking lot and just before I open my car door, he tells me that he enjoyed meeting me but he does not find me attractive enough. I have the wrong hair color and there will not be another date—with the caveat that he is okay remaining just friends. It takes everything I have to contain myself and not to burst out laughing.

The following Sunday, I go on what I have already decided will be my last and final date, figuring my self inflicted torture has come to an end. I have amassed more than enough dating "research" over the past few months with nothing much to show for it. This guy is another engineer. I meet him upcountry for coffee. He stares at me for over an hour, constantly repeating that I look like my picture, which he says is rare. Complimenting me on my fashion sense, my clothes, my jewelry and raving about my curly strawberry-blonde hair makes me nervous and terribly uncomfortable. I feel like a specimen in a Petri dish—yet he is very engaging, a bit more high strung than the low-key, what's-the-hurry Maui type I am used to. He presents me with two "avos," which is how he refers to the avocados he grows on his property. They are a real point of pride for him and expounds on the importance of eating them right away as they are perfectly ripe, After a few hours and several cups of coffee consumed, we part Maui style with a hug and say good bye.

The next day I receive a text addressed to "Miss Grace." I call a friend and tell her that even though the date was pleasant and went well, I am certain that it will not go anywhere; the guy is texting me by accident instead of texting his other date, Grace. I read my girlfriend his message and half way through I realize that it *is* meant for me. It is not for Grace but about how he sees me; it is a love poem. He and I have dinner out, the following week, enjoy drinks with my friends and take in a art gallery exhibit. He is sweet, very demonstrative, smart and interesting—not a bad combination—and he is also cute and in the best physical shape of all my dates so far. After three more weeks of ardent pursuit on his part, he finally convinces me to come to his house for dinner and to meet his father. I agree with some trepidation but all goes well. We prep and cook dinner together and predictably he asks me to stay over at his house. Maybe I should put an ad in the Maui News that I don't do sleepovers! He makes plans to visit his daughter in California and wants me to accompany him.

More gifts of prize avos, and then a week later he asks if we can talk, at my house, where I have finally moved after an overextended stay at the hotel. When I agree, he races over, bringing dinner for both of us. He has already declared his love and adoration for me and has been planning off-island trips together. But on this particular Friday evening, he has a different agenda.

"I think you are beautiful beyond what I could have imagined for myself," he begins. "You are super smart, super sophisticated, but there is a woman that I've always wanted to date. Our timing has always been off but I learned a couple of days ago that she is free. I'd like to be honest so would you mind waiting while I date her a couple of times and see how I feel about her?"

"What?" I stutter. Shock does not adequately express my feelings but I wish him well and tell him to find his happiness. A bit confounded, he asks for a hug and kiss so he can walk away with some closure. He was hoping that I would agree to wait for him and is disappointed. I pass on the hug and kiss and walk him to the door.

There must be something in the water here because this is the strangest group of men I have ever encountered. The one pervasive theme is the gift of avocados, apparently a token of affection and ultimately love. A close friend is grateful for the avocados I have been dropping off at his office but after receiving a half dozen or so, he asks me the obvious question. "Why do you keep buying avocados if you don't like them? Surely, not just to give to me." When I confess all, he asks me to stop. "That way, I won't have to imagine you out on yet another pointless date."

This is to be the last of the avocados and dates for a while. Maybe next time, if there is a next time, I will shoot for a strawberry papaya! Maybe next time, I will choose, rather than wait to be chosen.

Fooled

My son wanted to pack half his room and playroom into the two suitcases I allotted for him to take to Maui. It was December 15th and all I could think about was how this year I was truly on my own with my eight-year-old son. No husband, no father, no nanny. No one but my son and me on this long journey. I was still in shock after the unexpected breakup of my marriage so fear had not yet grabbed hold of me. We were leaving the cold, the snow, the grey skies, the city traffic—and the pain—behind us. I felt liberated, relieved that I was free. This was a new beginning, a new adventure for both of us.

When we landed, I took comfort in the fact that we were setting up house in the same condo complex we had stayed in so many times before and where we had established friendships with our neighbors. An older couple from Winnipeg, wintering here for a few months every year, had become surrogate grandparents and my son could hardly wait to knock on their door to visit, play Hawaiian Monopoly and eat the candies and homemade treats I forbid at home.

The neighbors in the condo above ours had two children with whom my son had bonded, and I had became very close to their parents. Even though they lived in Los Angeles, we stayed in close touch throughout the year. They would be arriving in just a few days, I reminded myself.

By now it was almost midnight. Exhausted after our fourteen-hour trip, I don't know how I managed to drive the forty-five minutes from the airport, drag in our six suitcases, put my son into his pajamas, drive with him to the all-night supermarket for necessities, drive back to the condo, put him to bed, and then unpack everything. The next day, we had breakfast together on our lanai, the sun glorious and warm on our faces. When I took in the view of Ulapalakula up the slopes of the volcano behind us and the ocean in the other direction, I wanted to live here forever. We had left abandoned, broken and confused but here on Maui we could heal, both of us. I felt grateful to be so far away from Toronto, in a place where no one could hurt us.

After breakfast my son, too shy to go over and knock on their door alone, badgered me to go with him to see the older couple. They welcomed us with open arms and hearts. My son and I took the next few days to swim, read stories, play smash ball on the beach and visit the grand oceanfront resorts. On the fifth day, our friends from Los Angeles arrived. Eager to see their children, my son ran upstairs and knocked on their door. A man he did not recognize let him in but by the time I followed a few minutes later, my son was already busy playing a video game with his friends, and the man was nowhere in sight.

My friends greeted me with warm hugs and we bantered about all being together again here on Maui. I had recently attended their son's *bar mitzvah* in Los Angeles and as we recalled the details of that special weekend, the man who had answered the door earlier appeared and sat down with the children. I recognized him; he had been introduced to me at the *bar mitzvah* as an old family friend. The children pounced on him, screaming in delight, "Your turn, Uncle Mikey."

When I gave my friends a quizzical look, they took me aside and explained that he was vacationing with them this year, as a sort of nanny. They assured me that he was harmless, great with the kids, was like an uncle, but not very sociable. "He'll probably stay home with the kids when we go out for dinner."

From that moment on, my son attached himself to Uncle Mikey, who was very warm and mentoring in return. The next two weeks were filled with laughter, good food, afternoon smoothies, group outings, days at the beach and water activities. When my friends packed up their SUV to leave after New Year's, I wondered how many times in a lifetime we say goodbye to the people we love. As they drove off, they called out to me. "Go out with Uncle Mikey, Heather. He is staying in our condo for another week. He'll be good company, for both of you, he's harmless!"

A few nights later, I knocked on the door upstairs. That was the beginning of a relationship that wreaked havoc with my emotions, my life, my health and my bank account. That knock at the door cost me a decade of palpable loneliness and financial ruin. Worst of all, it destroyed my self-confidence and my ability to trust anyone. I was robbed, pillaged and hung out to dry.

There was a silver lining ... of sorts. Once someone has taken it all—your heart, your soul, your money, your possessions, your trust and your self-esteem—you have nothing left to lose. You are free. Free to begin anew!

Love and Cracker Jack

One evening from my lanai, I watch spectacular fireworks crackle thunderously and shower the night sky with bursts of multicolored twinkling lights. They remind me of my childhood in Canada and how much I loved waving sparklers on the Victoria Day long weekend in May. When the light show is over, I am still feeling nostalgic, so I make some homemade popcorn, retire to the family room and put on one of my favorite films: *Breakfast at Tiffany's*. I have always loved Audrey Hepburn. She was so poised, so graceful, such a film and fashion icon, not to mention a incredible humanitarian.

A few weeks later, I am introduced by a dear friend on island to a very nice man visiting Maui for a few days sussing out his career opportunities. His blonde hair, the most beautiful ocean deep blue eyes and impish grin gave him a boy like quality even though he was in his mid fifties. Born on Oahu, he grew up as an island boy. Intent on seeing the world by the time he was in his late teens, he left Hawaii and joined the military. Ambition and hard work earned him a chemical engineering degree while serving his country. He eventually settled on the west coast in the United States, married and raised his family while building his career. While on Maui we tour the island, cruise the more remote beaches and explore the rainforest trails. Our first official date is dinner on the night of his arrival—a wonderful evening spent exchanging stories about our grown children, travel experiences and career goals.

After dinner, he presents me with a gift, the first of a series of gifts, he explains, one for each day of his visit on the island. I am baffled and uncomfortable at the prospect of accepting presents so soon in our platonic relationship. I gently remove the soft pink tissue paper to reveal a box of Cracker Jack—a mix of caramel corn and peanuts I have disliked since I was a child! I am more bemused than amused. Why on earth would he think I would want that? "There's a prize inside," he says proudly.

Not quite sure what is going on, I open the box and find the prize—a tiny paper tattoo wrapped in plastic. He seems delighted but I still do not get it. The next day we do the epic north west coastal of the island. Before nightfall, he hands me another box wrapped in pink tissue. Oh no, not another Cracker Jack box! Does he not understand that I detest this stuff? But I want to be appreciative so I thank him and pull out another prize—a paper cutout wrapped in plastic.

On the third day, he has business meetings so I assume that I will not have to contend with another box of that nasty caramel corn. But no such luck. He proudly presents me with the third box after another lovely dinner out. "These boxes come in a three pack," he explains. Thank goodness, we are finally done, I say to myself, but no, he has several three packs so I end up opening six more boxes.

With promising prospects for an executive level hotel position, he makes plans to return to Maui before he even boards his return flight back to the the mainland and we are both looking forward to spending more time getting to know one another.

Despite the geographic and time difference, once he leaves we begin to talk every day; a solid friendship develops.

A week and a half after he returns to the mainland, he asks me to FaceTime him. When we connect, I find myself looking at a large cardboard box. I watch his hand run a knife along the top to open it. When he does, I almost scream. Inside are a dozen more boxes of Cracker Jack. He laughs, reverses his screen on his iPhone camera so I can see his face and tells me that he has been waiting for this box to arrive. I am totally silent. What can I say? When I do not respond, he explains that he bought these 1970s Cracker Jack boxes

"I've been searching for one from the second I met you. Don't you know the deal with this?"

"No. I just thought you were crazy when you bought a dozen 1970s boxes."

"Sweetie, in 1950, Cracker Jack put a Tiffany's diamond ring in one, and only one, of their boxes. Haven't you seen the movie, *Breakfast at Tiffany's*? Holly Golightly, played by Audrey Hepburn, gets engaged with a ring out of a Cracker Jack box!"

I am speechless. I watched that very movie only a few weeks ago but never made the connection. He promises to bring the vintage 1950s Cracker Jack box with him on his next trip to Maui. "I've been waiting over forty years to open a box with someone I love and find a ring inside. That would be kismet."

Before he books his next trip over, I decide to put an end to this Cracker Jack nonsense once and for all. The next time we

FaceTime, I ask him to open the box. I watch him rip off the top. The caramel corn inside is discolored and as hard as rock. Near the bottom of the box is a small wormhole. We both laugh, speculating where that box has traveled since 1950. Then his face changes.

"What's in the box?" When he does not answer, I became anxious. "Is there a prize?" I am finally getting into the spirit of this whole thing. Still silent, he holds up a gold ring with a fuchsia heart-shaped stone. I almost fall over.

"So ... I guess this is it," he says.

What should I say? "I do"? One day, perhaps, but not now, and not with him. This year, the dress and the ring found me. Here's to hoping the right man is not far behind!

A Dance Partner

A few weeks ago, I got an email from the Maui Arts and Cultural Center (MACC) about their concert lineup. Their next concert scheduled is a performance by a group I have never heard of: Pink Martini. Online, I discover they play all my favorite kinds of music, which crosses the genres of classical, latin, jazz and classic pop and sung in different languages. I decide to buy a ticket.

"One, please," I tell the woman at the box office. I slip my ticket into my wallet and just as I am about to leave the MACC, I run into the theater director, who greets me warmly with a traditional Maui hug. When he asks me what I am doing there, I wave my ticket.

"We're trying something new for this concert Heather—a mosh pit for dancing! This type of is perfect for that." He is obviously excited about this new initiative.

The day of the concert, I shower, do my makeup and pull out a black body-fit dress I purchased in Italy but have not yet had an occasion to wear. This off-the-shoulder dress adorned with small black flowers across the bodice works perfectly with a pair of black suede heels with flowers that mimic the dress. A coordinating black evening bag finishes off my ensemble. I make sure to tuck my ticket and red man-catcher lipstick into my bag and drive to the theater in town.

As I pass the box office, a friend who works there stops me and asks who is joining me at the concert. "I'm on my own," I tell her, my all too familiar response.

"You look beautiful, Heather," she says, shaking her head. "You really should have a date." I am delighted when she offers to exchange my ticket for a better seat, closer to the front and one over from the aisle. "Someone bought the aisle seat but hasn't picked it up. Since it's almost show time, you might as well sit there. I know you prefer the aisle."

With the concert about to start, I walk as quickly as I can manage in heels and take my seat just as the bell rings. Seconds later, after the theater darkens, I silently move over to the aisle seat next to mine. As I sit down, I feel two hands wrap around my waist. I jump, turn sharply and see a man seated below me. "So sorry! Please excuse me," I stammer in a whisper as I hurriedly return to my own seat.

"No problem," he whispers back. "I snuck in after the lights went down. You can sit in my lap anytime."

Hugely embarrassed, I suddenly recall another similarly awkward moment when my aunt and I entered the cruise ship's theater in the middle of the terrorist's performance and he stopped playing and watched in silence as we walked to our front-row seats in full view of the entire audience.

As the Pink Martini plays "La Soledad," the man in the isle seat asks if I understand the Spanish lyrics. "Yes," I whisper back. The band plays on and the mosh pit soon fills with dancing couples but I decline when he asks me to dance,

Not long afterward, to the romantic strains of "Aspettami," he asks me again. I decline once more. "Perhaps you'll feel more comfortable with me after intermission," he persists. "I'm no Fred Astaire but I can move you around the dance floor." I smile but say nothing.

When the house lights come up for intermission, I discover that the man in the isle seat is handsome, with a full head of grey hair, tall and well built and seems about my age. He follows me out and asks if I'd like to accompany him to the bar and have a glass of wine. "You are the most beautifully dressed woman here. You must be from Europe. No one on Maui knows how to dress." I decline his offer to buy me a drink, feeling a bit panicked and terribly uncomfortable by his attention, still that shy little girl inside, after all he is a stranger.

After intermission, once I've returned to my seat an older couple seated behind me taps me on the shoulder and hands me a credit card. "Your boyfriend dropped this under his seat."

"He's not my boyfriend. I don't even know him!"

"Well, he certainly seemed enamored with you, so we assumed …"

When my seat mate returns, I hand him his credit card. "I was thinking of keeping it and charging some European dresses and shoes," I tease.

He laughs and tells me that he is a general contractor living upcountry. He gives me a quick synopsis of his family history and business. "Will you dance with me, pretty European girl, now that you know a little about me?"

"Not yet," I reply.

When the concert ends, I am relieved that I have managed to fend off his repeated entreaties to dance. As I walk up the aisle to leave, he calls out, "How about dinner at The Four Seasons Hotel, do you like Spago?"

Despite dangling the enticement of the island's most upscale restaurant—and everything that accepting that invitation implies—this man at first meeting appears to be different from the others I have dated on island, a bit more sophisticated and evolved, so I turn, pause and, unaccountably, give him my home phone number.

As I drive out of the lot with the top down, the constellations twinkling brightly in the sky, I am forced to admit to myself that I do, in fact, want a dance partner. I even dare to articulate those very words aloud in an effort to put my desire out into the universe.

By the time I get home, the light on my answering machine is blinking. There is only one message; it is from my theater seat mate. "Call me. I want to take you out to dinner." Of course, he neglects to leave a return number and the caller ID reads "Unknown Name. Unknown number." What is it with these island men? Spontaneous but no critical thinking or follow-up. I must have overestimated him. Oh well, no matter!

When I recount my encounter with the handsome contractor, my friends insist I look him up, reminding me that Maui has a "coconut wireless" and surely someone will know how to reach him. I decide not to pursue it and he does not call again.

A few months later, Julia comes from Toronto for a visit and insists on driving upcountry to locate the contractor just for sake of a laugh at my expense. "You're being ridiculous," I scoff, but off we go. We drive around the beautiful countryside and, much to my surprise, she finds his mailbox. She tears a page out of the driver's manual in her rental car and instructs me to leave him a note. I must be crazy, I think, as I write, "You left me a voice mail asking me out to dinner but never left your number. I am the girl who sat in your lap at the Pink Martini concert and if you are still interested in going to dinner you can call me at this number." I hesitate to leave the note in his mailbox but figure I will not hear from him anyway so no harm done. This is a familiar pattern among Maui men so it's a non starter. Three months later, the phone rings as I am making dinner at home. It is the contractor! "I was going through my son's knapsack after school and found a note with your phone number. I'm not quite sure how it got in there." He sounds perplexed. I am stunned by this odd turn of events but upon his request agree to meet him for a drink at a nearby restaurant the next evening. "It has a great bar and live music so we can finally dance," he says.

Ever the optimist, I am willing to give him the benefit of the doubt but not long into our date, it becomes clear that we are not a match. He is a seasoned dancer, true, but frenetic, quick paced, much like the jive, whereas I prefer the slow romantic glide of the waltz. Not the dance partner I am looking for after all!

Farfalle

"Header, I'm coming," the email reads. My heart all a flutter, I immediately know without glancing at the sender's name that it is my marine biologist. Who else calls me "Header"?

I giggle and write him back. "When, when?" I know the answer to my question even before I ask it. I count to ten. As expected, his reply appears. "Soon Gingy, soon Gingy!"

Why do I bother asking when I know that despite my adoration and longing for this man, he is a free spirit, committed to remaining unattached and unencumbered. His attraction to me, he tells me often, is that I am like him, a *farfalla*, a butterfly who flits and soars and resists capture, most beautiful when it spreads its wings in flight. His assessment of me is true to a point, but after much soul-searching, traveling and self-reflection, I am ready for a partner and an intimate, loving, respectful and mature relationship of substance. That is where he and I differ.

Weeks of silence from the marine biologist follow. One evening, after I have dragged myself home from a long day at work, bantering with and dressing more shoppers than I can count, the phone rings. It is after nine o'clock. Reluctantly, I pick up.

"Gingy, what are you doing? Come have a mojito. I am here waiting for you."

His accent and voice is so distinctive that I know it is my marine biologist even though the caller ID reads "Unknown Name."

"Where are you?" I have told him repeatedly that I have no taste for mixed drinks and have difficulty staying awake past eight o'clock but I decide that it is easier just to acquiesce and meet him. I wash my hands and face in an effort to freshen up, slip into my jeans and off I go. Along the way, I wonder why each and every time this man lands on the island, I always jump at his command.

I walk into the bar where he has told me he is waiting with mojito in hand, but no one is there except the bartender. It is a Sunday night and almost everyone on Maui is at home, sound asleep by now. Frustrated and angry with myself for running the minute he calls, I decide to walk once more through the bar area. I hear my name being called and turn, hoping it is my marine biologist but simultaneously doubting it since I am being hailed as "Heather."

When I turn toward the voice, I discover it is my family physician standing behind the bar, smiling. "What are you doing there?" I ask him, puzzled.

"I do this bartending gig on Sunday nights for extra money. The tips are good. By the way, your date is looking for you. He told me a girl with golden curls ran past him but he didn't realize it was you until I called out your name." Only on Maui is your doctor a part-time bartender!

Sure enough, the marine biologist appears behind me as I chat with my doctor. He hugs me and as usual tells me I look beautiful, like a young girl. The chemistry between us is undeniable. He sips his mojito and orders me a glass of Merlot. We catch up on our latest news, holding hands from the time I sit down until he walks me to my car. Reluctantly, I say good night and open my car door. He walks towards me and kisses me tenderly a few times. "Can I come to see you, Gingy?"

"When?"

"We will keep in touch, baby. I will call you."

A few days later he calls and asks if he can come by for coffee. I give him directions to my house and wait for him on my driveway as he has a tendency to get lost, the proverbial genius with no sense of time, space or direction.

"Cappuccino?" He nods and smiles. He gives me a quick summary of his itinerary and, true to form, suggests that I join him in Europe. He has extended the same invitation before but I now know the score: a proposal with no follow through. God bless this incredible, intelligent, warm and well meaning man who is so attentive but only when he is in attendance.

Unlike anyone I have ever known, he has the ability to make me feel adored. But I finally understand that he bestows his love and adoration on all his women around the globe. After his cappuccino, I tell him how much I love seeing him and will miss him. I walk him to his car and after he kisses me, he confesses that he loves spending time with me, too. He will always come to see me but he will always leave. "We, Gingy, are the same. We are *farfalle*."

As he pulls away, the monarchs are dancing around the butterfly bushes that line my driveway. Inside, I feel both filled up and empty, all at the same time.

Always Wear Clean Underwear

I cannot believe that I am sitting on a gurney in Toronto General Hospital without my underpants. Like most little girls, I was told growing up to always wear clean underwear in case I ever needed emergency medical attention. But now, at eighteen, I find myself wearing no underpants at all. I wish I were wearing my bikini panties with the day of the week sewn onto the backside like I did as a little girl. Today, I should be wearing my "Friday" panties. They would have helped avoid the humiliation of being examined naked by the nurses and doctor.

I was brought into the emergency department of this downtown hospital in my swimsuit. I had been in a car accident. It all happened in a flash. My mother and I were suddenly spinning out of control in her brand-new shiny pewter-colored sedan. We crossed the centre line into oncoming traffic and were hit first from behind, hard, then clipped on the front passenger side, propelling us into a tailspin. I hope that we have not broken any bones.

My mother was driving me to the swimming pool of some close family friends to celebrate the removal of a cast from my leg that morning. I had been laid up for weeks with a heavy cumbersome plaster foot and leg cast after extensive foot surgery —and I was so looking forward to a swim. As I ponder the curious timing of the accident, the doctor delivers the disappointing news: not only is my foot broken again but my right shoulder is cracked, too. I get a cast and a sling—not conducive to get a hot date.

Fortunately, my mother was not injured. She is so lucky, I tell myself. But truth is she is anything but lucky. That accident marks the beginning of her end. Her excruciating back pain, the doctors say, is cause for concern.

I can still hear her words, "Make sure you always wear clean underwear," yet both of us were panty-less.

The Beginning of The End

I am standing in the lobby of the community center of Bayview Avenue and John Street in suburban Toronto. The center is crowded with people bustling past, yet I feel completely and utterly alone. I am holding the chrome payphone receiver in my hand, afraid to hang it up because if I do, then what I just heard will be real, true. It is 8:30 a.m. I have driven to the center in my mother's car to make this phone call because the doctor had asked me not to call him from home. He does not want anyone in my family to overhear our conversation.

Last night, I took my mother to the hospital where she was admitted for some preliminary tests. She had been wracked with back pain for most of the year. Doctors could find nothing physically wrong and diagnosed her pain as stress. I was skeptical because my mother never complains or lets stress affect her.

This morning, our general practitioner has just finished telling me that my mother has cancer and "not the good kind." Funny … is there a good kind? Turns out she has the type of cancer that kills you, the no-treatment kind of cancer.

"Best not to tell anyone in your family, Heather. Your mother is going to need you to be strong because she has to have a battery of tests before we can conclusively diagnose this beast. I've known your father for years and he will never be able to handle this, and your brother and sister are far too young. Keep this to yourself for the next month or until we know exactly how we will deal with this. We need to map out a protocol just to manage her pain."

What now? All I can do is walk mechanically to the car, drive to the hospital, pick up my mother and drive her home. I vow that when I go to bed, when I recite my Hebrew bedtime prayer as I do every night, I will pray like never before that the doctors are mistaken. When the sun finally sets, I will go to the place my mother always speaks of, somewhere over the rainbow, and find a wizard or some other magical creature to wave a wand, create a potion or simply erase the words that I have heard today.

"Get your financial affairs in order, update your will and decide on a resting spot" That is what the oncologist at the Princess Margaret Hospital is telling my mother. I cannot help but fixate on the nameplate on the office door: "Dr. Pain." Odd how often people's names reflect their jobs. Refocus on the situation at hand, I scold myself. But it is too much to take in.

My mother, father and I sit motionless. There is no mistake here, we are told; the tests are conclusive. There is no treatment, no procedure, no hope ... just death.

This is not acceptable, I tell myself. I never give up, so we need to leave and find someone who can do something to change the outcome. "I'm not worried, mom, so don't you worry ... I can find a way to fix this." I squeeze my mother's hand reassuringly. My father sits in silence, expressionless. Then he stands up, robotically picks up his leather jacket splayed across the back of his chair, very slowly puts it on, winces and simply walks out.

In an attempt to distract attention from my father's abject behavior, I ask the doctor a few more questions. I take my mother's clammy hand and walk her down the dreary hospital corridor, through the emergency department and out into the parking lot. Once we are in the car, I try to soothe her by playing her favorite music cassette. I dare not speak. When I glance at her, sitting so demurely, looking so small and diminished, I understand for the first time what real heartbreak is as a single tear rolls down her sun-kissed cheek. I take one hand off the steering wheel and gently wrap her hand in mine. In that moment, I realize that my role has changed. I am now the mother and she, the helpless, sick child.

Later that evening, when my father finally returns, he announces, "This is too much for me to deal with."

The Secret

"Come sit on the bed, Heather; we need to talk," my mother says. I have been back only four months since my honeymoon. I sit close to her frail, skeletal body and hold her hand. My mother's hands, ever since I can remember, have always been perfectly manicured and even now she is wearing the apple-red nail polish that looks so glamorous against her olive skin.

"I've decided that this is no way to live. If you love me, you will let me go. I'm tired and I don't want to do this anymore. Tomorrow you will tell everyone I am having surgery again to cut back the tumor in my esophagus. Be there to witness my request, assist me to remove the helix tube, the respirator and the rest of the equipment I'm hooked up to. Then bury me in something warm because you know how I hate the cold and in a spot where the sun shines on my grave."

I have no words. I cannot speak. I am screaming, crying inside, but silent. I somehow fall into a deep sleep in the chair beside her hospital bed. Hours later, I feel the doctor lightly touch my shoulder. Although my brain has stopped functioning, I walk out to the lounge where my father, sister, brother, aunt, uncle and some family friends have assembled. They are happy because they have been told that this surgery will give my mother some relief and more time. I know better. I smile when they tell me that this is such good news, all the while feeling numb inside. I can almost taste the bile in the back of my throat.

Moments later I am sitting in the hideous mustard-and-sage green tiled operating room. The temperature is frosty and I am chilled to the bone. I stand next to the gurney on which my mother is wrapped like a mummy in a white flannel hospital blanket. She and I are holding hands and I am clutching at her for dear life. Please, please, please don't die, I beg her silently. I need you. Don't leave me. It's too soon. Please don't go.

In an almost inaudible whisper, she says, "Heather, you need to take care of your father. He seems strong but he will never cope with this. Your sister will need you to watch over her. Your brother will have the hardest time. You are in charge now. You are my girl, the one I am counting on to look after them.

"You've inherited the best and worst of me. Like me, you feel too much. If one day you find yourself lost and unsure of what to do, if you are exhausted and broken, you must go and find your life like I told you as a little girl. You will find it somewhere over the rainbow, and I will be there. You are a special girl, a magnet, the light. Find your happiness and I will know.

"I will always be with you … when you are sad, when you are happy, when you birth your first child, when you celebrate your anniversary, your birthday, every holiday, no matter where you are. But for now, you need to be strong, you need not to cry, you need to say 'See you soon,' and sit by my side until I'm gone. Then go back upstairs and let everyone know that all is well. The doctor will be the one to tell them that he lost me in surgery. This is our secret, ours to keep, to hold."

With my mother's assistance, I pull out the helix tube and shut off the machines. I sit motionless, tearless, empty, sick inside, tenderly holding her hands. She whispers one last time, her eyes transfixed on mine, "See you soon, my big girl." And now she is somewhere over the rainbow.

My mother's fears came true years later as my brother and father floundered, anguish and darkness engulfing them both and so my life changed forever.

Tsunamis

The day after arriving on vacation in Maui with Julia, I am determined to get back to Toronto in time for my father's funeral. In the Jewish tradition, people are usually buried within a day or two of their death, barring the Sabbath or some other holy day. It is high season on Maui in mid-February and Air Canada keeps repeating that no seats are available for a week. "Try again," I insist and hang up to wait for the coroner to fax me a death certificate to the hotel.

I manage to locate the Air Canada manager in Montreal. Despite my full-fare business-class ticket and the airline's own policy clearly stated on its website that it is obliged to get me back due to the death of an immediate family member, she refuses to help. I offer to buy a new ticket but to no avail.

Resolved to get on a plane even if it means camping at the airport, I pack a small suitcase, drive to the airport with Julia and head to the counter of United Airlines, which code shares flights with Air Canada. When I explain the circumstances, a compassionate ticket agent finally tells me what I have been hoping to hear. "Don't worry. We'll get you both out on a flight today. Come back at nine o'clock this evening as the flight departs at ten fifty." He asks if we need return flights to Maui. "What day are we going to the Elton John concert at the MACC?" I ask Julia, who reminds me that it is in six days' time. I turn back to the ticket agent. "Can you get us back by 6 p.m. on that day?"

I call my sister with my arrival time and suggest a private *shiva* at her house. Before I left Toronto, I cleaned out my fridge and freezer in case I extended my month-long stay in Maui. I remind her that I am not prepared to receive mourners at my house.

Julia and I return to the hotel where I change into black capris, a black t-shirt and black sandals. In my agitated, foggy state my outfit seems like appropriate mourning garb for travel to Toronto in mid-winter. Then I grab my small packed bag and we head back to the airport.

I have unwittingly become "funeral queen"—a title I detest—having singlehandedly organized the burials of my mother, two grandmothers and my infant daughter. Now, I am forced to do it again, this time for my father. After the death of his mother, the marine biologist told me that he was done with funerals. I feel exactly the same way but my hands are tied. I have a daunting feeling my father's funeral arrangements may fall into my lap regardless of being on the other side of the world right now. Before we board, I call a girlfriend, a practicing rabbi in Toronto. Recalling that my father has no reserved plot, I ask her to get him one on my behalf, at the same cemetery where my mother is buried. Despite being told the cemetery is full, she somehow manages to secure a plot and agrees to officiate at the funeral.

I arrive in Toronto the next afternoon and that evening we meet the rabbi at my home to help her prepare the eulogy. When my siblings and uncle fail to come up with anything complimentary to say about my father, I tell the rabbi, "He adored his grandchildren" and she builds her eulogy around that. I also come up with the tellingly curt epitaph for his headstone: "Loving and devoted grandfather."

Soon after my arrival, I discover that my sister has sent out an email blast inviting everyone she knows to four days of open *shiva* at my house. I have no choice but to order what is needed and prepare for the hordes of people bound to arrive.

After the funeral service, we drive to the cemetery, recite the mourner's *Kaddish* and lower my father into the ground. Feeling ill from exhaustion, jet lag and the bone-chilling temperatures, I put my head down and only then realize that my mother's grave is directly behind and slightly to the right of my father's. How ironic! My father had superstitiously refused to buy a joint plot when my mother died yet, decades later, with the cemetery filled to near capacity, the one available plot happens to be adjacent to hers. I go over my mother's plot and apologize profusely. Even in death, she cannot escape him.

After four exhausting days of running a hot-and-cold food service in my home for the endless crowds, Julia and I get back on a plane and arrive in Maui at 6:45 p.m. We pick up our rental car and head directly to the MACC. We make it to our front row seats in time for the pre-show and enjoy every moment of Elton John's performance. I feel no guilt, merely a feeling of lightness and release.

Legacy in Death

The night of my father's funeral, I cannot sleep. I climb out of my toasty bed and bundle up in a long shearling coat, gloves, scarf and winter boots. I step outside of house and carefully navigate down the icy, snow-covered steps to the driveway . My car is covered in a dusting of powdery snow. The streetlights illuminate the flurries of snowflakes landing on the tree branches. It looks like a winter wonderland but having just returned to Toronto from Maui, I feel the bitter cold all the more intensely. I unlock the car door and hit the lds and wait until the car heats up.

How I do not miss this! After a large piece of crystalized ice slides down the front windshield and I can finally see. I drive to my father's condo in the silence of the night. Oddly, I have no idea why I am going there or what I expect to find. Something is compelling me to look for clues, to make sense of his sudden death, given that two weeks before I left for Maui, the doctor had not only gave him a clean bill of health but authorized the reinstatement of his driver's license. His words to my father are still fresh in my mind: "You've never been so well but you must take the medication as prescribed to prevent heart attack and kidney failure. That's crucial."

I drive past the gate of his condo building, waved on by the security guard, park in guest parking, trudge through a pile of snow and walk into the building with his keys in my hand. The lobby is totally empty as it is almost midnight. The elevator door opens immediately when I press the button. How strange to be in this building after so many years of wondering why I was never allowed or welcome in my father's home. No point in dwelling on the inexplicable, I tell myself. The elevator stops.

I walk down the hallway, slip the key into the door and step inside. A wave of nausea overcomes me. I rush to the bathroom, sit on the floor in front of the toilet and put my head down, hoping it will pass. After a few minutes, I look up and realize that I am sitting near where my father was found after he collapsed and gashed his head. I can see the blood stains on the floor, which has been only superficially cleaned.

When I am able to stand, I open the small medicine cabinet above the sink, unsure of what I might find. Nothing, nothing but aspirin, toothpaste, shaving cream and a few band aids. Next, I walk through his bedroom, living room, office, dining room and lastly, into the kitchen, the room where I first realized that my father had serious mental and physical problems. I remember opening the kitchen cabinets and finding glasses half full of soda pop.

Tentatively, I open the cabinets and pull out the blister packs of medicine that I was authorized to pick up from the pharmacy. Before leaving for Maui, I had picked up a two-week supply of his heart and kidney medication, enough to last him until he could pick it up himself. I had labelled the dates with a marker and left him clear instructions about taking his pills and the importance of never missing the prescribed daily dose.

I lay the packages on the kitchen counter and examine the dates on the packs. Disbelief, anger, guilt and grief: how can I be feeling all of this simultaneously but I do. Almost a week's worth of medication is still in the blister packs. I run to the bathroom again, this time knowing I am going to vomit. I weep and rinse out my mouth, grab the blister packs, my purse and leave.

The next morning, I check my cell phone and see that I have a missed call from a few days earlier. There is a voicemail message from my father. He sounds despondent, desperate. "Heather, come home. I know you've just left today but I can't do this on my own. I want you to come home. I need you to come home now or I won't ,make it." It is difficult not to choke on all this, now that I realize that he stopped taking his medication on purpose.

My father held me hostage with his selfishness and emotional abuse during his lifetime and he is doing it again in death. That is his legacy, along with blame and guilt, and the debts that he left me to settle. The monumental task of unshackling myself from all of it is up to me. For now, all I can do is get back on the plane to Maui.

Less than two weeks later, after Julia has returned to Toronto, a tsunami hits Maui, cutting power to the entire island. Helicopters drop flats of drinking water and the population is warned to stay off the roads, many of which are flooded.

Amidst the confusion, I meet the hotel's general manager. "So sorry, but we have to evacuate you from your beachfront suite. I'll send the valets to pack you up and move you. Is there anything you want?"

"I'd love a cup of coffee but everything is *pau*."

I listen as he instructs the operations manager over his two-way radio. "Ms. Samuel wants coffee. Open Starbucks and keep it open all night for her."

All the guests are moved into the ballroom, given beach towels and blankets and instructed to hunker down on the floor for the night. Thanks to the emergency generators, we have air conditioning and can follow the news from Guam on the ballroom's oversized TV.

The GM takes me aside, asks the hotel staff to escort me to his executive office. He instructs one of his assistants to prepare the pullout coach and bring me some food. It takes three golf carts to move all my belongings. I stay there until eight o'clock the next morning. At nine o'clock, when we are told that it is safe to go outside, the ocean is eerily calm, so glassy that it looks more like a massive lake than the Pacific. The air is still, the sun is shining brightly and the sky is a clear blue once again.

Despite the special attention I received at the hotel, I cannot help thinking that my whole life has been a series of tsunamis. There is great comfort in seeing that after the worst storm there always sunshine...and hope.

Walking Away

"He's not for you, Heather," warned the sage, but I did not listen. Of course, he was right. He has an uncanny knack for always knowing what is right for me, especially when it involves my fragile heart. "He may be able to spell the word love but does he understand it requires action, it's not just a four letter word on paper!" But it takes five months and another few month of self-recrimination and guilt to figure out that I have given my heart to the wrong man, a man who turns out to be much like my father, even to their preferred brand of alcohol.

It all begins almost a year earlier when I find myself "homeless" again, an especially unbearable condition because of my past history: almost every home I have lived in has been taken away from me. Consequently, what I crave more than anything is to root, to nest, to create a beautiful harmonious environment for myself; I need that for my well-being, to function at my best. Unfortunately, the fates seemed to be conspiring, or maybe laughing at the irony. Here I am looking again for a home, after a career of renovating and designing a series of upscale homes in Toronto. The shoemaker with no shoes—a poor analogy, perhaps, given my extensive shoe collection!

After being forced out of my south Maui home of three plus years when it goes up for sale with very little notice, I find myself out of options. Despite my diligent efforts and employing the assistance of several rental agents, we can find nothing due to an impossibly tight rental market that is even more skewed than when I arrived more than three years earlier. However, I never stop looking, praying that something, anything, will miraculously turn up before I run out of time. Nothing does.

As the last day of my tenancy approaches, I reluctantly accept an interim locale. My misgivings turn out to be prescient when disaster strikes: an out-of-control termite infestation makes this place uninhabitable. Only three weeks after moving in, unpacking and setting up house, even going so far as to hang my artwork on the walls, I am forced to pack up again and move out, this time putting everything into storage, a feat in itself as storage lockers are also in short supply.

By then, I am utterly discouraged, frustrated and beyond exhausted. For the first time on Maui, I am ready to crumble and admit defeat, pack up and leave for good. Fortunately, first couple of weeks for no charge. Back I go to my-home-away-from-home — to regroup, regain my strength and carry on the fight to find a nice home to live on Maui. My girlfriends keep asking how long I can keep this up before admitting I am totally spent, and crawling back "home" to Toronto. "I don't know, don't ask me, I have no answers, I have never been one to cave in defeat, I have to dig deeper and find a way," I repeat over and over. "Home" — what an imponderable concept, given my history.

Can't Go Home Again

A few months after my mother's death, my father sold our family home without consulting us, walked away from his children and moved into his own luxury condo. My siblings each forced to move in with family friends and I luckily had secured a tiny midtown apartment with my husband. Bizarre as that was at the time, it was only after my father's death that I realized how absurd it was that he had also given away all my mother's possessions and everything in our family home without consulting or considering his children.

My mother had squirreled away a few dollars from her part-time administrative job and given me her banking information. She instructed me to use her money to cover the expenses I incurred going back and forth to the hospital during her lengthy illness. When I went to her bank a few months after her death, the bank manager told me that my father had withdrawn all the funds and closed her account. I never questioned my father or even spoke of it. I simply buried my disappointment, as always.

One snowy day shortly after my father had been buried deep below ground, nostalgia and curiosity induced me to drive by our old family home in Toronto. The house appeared unchanged, but for the three beautiful birch trees that had grown almost as tall as the roofline. The brass eagle ornament, a symbol of strength and protection to my father, still hung over the double garage doors. My intention was simply to drive through my old neighborhood but something compelled me to pull into the driveway of our former family home. I got out of the car and walked to the front entrance, not even sure what I would say if someone answered the door. I rang the familiar doorbell and a woman opened it slightly, peered out at me.

"I used to live here. I mean, this used to be my house," I stammered, fumbling my words because I was transfixed by the familiar paisley wallpaper in the hall. "My mother decorated this house ... the kitchen has an exposed brick wall ... well, it used to ... I was wondering if I could have a quick look?" I hoped she did not take me for a prowler or a nutcase.

"Your mom died when you were young, right?" I nodded, holding back tears. "When your father showed us the house, my husband and I fell in love with it and everything in it. Your mother had such good taste, a flare for decorating. We made your father an offer on the spot." I sheepishly asked if I could see my old bedroom. "Come in," she said, and moved aside.

As I walked from room to room, I was assailed with flashbacks: my young mother, my siblings, a holiday, a dinner, a moment, a lifetime—all of it overwhelming. My bedroom walls were still covered in the pale peach-and-lemon cabbage-rose wallpaper she and I had chosen together. The light fixture that she had made in a ceramics studio still hung from the floral plaster medallion in the centre of the ceiling over my queen-size bed. I felt ill. But it was when I walked into the kitchen that I was consumed with hatred toward my father. All the copper pots that my mother had so carefully chosen together on a trip to the Carolinas were still hanging in the exact same spots. The brass hooks that she had so painstakingly handpicked, the furniture—nothing in the house had been changed in thirty years! Even the monogrammed towels in the powder room bore my parents' initials. How could my father have left everything to strangers and not given his children a single keepsake to remind them of their mother? Unfathomable!

This was more than I could bear so I thanked the woman and asked her if I could take some small object with me, a brass hook, a towel, some token to remember my mother. She would give it some thought, she replied, but as my father had sold it all to them, she really did not want to part with a thing.

As I drove away, I once again willed myself to bury my disappointment and despair. "They are just things," I reminded myself in a whisper. After all, I had been left with something that no one can give or take away from me; my memories and her soul that lives and thrives within me.

Ordinary Girl

At the hotel, I do my best to make my provisional residence feel homey. I place framed photos of my son on my bedside table, set up my computer and favorite coffee mug on the desk, position all my perfumes, hair accessories and jewelry in the bathroom along with a vase of fresh flowers, and spread my books and magazines strategically around the suite. I fill the closet with rows of shoes and clothes appropriate for working in the store.

I ask for a bowl of Granny Smith apples to be delivered weekly to my makeshift kitchen area, which consists of an oversized microwave, a mini bar fridge stocked with bottled water and leafy greens, a small coffeemaker and a few plates and some cutlery. I become expert at "sink salads," prepping and assembling my leafy meals in the bathroom sink. I look forward to my workdays at the store, just a quick walk away. Being productive, contributing to the store's bottom line and talking to interesting shoppers is my salvation.

My morning ritual before work begins with a quick stop at the coffee shop in the hotel lobby before heading to the gym for a short workout. Then I attend a pilates and a yoga instructional class on the hotel lawn overlooking the ocean. The exercise keeps me in shape and the yoga keeps me balanced, figuratively and literally. At the end of my workday, I usually stop to sit in the lobby outside the closed coffee shop to read my email and write, to unwind and decompress after non-stop chatting with shoppers all day.

One evening, after I have settled into a chair, a tall nice-looking man walks over to me. "It's late and the coffee shop is closed," he says. No kidding, Sherlock, I think grumpily to myself. He then offers to walk me to my car in the parking lot.

"No thanks, I'm okay," I reply, hoping he will read my dismissive body language and leave me alone. But he persists, asking me more questions, trying to figure out what I am doing here. Finally, frustrated by his persistence, I turn it around: "Don't *you* need to go home? Can I walk you to *your* car?"

Bemused, he explains that he is on his way home to have dinner with his family. He introduces himself and hands me his business card, which I quickly drop into my purse, the equivalent of the Bermuda Triangle, though not before noting that he is an architect, presumably working on a project at the hotel for a brief stint. When he asks again if he can walk me to my car, I finally blurt, "No thanks, I *am* home." He still does not get it so I explain that I am a hotel guest, albeit for an extended stay.

After that first meeting, I keep bumping into the architect on and off the property and always rejected his overtures. I have no interest in the architect. When he offers to take me out on a stand-up paddling excursion, I tell him, "I don't swim so no thank you."

"I can teach you and I'd only take you in calm waters," he counters.

"Haven't you seen the movie, *The Other Side of Midnight*?" I quip. He has not and appears perplexed by the reference to the movie, so I explain that there is a scene in the movie with two people going out in a boat and only one comes back, and it is not the woman, "so, no, I'm not interested in going stand-up paddle boarding." Undeterred, he suggests hiking. "There's no water involved." I do not respond. Surely, by now, he will have figured out that I am not interested!

A few days later, as I dress for a dinner date, I realize that I need help tying the back of my new long white halter dress. I grab my room key card, purse, my new white sandals and head out to look for the housekeeper, who happens to be standing in the corridor with her restocking cart. Just as I am about to thank her for assisting me, the architect walks by and stares at me. I must get away from this guy, I tell myself. He turns up everywhere; it is very unnerving.

A month later, after a difficult search, I finally find the perfect house. It is brand new, beautiful and in a gated community where I feel safe. On moving day, I work like a machine through the night to unpack the one hundred and eighty boxes that the movers have neatly piled in the garage. After only a few hours of sleep, I walk into my new kitchen and groan. I have neglected to buy coffee and cream for my morning java jolt. I quickly change into yoga pants and top, pick up my flip-flops and keys and drive back to my regular coffee hangout at the hotel.

Unbelievable! I have left the hotel yet there he is again, standing in line at the coffee shop. "Give me a call if you ever want to go in the water," he tells me, delighted to have bumped into me. "You've got my card."

He must be obtuse. "I threw your card in the trash and for the last time, I don't go in the ocean!" The girls who work in the coffee shop know me well and are shocked by my uncharacteristically rude reply, but he does not flinch. He simply reaches for his wallet, extracts another business card and hands it to me.

I walk out of the shop, shaking my head, wondering what it will take to convince him that I am not interested. I stop to chat with some hotel staff and when he crosses my path yet again in the lobby, I impulsively call out, "Hey, do you have a pen?" When he shakes his head, I run and borrow one from the sundries shop, scribble my cell phone number on his business card and hand it back to him. "Now you have my number, but don't call me to go in the ocean." I smile smugly as I drive home. I am sure that I have gotten rid of him for good because I took charge, convinced that he is more interested in the chase than in me. How wrong I was.

The very next evening, he begins an ardent but confusing courtship: months of constant texting, bouquets of long-stemmed roses, gifts of gelato, champagne and cards, all of which he brings to my door as an excuse to stay just to talk. I am oddly comfortable with his formality and old-school approach but secretly wonder where this is going since we have only been out once—for a very awkward lunch early on when I mistakenly assumed he was simply networking for professional reasons.

What truly captures my heart, however, is how invested he appears to be in his children, whom he has raised on his own. From everyone's account, they are great kids, polite, respectful and star athletes thanks to his coaching and attention. My mother's words still ring in my head. "The measure of a man is in the way he loves and raises his children and in the way he loves, protects and cherishes his partner." In my books, a good father can do no wrong. A "good father" was what I had longed for growing up.

More texts, more long conversations into the night, and finally, a romantic dinner at one of the island's iconic restaurants. Lightening flashes, thunder rumbles and fat raindrops pound the windshield as he drives me home, both of us quiet, deep in thought. When he pulls into my driveway and gets out of the car to open my door, I feel comfortable enough with him to invite him in for a n after dinner cappuccino since he has been a perfect gentleman thus far—sweet, kind and respectful. That night we became lovers.

Before dawn the next morning, as the roosters crow, I feel him kiss me lightly on my cheek and cover me with the duvet. Still groggy, I ask him where he is going so early. "To look after my children," he says. Disappointed that we are not going to spend the morning together over a leisurely Sunday brunch and perplexed because his children are young adults, I do not protest, merely say goodbye.

I may act like a runaway bride when I feel that a relationship is moving too quickly, is threatening or going nowhere, but I had no inkling that the architect is a runaway cowboy. After a week goes by after our intimate evening and I have still heard nothing from him, I vow to walk away. Talk about a message! I am very hurt and disappointed, mostly with myself, but when I look dispassionately at what has transpired between us over the course of four months, I realize that our so-called relationship has been limited to two dates, long and numerous conversations, most of them on the phone late at night, infrequent visits from him at my house, and one sleepover.

My modus operandi is *never* to contact men, to always wait for them to contact me. I have never been comfortable as the aggressor. Why would I want to be with someone who does not want to be with me? When I sense disinterest, I simply walk away. This time, however, I do something totally out of character; I decide to take a stand. If I am ever going to have a secure, happy, committed relationship, I must speak up and communicate what it is I need and expect. Perhaps I have not been clear enough with the architect. It is foolish to expect him to be clairvoyant. Now is the time to set aside my usual reticence and risk rejection.

When he finally turns up at my door a week later, admitting had no idea why I was upset, we sit down on my living room sofa. I suggest he get comfortable because it is time for a straightforward forthright talk. I give him a short list of my non negotiable and let him know what triggers my insecurities. "If we are going to continue to see each other and see where this goes, then I need you to show up, emotionally and physically." Despite my serious attraction to him, I admit that I am prepared to walk away today if showing up and making me feel considered and appreciated is not something he is willing or able to do. "I don't want to feel like I am on your to-do list." He listens intently, seems to understand and agrees to work at making me feel secure. I explain after much soul-searching that a real and honest relationship is what I am looking for not an arrangement. I am very specific explaining that I am very independent but consistent communication is key in the kind of relationship I am looking for. He makes it very clear that he has no interest in ending a relationship that is just beginning, adamant that I am everything he wants in a partner and understand what I need, is willing to do better, his words not mine.

Before leaving on a family vacation off-island over Christmas, he comes over frequently relaxes on my lanai, reads, talks and just spends time with me. By then, as much as I hate to admit I am smitten. I can envision a life with him; I can see exactly what it could look like. He constantly tells me that he is genuinely serious about me. "Now that I've got you," he says, "I have to figure out how to keep you with me for the next few decades." Yet, at the same time he keeps voicing nagging concerns about the differences in our backgrounds, education and lifestyles. To allay his fears that I am "too sophisticated" for him and to express my feelings of love and adoration, I hand him a handwritten note that I ask him to open over the holidays. He opens it on the spot.

When we first met, you told me that you are a simple man. I told you that I am just an ordinary girl. There is no denying that our paths thus far have taken each of us to very different places. We have experienced different cultures, passions and chosen different career paths. The gift that we can now bring to one another is to share those experiences. Together we can create new ones as we are walking today on the same path in a place we both love.

You are anything but a simple man. You are complex, intelligent, curious, articulate, focused, a man of substance. That is hardly simple. That is the man I love with my whole heart. I, on the other hand am just an ordinary girl. Consistent, loyal, attending, measured, dependable, loving, trustworthy is who I am . It's rare in this world to find someone you are proud to walk beside physically and metaphorically, wanting to do it today, tomorrow and the tomorrow after that.

So simple man, this ordinary girl will proudly walk beside you, love you, hold you up when you are exhausted, be your cheerleader, you voice of reason, your partner, your support, your co- parent of our adult children, your sous-chef, your champion and everything in between. All I ask is that we love one another and appreciate how lucky we are to have been fated to have met at this time in our lives. All you have to do is show up, have my back and stand by me.

As he puts my note back in the envelope, he is visibly shaken. "Oh no, I told you to read it after your left on vacation. Did I say too much?""No. It's the most incredible letter I've ever received. I don't know what to say."

Over the next ten days, I have never dared to dream of what ensued. He calls and texts constantly, professing his love and telling me how much he misses me; that we are finally on solid ground and moving forward to build a life together. I am elated and long for his return.

What I fail to see is the pathology: the perpetual push-pull that keeps me continually off balance and second-guessing everything. Shortly after he returns from vacation, more than a week goes by with no communication, leaving me consumed with self-doubt and confusion. The silent treatment is the most emotionally damaging to ones psyche and self esteem, worse that being physically abused. I spent my childhood listening to my mother beg my father to pay attention to her, to talk to her instead of shutting her out and constantly insisting that he needed his space. Then I found myself in a marriage where much of the same obtained, although, unlike my mother, I was far too proud to beg or ask for anything. Questioning whether I fallen into in the same kind of untenable relationship, my gut tells me to walk away. After another month of the same disturbing pattern of constant attention, professions of adoration, love bombing followed by silence, I realize that I have to do something drastic.

I cannot bear the thought of walking away after a five-month investment of emotional and physical intimacy, so I do what I always do when things need fixing: I try harder. It is time to double down and finally meet his children in his home, something he has been hinting at but also resists, perhaps sensing the risk he is taking. I find his ambivalence curious, and troubling but I broach the subject again. Aha, that is the rub, finally he admits that he needs the assurance that his children will be onside with our union.

A few days later, I am finally sitting at his dining room table. When his children join hands and he holds his out to me, I am momentarily perplexed. Is this a séance? I smile inwardly when I realize this is just grace before the meal.

I engage in a flurry of chatter with his sweet, intelligent and well-mannered grown children, who speak so lovingly to one another and with great respect to their father. I am impressed.

One of his daughters takes me aside to confide her anguish about a recent break up with her boyfriend. In a flood of tears, she admits her lack of self-confidence and her self-doubt. Although she is thrilled to be able to unburden herself to me, another woman, about matters of the heart, she relays her father's protective love, his understanding and support in comforting her. I am taken aback, never having experienced growing up that a father's love could be nurturing.

He calls the next evening, overjoyed that everyone has gotten along so well, his fretting about the differences in our homes and lifestyles momentarily put to rest. When the daughter asks to spend the next Friday with me and stay over, I am touched and arrange a girly-girls' evening: mani-pedi, followed by pizza, ice cream and girl talk while baking cookies together. The architect and his other children join us the next day and they all stay over for the rest of the weekend. I bond with his children, doing a jigsaw puzzle with one, spending time at the pool with the others.

My vision of our life together is now becoming bigger and more complicated but I can still see it, and it also includes my son, perhaps a dog or pair of golden retrievers (on my wish list, not the architect's). Two more busy family weekends at my home follow, moving the relationship forward at warp speed—with his children! The architect, however, is still floundering with his own self-doubts, his insecurities. He says he feels pressured and worried that he is going to let me down, hurt me but I only ask for his presence and not even that with any regularity.

On the last weekend we spend together at his house, I feel less tenuous. His house is now familiar and his children are so welcoming. When I offer to help prepare dinner, he insists that I relax. We chat through dinner and the children tidy up. After dinner we watch the news together, which has become somewhat of a ritual, and then I excuse myself to shower before bedtime.

I recall that the shampoo and soap in the shower stall are set on a very high window ledge way beyond my five foot something reach. Reluctant to ask the architect for help out of fear that he will interpret my request as an implied criticism of his home. He is concerned that his house is not at same level of luxury as mine. I quietly head upstairs into the kitchen and take a long-handled wooden spoon and head downstairs to the bathroom. This will work, I think, as I tuck it in my yoga pants. However, once in the shower, I realize that I have miscalculated the length of the spoon and my reach. After a few tries and misses jumping up and down, the shampoo comes crashing down. I ignore the architect's query from the master bedroom next door about the loud noise. The shampoo will have to do double duty since I am not going to keep jumping for the soap, too.

After towel drying my hair, I dress in clean yoga pants and a fresh t-shirt. Then it occurs to me that I have to do something about the spoon, so I hide it in my yoga pants and position it toward my left leg. It is chilly evening so I climb into bed with the architect, wrap myself up in the duvet to get warm, lie on my left side, hoping he will not pull me close. How will I explain the wooden spoon tucked into my tights? Just before he dozes off, he offers me one of his large long-sleeve tops as a makeshift nightshirt. "I'm cold so think I'd rather keep my yoga pants on," I reply. Thankfully, a few minutes later, he falls into a deep sleep.

I carefully peel off the covers, tiptoe out of the bedroom and upstairs to the kitchen to return the spoon. The next morning I awake and head up to the kitchen. The architect is busy preparing breakfast and mixing up pancake batter with the same spoon I used the night before. My god if he only knew!

The following week, all it takes is a trivial change of plans by me to precipitate the crisis from which we will not recover. The safe and caring place I thought I had found in his home suddenly becomes cold, unwelcoming and for the first time it's clear that there is no fixing this. As much as he seems to want the relationship, his fear of intimacy and commitment pushed it away as we grow closer.

I have already witnessed enough interactions with his children to see that what I initially interpreted as respect is, in fact, fear of disappointing him and of breaking the rules; his children dare not question or cross him. My heart aches for these children; for his household is eerily similar to the one I grew up in as a child. The worst part is that I know he loves his children and is totally unaware of the way they perceive him. In fact he lacks empathy and consideration for people, and has an excessive need for constant praise and admiration. I realize when the attention is not focused on him, all hell breaks loose. I witnessed his childish random outbursts, pouting and brooding over the most ridiculous things and now understood why his children chose silence as their best survival strategy in that household. When he shuts me out, at the beginning of our relationship, my automatic reaction is to send apologetic texts, pleading for him to call and tell me what I have done wrong. I feel as if I am reliving my life with my mercurial, narcissistic father—apologizing, afraid that I am not good enough, not worthy. Valentine's Day, the architect finally calls me late at night, and I can hear ice clinking in a glass. "You are the most beautiful and intelligent woman I've ever known, but we are not in the same place. This is too much pressure. It's too serious. It's moving too fast. I need space!" All I can think of is that perhaps it's February 14th, not the best day to break the news to me!

However, that is when I realize that he is a troubled, elusive man, struggling with more than low self-esteem issues, or someone who lives at an emotional distance. I decide then that this angst-ridden, rollercoaster of a relationship must come to an end. Before I have a chance to tell him it is over, he interrupts me. "It's not you, Heather, it's me. I have been having trouble dealing with things for a while now. I hope if I call you at some point, you will pick up the phone and talk to me." Now I know he is off his rocker!!

A few days of deep, palpable heartbreak and a sea of tears later, I pick myself up and carry on knowing I will never make sense of his behavior. Thinking back on what transpired, I regret having projected my ideal of a partner on him. That was not fair; living up to an ideal is impossible. The only consolation is that I have done some good for his children. When I reluctantly admit to one his daughters, wise beyond her years, that her father and I are done, she tells me, "You've shown me how to hold my head up high, respect myself and value myself when I was at my lowest point and lacking self-esteem. You are a role model for me and my siblings, who love you. You've done nothing wrong, nothing to feel badly about."

Overwhelmed by her words, I weep silently, not because the relationship has failed, but because she is walking in my shoes. Like me some thirty years ago, she is dealing with a commanding and emotionally limited, narcissistic father and struggling with her sense of self. The difference is that she is not alone; she has me.

I will continue to show her how special she is; that no one can take that away from her; that she need never fear or doubt herself; that she must stand tall and respect, value and validate herself. I will teach her these things—because that girl is me

Epilogue

A few months later, my cell phone rings at 9:25 p.m. and then again five minutes later. I let it ring. It is the architect; he does not leave a message. Several more weeks go by and then, by chance, I run into him. He is very friendly; I am very reserved. When we part, I know that nothing has changed for me; I am still in love with him. Move on, I coach myself every day, hoping that time will lessen the emotional connection.

The next time we accidentally meet, we exchange pleasantries. I attempt to keep some physical distance between us, but he moves closer and takes my hand. He tells me how much he has missed talking to me, missed seeing me, needs me. . I am taken aback, surprised that he is suddenly so forthright. He hugs me tightly and kisses me softly. My heart pounds; I find myself melting into his embrace and kissing him back. I know I should leave. Nothing has changed except his determination to articulate and demonstrate his affection.

"When everything has fallen apart and there's nothing left but pain and heartache, take the lesson and drop the rest," the sage had advised me on one of our recent walks. So I take his advice and get into my car to leave. Before I can drive away, the architect asks if he can call me later that evening. When I do not reply, he asks again. Despite my longing to hear from him, I find the words, "Please don't. There's really no point."

At 3:30 a.m. that night, my phone starts pinging with a series of texts. I ignore it until it rings minutes later. "Why are you calling me at this hour? What is wrong with you?" I am frustrated and upset. He is so mercurial!

"I can't sleep. I can't stop thinking about you. I need you to talk me back to sleep." An hour later, he is at my front door, offering his affection, holding his first and real love, the mistress I can not compete with, his vodka bottle and hoping to rekindle our former intimacy. With heavy heart, I send him home.

When you open your heart to an empty vessel, you can pour love in the form of praise, love, tender touch, an embrace, a tender kiss,

But no matter how you give, turn yourself inside out, lose yourself in building him up, you are bound and sure to hit a miss.

He is broken, has a severed heart, but blind to his own limitations, his reality, conflicted by his need, wanting and not at the same time,

Posing as someone, a stranger reflected back when he dares to face a mirror,

But too frightened by the pathology of his own self destructive crime.

Heartbreaking, palpable and no sense of justice but the only sanity is in walking, running far and away,

The collateral damage, a small piece of self-worth robbed, unanswered questions and a wonder if giving love will always lead to dismay.

Fractures heal, cracks fill in, and over time the warmth of the sun and kindness that even comes at the hand of a gentle stranger gives hope,

Finding a balance, having a tall and strong rooted frame that stands behind you for support, empathy for lost and wounded is the only way to cope.

We pray for these lone souls, we grieve love lost, we dream of the day when the light ignites within this half a being,

And we go on sewing our own seeds, planting our own garden, reaping the beauty in the flowers that bloom with careful tending and seeing.

Answers and love come when you ask not, they appear like magic and wrap you up in a blanket of security,

These moments, hours, days in our life are meant to forge, serve a higher purpose and we grapple but in the end we are rewarded with purity.

Love hurts, love heals, love holds, and above all love hands you the hope of a whole heart again!

In my lifetime, I have rarely admitted defeat. I have always believed that if I just try harder and work smarter, I will eventually prevail; that love, kindness, loyalty and compassion can fix anything. I now understand that love is not enough to build and sustain a healthy relationship; that I can only fix myself, not anyone else. I must admit and accept my limitations.

Although my life has been less than idyllic, I am not what has happened to me but what I chose to become. I in the end, I am just an ordinary girl, albeit one who will continue to water her garden.

Perek Bet….The Next Chapter……

ABOUT THE AUTHOR

Born and raised in Toronto, Canada, H. J. Samuel is an and loves to travel , write and is an entrepenuer at heart.

A multi-talented polyglot and trained pastry chef, she has owned, operated successful retail, catering/event and design ventures. She lives in Maui, Hawaii and spends her summer months in Florence, Italy. Follow H. J. Samuel on her *Wailea Girl Living the Dream* blog at waileagirl.blogspot.com

CPSIA information can be obtained
at www.ICGtesting.com
Printed in the USA
BVHW042159270819
557006BV00007B/115/P